D0208602

Learning Resources Center
Santa Fe Community College
P.O. Box 4187
Santa Fe, New Mexico 87502

Myth and the History of the Hispanic Southwest

Myth
and the
History
of the
Hispanic
Southwest

Essays by

DAVID J. WEBER

Published in observation of the 500th anniversary
of Spain's discovery of the New World

The Calvin P. Horn Lectures
in Western History and Culture

University of New Mexico
November 8–11, 1987

UNIVERSITY OF NEW MEXICO PRESS, Albuquerque

Library of Congress Cataloging-in-Publication Data

Weber, David J.
  Myth and the history of the Hispanic southwest : essays
/ by David J. Weber.—1st ed.
    p. cm.—(The Calvin P. Horn lectures in western history
and culture)
    "University of New Mexico, November 8–11, 1987."
    Includes bibliographical references and index.
    ISBN 0-8263-1094-X
    1. Mexican-American Border Region—Historiography.
2. Southwest, New—Historiography.
3. Southwest, New—Ethnic relations—Historiography.
I. Title.
II. Series.
F786.W365   1988
972'.1—dc19   88-12035

To Carol

Contents

Learning Resources Center
Santa Fe Community College
Santa Fe, New Mexico
(505) 471-8200

Introduction

Conventional wisdom in the United States suggests that a sharp line exists between history and myth. History seems to represent a "true" account of past events; myth seems to represent a fictional construction. Scholars who have taken pains to define history and myth have often pointed out that no sharp line divides the two. History contains mythic elements, and myth contains historical elements. To suppose otherwise is to place too great a faith in our ability to reconstruct the past through *logos*, and too little imagination to seek the truths inherent in *mythos*.

Implicitly and explicitly, the essays in this book consider some of the myths inherent in the writing of the history of Spanish-Mexican peoples in what is today the American Southwest. In this century, the effort to reconstruct the history of Hispanics in what is today the United States has itself developed in part as a response to myths. Historians interested in America's Spanish-Mexican heritage have found it difficult to accept the popular reconstructions of the American past that place America's colonial origins entirely within the thirteen English colonies, or that omit Mexican Americans from historical narratives. Instead, historians of the Spanish-Mexican Borderlands have seen the nation's origins as multiethnic, and the diverse stories of *hispanos* and *mexicanos* in today's Sunbelt states as an essential part of the American story—if it is to be told more fully and truthfully.

Historians of the so-called Borderlands school, writing in the tradition of Herbert Eugene Bolton, the field's founder, have in large measure used traditional Anglo-centered American history as a foil against which they could more clearly define or invent their own field. This has shaped the historiography of the Borderlands school and contributed to its confusion over self-definition. I explain these problems more fully in an essay in this volume, "John Francis Bannon and the Historiography of the Spanish Borderlands." Even as historians of the Borderlands have defined themselves within the framework of American history, however, they have resisted applying to the Borderlands one of the most powerful paradigms of American historiography—the famous thesis of Frederick Jackson Turner. As I explain in another essay in this volume, "Turner, the Boltonians, and the Borderlands," America's mythic idealization of its frontier life—a myth that gave power to Turner's construction—had no counterpart in northern Mexico and little utility, then, for historians of the Borderlands.

Although historians of the Spanish-Mexican experience in America have sought to counter myths, they have inevitably invented new ones—sometimes egregiously as I suggest in two other essays in this book, "Reflections on Coronado and the Myth of Quivira" and "Fray Marcos de Niza and the Historians." Whether new or old, myths are often as harmless as Dr. Joseph James Markey's ill-advised search for a missing Spanish ship (a story that I retell in my essay, "Reflections on Coronado . . ."). Other times, however, myths hold potential for great harm, as I note in "Refighting the Alamo: Mythmaking and the Texas Revolution," and in "'Scarce More Than Apes': Historical Roots of Anglo-American Stereotypes of Mexicans."

Like other historians who work in the Spanish-Mexican Borderlands, I too have sought to tell the Hispanic sides of American history and have doubtless contributed myths of my own. Throughout this book, but rather directly in three essays, I attempt to counterbalance what I see as one-sided, Anglophile versions of aspects of America's westward expansion: "Mexico's Far Northern Frontier, 1821–1854: Historiography Askew," "'From Hell Itself': The Americanization of Mexico's Northern Frontier, 1821–1846," and "American Westward Expansion and the Breakdown of Relations Between *Pobladores* and *'Indios Bárbaros'* . . ."

Historians' abilities to reconstruct the past are, of course, bound by culture and limited by their angle of vision. The story is told of a Cree hunter asked to testify in court. Could he describe the impact of a hydroelectric dam on his way of life? The Indian said that he could. When asked, however, to tell the truth, he balked. "I'm not sure I can tell the truth," he replied, "I can only tell what I know."[1] None of us can tell more than we know, but through the study of history we can make an effort to know more—to rise above our time and place and to broaden our angles of vision. In the southwestern corner of America, where myth and history have so long intersected, more careful study of *hispanos* and *mexicanos* may help us to untangle history and myth. In so doing, we should have no illusions that we will banish myths, or that such an end would be either possible or desirable. Our purpose should not be to eliminate myths, but to illuminate them. Toward that end, I offer these essays.

This book had its genesis in the Calvin P. Horn Lectures at the University of New Mexico. The four Horn Lectures appear in this volume: "Reflections on Coronado and the Myth of Quivira," "John Francis Bannon and the Historiography of the Spanish Borderlands," "The Americanization of Mexico's Northern Frontier, 1821–1846," and "Refighting the Alamo: Mythmaking and the Texas Revolution." This volume contains five additional essays. All are arranged in rough chronological order, according to the topic that they treat. The provenance of essays that appeared previously in print has been indicated. I wrote each of these works for a specific purpose or occasion, hence the length of each piece and the extent of its documentation varies.

Some of the intellectual debts incurred in preparing these essays go back over many years and are too numerous to mention. In this last year, however, I have profited especially from the insights of Ramón Gutiérrez of the University of California at San Diego, and from good conversations with colleagues at the Center for Advanced Study in the Behavioral Sciences at Stanford, where I spent 1986–87 as a Fellow. I am grateful to the Center and *all* of its gracious and helpful staff, but especially to Leslie Lindzey, Kathleen Much, and Rosanne Torre. Financial support provided by the Andrew W. Mellon Foundation and my own institution, Southern Methodist University, made a year at the Center possible.

Finally, I wish to thank Calvin Horn, who has sponsored the Horn Lectures and their publication. I first met Calvin Horn in 1966. That year he entered my life in two important ways—as a philanthropist

1. This story, apparently apocryphal, is told by James Clifford in Clifford and George E. Marcus, eds., *Writing Culture: The Poetics and Politics of Ethnography* (Berkeley: University of California Press, 1986), p. 8.

and as a publisher. First, Calvin Horn the philanthropist had established a scholarship for a graduate student at the University of New
Mexico in the name of John F. Kennedy. I had the good fortune to
become its first recipient, along with the special pleasure of receiving
the award directly from Ted Kennedy. Second, with more faith than
prudence, Calvin Horn the publisher trusted me to edit and write an
introduction to a rare volume that he was reprinting, even though I
had not yet finished my doctorate. I completed the work in the early
summer of 1967, just after turning in my dissertation. Later that year,
Mr. Horn published a handsome reprint of Albert Pike's valuable *Prose
Sketches Written in the Western Country,* a book that had first appeared
in 1834. Meanwhile, I had moved to San Diego and gradually lost
contact with Calvin Horn.

Two decades later, Calvin Horn entered my life again—as publisher and philanthropist. First, although Mr. Horn had long since
ceased to publish books, in 1986 I got in touch with him to seek his
permission to allow Texas A&M University Press to reprint Albert
Pike's book in their *Southwest Landmark* series. Mr. Horn graciously
agreed, and a few months ago *Prose Sketches and Poems Written in the
Western Country* came back into print. Second, Calvin Horn the
philanthropist reentered my life through sponsoring a series of lectures
in western history and culture at the University of New Mexico. As
I worked to prepare the Horn Lectures over the last year, I could not
help but reflect on the coincidence of returning to the University of
New Mexico at the instigation of Calvin Horn. I am honored to have
been one of the Horn Lecturers, and delighted to have had the chance
to come back to the university whose rich human and scholarly resources
in Latin American and southwestern history first kindled my interest
in the Hispanic experience in North America.

1

Reflections on Coronado
and the Myth
of Quivira*

In 1984, public discussion in Texas turned to the subject of myth almost as frequently as it did to George Orwell. The catalyst for the frequent appearance of myth in public forums in this state was the Texas Committee for the Humanities, which had invited proposals for projects on "Texas Myths." There is a saying in the West that water does not flow downhill, it flows toward money. So it is with many intellectuals. Although Orwell would hardly have approved, federal dollars shaped the contours of public discourse in 1984 and "Texas Myths" became the topic of choice for a number of essays, lectures, symposia, and exhibits.[1] There were some among us who counseled caution. Even as he wrote about myths in Texas, historian T. R. Fehrenbach wondered if the Texas Committee intended to foster "a scholarly pursuit for knowledge, or a sneaky form of demythologizing?"[2] Others, untroubled by conspiracy theories, plunged ahead to meditate on aspects of the mythic past and present of the Lone Star State. For

*This essay represents an expanded version of a lecture given in the autumn of 1984 at a symposium in Canyon, Texas, sponsored by the Panhandle-Plains Historical Society and Museum: "Myths that Made Texas: Coronado and the Myth of Quivira." It was published as "Meditations on Coronado and the Myth of Quivira," in Dianna Everett, ed., *Coronado and the Myth of Quivira* (Canyon: Panhandle-Plains Historical Society, 1985), pp. 59–69, and in *Southwest Review* 70 (Spring 1985): 230–41. This version appears here with permission of the Panhandle-Plains Historical Society.

1. One result of the "Texas Myths" project has been a book of interesting essays, Robert F. O'Connor, ed., *Texas Myths* (College Station: Texas A&M University Press, 1986).

2. T. R. Fehrenbach, "Demystifying Texas Mythology," *Dallas Times Herald*, September 23, 1984.

my part, attracted by a paltry sum, I found myself heading toward Canyon, in the Texas Panhandle. There, the first white man to be drawn into Texas by myth, the young Spanish explorer Francisco Vázquez de Coronado, had camped on the edge of Palo Duro Canyon in 1541. In 1984, it was my task to talk about "Coronado and the Myth of Quivira" at a symposium sponsored by the Panhandle-Plains Historical Society, with a grant from the Texas Committee for the Humanities. I was to explain to a general audience "the impact of the Spanish conquest, and surrounding myths, on the Southwest, its people, and its history"—in thirty minutes.

Myth is, of course, a slippery word that has come to have many meanings. In the classical sense, myths usually tell of the exploits of gods and heroes, or employ narrative form to explain some phenomenon of nature or the origins of a society's beliefs or institutions. In another sense of the word, it might be said that every age has its own myths—some based on fact and some derived entirely from the imagination. Some of these myths embody a people's cultural ideals and incite them to action or to a certain kind of behavior—as did the Nazi myth of so-called Aryan supremacy. In still another sense, we use *myth* quite simply to refer to any imaginary person or thing. Finally, we use *myth* as a synonym for those stories that we also call legends or folktales. I take these multiple meanings as license to use the word imprecisely, but hope that the context in which I use *myth* will make my meaning clear.[3]

Like many of his countrymen, thirty-year-old Francisco Vázquez de Coronado, the premier Spanish explorer of what is today the American Southwest, found the myths of his time and place irresistibly seductive. In 1540, Coronado left a high government position and a wealthy wife in New Spain, as Mexico was then called, to venture into the unexplored interior of North America. Rumors of the existence in the north of the mythical seven golden cities of Antilia (believed to have been founded by seven Portuguese bishops who had fled across the Atlantic during the eighth-century Moorish invasion of Iberia), drew Coronado into present-day Arizona and New Mexico. At Zuni, which the Spaniards had come to call Cíbola, the sight of

3. This question has been discussed in many sources. See, for example, G. S. Kirk, *Myth: Its Meaning and Functions in Ancient & Other Cultures* (Cambridge University Press, 1970), pp. 1–41 and especially pp. 11 and 28.

the humble mud-walled villages should have awakened him from his dream of Antilia. But Coronado expected to find seven cities, and he refused to be disappointed. He reported to the viceroy that seven towns existed at Zuni, although archaeological evidence suggests only six Zuni pueblos in Coronado's day.[4] Antilia itself, however, must lay beyond. Reports of the existence of still another rich kingdom, this called Quivira, permitted Coronado to dream again, and drew him onto the Great Plains, farther into the void.

Coronado was only one of the many Spanish explorers who engaged in what historian George Hammond once termed "the search for the fabulous."[5] Stories of mythical peoples and places, such as El Dorado (the gilded man), the lands of Amazon women occupied by Queen Calafia (from which the name California derives), or the Strait of Anián (known to the British as the Northwest Passage) were among the many motors that propelled Spanish adventurers both before and after Coronado's fruitless probe into the unknown. Perhaps the ultimate myth of the age of exploration was one in which Columbus came to believe—the ageless and enduring myth that a utopia exists on earth. On his third voyage to America in 1498, Columbus became convinced that the Terrestrial Paradise, the Garden of Eden, was somewhere in northern South America, and that he had sailed near it. The earth, he had come to believe, was not round, but pear shaped. It contained an appendage much like a woman's breast, he said, with the Garden of Eden located at the nipple—closest to heaven.[6]

Although Columbus's Terrestrial Paradise and Coronado's Quivira

4. Coronado to the Viceroy, August 3, 1540, quoted in Hammond and Rey, eds. and trans., *Narratives*, p. 170. F. W. Hodge, "The Six Cities of Cíbola," *New Mexico Historical Review* 1 (October 1926): 478–88. Hodge's view that only six pueblos existed in 1540 seems to be sustained by current scholarship. See, for example, T. J. Ferguson and E. Richard Hart, *A Zuni Atlas* (Norman: University of Oklahoma Press, 1985), p. 29 and Richard B. Woodbury, "Zuni Prehistory and History to 1850," in Alfonso Ortiz, ed., *Southwest*, vol. 9 of the *Handbook of North American Indians*, William C. Sturtevant, ed. (Washington: Smithsonian Institution, 1979), p. 469. Keith W. Kintigh, "Settlement, Subsistence, and Society in Late Zuni Prehistory," *Anthropological Papers of the University of Arizona*, 44 (Tucson: University of Arizona Press, 1985), pp. 5, 6, suggests that the question has not yet been settled.

5. George P. Hammond, "The Search for the Fabulous in the Settlement of the Southwest," *Utah Historical Quarterly* 24 (1956): 1–19.

6. Samuel Eliot Morison, *Admiral of the Ocean Sea: A Life of Christopher Columbus* (Boston: Little, Brown and Company, 1942), pp. 556–57. See, too, Henri Baudet, *Paradise on Earth: Some Thoughts on European Images of Non-European Man*, Elizabeth Wentholt, trans. (New Haven: Yale University Press, 1965).

proved to be fantasies, both explorers had every reason to believe in their existence. Oral traditions and books, the so-called romances of chivalry, had fired the imaginations of Spanish *conquistadores* with tales of Seven Cities and of Amazons, blurring the line between fact and fantasy. These "lying histories," as some critics termed the popular romances of the day, assured Spaniards that "easy wealth . . . abounded in these remote corners and exotic lands of the globe."[7] Moreover, Hernán Cortés and Francisco Pizarro had proved the existence of great kingdoms and extraordinary wealth. Coronado had ample precedent to follow.

Historians and folklorists have taken delight in telling and retelling the stories of the Spanish search for the fabulous. When Spaniards failed to locate treasure, modern writers have alluded to their search for mythical or imaginary places. When, on the other hand, the Spaniards did stumble onto a fabulous place, as Cortés did in the halls of Montezuma, or as Pizarro did in the Inca strongholds of Cajamarca and Cuzco, then we seem to leave the realm of myth and enter the world of reality. The line between myth and reality, however, is not as sharp as we often choose to believe.

In Mexico and in Peru, Cortés and Pizarro discovered treasure beyond imagining—and yet, this treasure existed only because of their imagining. Gold, the principal commodity that the Spaniards valued, has no intrinsic value in and of itself. Unlike essential commodities, such as food or shelter, whatever value gold held for the Spaniards was the value they invested in it through their own beliefs, or myths. But myth can be as powerful as reality, and Cortés exaggerated only slightly when he sent a message to Montezuma saying that the Spaniards had a disease of the heart that only gold could cure. The Aztecs, who apparently valued quetzal feathers as much as they valued gold, expressed amazement at the Spaniards' greed for gold and how, at the sight of it, the Spaniards "grinned like little beasts and patted each other with delight." Similarly, Arawak Indians in the Caribbean, to whom gold appears to have held little value, seemed astonished that Columbus and his followers wanted them to work for it.[8]

7. Irving A. Leonard, *Books of the Brave* (Cambridge: Harvard University Press, 1949), p. 53.

8. The quote is from Miguel León-Portilla, *The Broken Spears: The Aztec Account of the Conquest of Mexico* (Boston: Beacon Press, 1962), p. 68. For the Arawaks, see Carl Ortwin Sauer, *The Early Spanish Main* (Berkeley: University of California Press, 1969), pp. 61–62.

But we should not suppose smugly that the search for Quivira and other fabulous places was limited to credulous Spaniards. Contemporary Anglo Americans, and their English forebears, have also sought Quivira with as much fervor as any Spanish conquistador. In the Elizabethan era, early reports of America reached England in dulcet tones. With what one historian has called "tedious regularity," early English visitors to America "referred to it as the . . . 'garden of Eden,' 'this earthly paradise,' and this paradise of the worlde.'"[9] Englishmen were well aware of Spaniards' successes in extracting gold from this paradise. Indeed, reports had it that Spaniards had found gold everywhere. "No river, nor mountaine, and but few plaines . . . are vtterlie without it," one English chronicler noted.[10] Many Englishmen subscribed to the myth that gold existed only in warmer regions of the hemisphere, where the golden rays of the sun had greater power to work its alchemy. Unfortunately for Englishmen, by the time America beckoned them, Spaniards had already swarmed over the tropics. But Englishmen expected to find gold in North America, too. The gentlemen who planted English outposts at Roanoke and Jamestown searched vigorously for mines. "In the ende," however, as one Virginia colonist wrote, "all turned to vapore."[11]

Subsequent searches for gold in North America by Englishman and Spaniard alike also turned to "vapore," until the mid-nineteenth century when Anglo-Americans reached California's golden shores. Then, the treasure of the Sierra Nevada sent a new wave of dreamers westward. And on into our time, some continue to dream. No one who has lived long in the Southwest can remain oblivious to stories of seekers after buried treasure and lost mines. The searches for the lost Peg-leg mine in southern California, the lost Dutchman in the Superstition Mountains of Arizona, and the treasure of San Sabá in Texas come readily to mind. Legend has it that Palo Duro, through which Coronado passed, once yielded to treasure hunters a buried trunk of Spanish coins.

At times, modern-day treasure seekers have had fabulous success,

9. Contemporary accounts, quoted in Bernard W. Sheehan, *Savagism and Civility: Indians and Englishmen in Colonial Virginia* (Cambridge: Cambridge University Press, 1980), p. 11. Sheehan provides a succinct discussion of this question, and a guide to other sources.
10. Quoted in ibid., p. 14.
11. Quoted in ibid., p. 16.

especially when informed by facts. In one of the most celebrated cases,
Mel Fisher, assisted by historian Gene Lyon, found wreckage of the
Atocha, which sank in 1622 off of Florida's Marquesas Keys.[12] On the
other hand, less informed enthusiasts, who have taken at face value
oral traditions as fantastic as those of Quivira and Antilia, have squan-
dered treasure instead of finding it. For nearly two decades, for example, thousands of dollars and considerable human energy has been
expended in a futile search for the *Trinidad,* a vessel that probably
disappeared off the coast of Baja California early in 1540—the same
year that Coronado set out to explore the Southwest.

The *Trinidad* was one of three vessels sent out by Hernán Cortés
in 1539 to investigate rumors of wealth to the north of Mexico. Led
by Francisco de Ulloa, the *Trinidad* sailed up to the head of the Gulf
of California, where Ulloa discovered that Baja California was not an
island but a peninsula connected to the mainland. Ulloa piloted the
Trinidad southward along the peninsula, rounded its tip, and headed
north along its outer coast, vanishing somewhere north of Cedros
Island. Among historians of the expedition, Joseph James Markey, an
ophthamologist and amateaur archaeologist, stood alone in asserting
that Ulloa led the *Trinidad* as far north as the coast of present-day
California. Privy to documents that only he had seen, Markey knew
that the *Trinidad* came to an unhappy ending near the San Luis Rey
River—coincidentally the site of Markey's hometown of Oceanside.

Although Dr. Markey produced no convincing evidence to support
his position, beginning in 1968, if not before, a series of adventurers
and treasure hunters began to scour the ocean floor off the coast of
Oceanside. In fits and starts, the search has continued to the present
day. The hunt has gone on despite substantive doubts raised by professional historians about the soundness of Markey's position. It has
continued despite the fact that the artifacts that Markey presented to
support his case included a faked photograph of himself in a cave near
Oceanside (it was actually a mirror image of a photograph that he had
earlier claimed to have taken in Tahiti). Searches have continued
despite Markey's feeble defense of his position, which counted among
his stronger arguments the boast that the length of his entry in *Who's
Who in America* exceeded that of Richard Nixon. Finally, searchers
have continued although Markey died in December of 1985 without

12. Eugene Lyon, *The Search for the Atocha* (New York: Harper and Row, 1979).

producing the documentary evidence that he claimed to have discovered in Spain in 1951 and that he described in detail in numerous interviews with the media.[13]

Although the names have changed, then, the search for Quivira has continued. Yesterday's myths, legends, or stories—whatever we choose to call them—continue to lure today's treasure hunters into remote corners of the continent and under the waters of the Atlantic, the Pacific, and the Gulf of Mexico. With his customary combination of percipience and poetry, J. Frank Dobie aptly described those modern seekers after the fabulous as "Coronado's Children."[14]

Literally as well as figuratively, Coronado's children have sought Quivira. Full of hope and unencumbered by research, treasure hunters in the late nineteenth century mistakenly identified the ruins of two Franciscan missions, located in New Mexico on the edge of the high plains, as Coronado's Quivira. As a result, the abandoned seventeenth-century missions of San Isidro and San Buenaventura came to be called Quivira, and zealots tunneled under the ancient walls in a fruitless search. The power of the myth soon transcended the facts. When the ruined missions and the area around them fell under federal protection in 1909, the government dedicated the area as Gran Quivira National Monument, although the Quivira that Coronado sought was apparently a village of Wichita Indians located hundreds of miles away in present-day central Kansas.[15]

If the hope of finding fabulous places and scarce metals that they

13. The story is told in broad outline in Stephen T. Garrahy and David J. Weber, "Francisco de Ulloa, Joseph James Markey, and the Discovery of Upper California," *California Historical Society Quarterly* 50 (March 1971): 73–78, which was reprinted in the Southwest Section of the *San Diego Union*, July 11, 1971, along with photographs of the cave in Tahiti (full copies of each photo are in my possession). Markey's reply, with his quip about *Who's Who in America*, appeared the next week, in the *San Diego Union*, July 18, 1971. For a summary of efforts to find the *Trinidad*, and an interview with the head of the current crew, see two articles by Gordon Smith, "The Treasure Trove of the Trinidad," and "Some Experts Discount Tale of Gold Ship," *Los Angeles Times*, January 8, 1987.

14. The mystery of Palo Duro is discussed in J. Frank Dobie, *Coronado's Children: Tales of Lost Mines and Buried Treasures of the Southwest* (Dallas: Southwest Press, 1930), pp. 289–94.

15. *New Mexico: A Guide to the Colorful State* (New York: Hastings House for the Coronado Cuarto Centennial Commission, 1940), p. 339, Gordon Vivian, *Gran Quivira: Excavations in a 17th-Century Jumano Pueblo* (Washington, D.C.: National Park Service, 1964), pp. 31–33.

imbued with mythic value drove Coronado toward Quivira, so too did other Spanish beliefs and values that we might call myths. In 1540 when Coronado approached the Zuni town that he had believed would be one of the mythical Seven Cities of Antilia, but was known to his Indian informants as Cíbola, he found the natives prepared to resist him. They had removed the women, children, and elderly men to a safe place, and had hidden their most valuable moveable possessions, including turquoises but not gold, for they had none. As the Spaniards approached, Zuni warriors met them outside of the town and drew lines on the ground, ordering the Spaniards not to pass beyond them. The warriors drew these lines with sacred corn meal in the same manner, it would appear, as Pueblos do today to indicate places beyond which strangers may not pass during ceremonies.[16]

While the Zuni defenders waited to see if their sacred corn meal would be efficacious in turning back the unwelcome strangers, the Spanish warriors resorted to devices springing from their own myths. They read a statement to the Zunis, which learned men in Spain had prepared. This document summarized Spanish creation myths and explained how Spain's monarchs had indirectly received temporal power from a deity through one they called Pope. But the words in this *requerimiento,* or summons, spoken in prescribed form and attested to by a notary, failed to win the Indians' friendship. Thus, the Spaniards attacked the natives, crying out the name of Saint James, the Killer of Moors—"Santiago Matamoros!"—as an incantation.

Here, in this confrontation between the mythical power of the golden corn meal of the Zunis and the mythical power of the words brought by the golden-helmeted Coronado, two systems of signs and of religious thought, or what we might call myths, collided with one another. Spaniards of Coronado's day who subscribed to official Catholic doctrine believed in the existence of a single supreme being who was not of this earth, but who resided in an extraterrestrial place called heaven—a place that no living Spaniard had visited. The Spaniards' single god consisted of three persons surrounded by beings called angels and saints. Fiercely committed to religious orthodoxy, Spaniards officially held to the myth that their conception of the supernatural world was the only true one and that all others must yield to them (although

---

16. Herbert Eugene Bolton, *Coronado: Knight of Pueblos and Plains* (Albuquerque: University of New Mexico Press, 1964), pp. 119–20.

many Spaniards simultaneously engaged in religious practices that resembled those of Indians, including pantheistic worship at pre-Christian shrines).[17] In the *requerimiento,* drawn up about 1513, Spaniards asked indigenous peoples in what came to be called America to "acknowledge the [Catholic] Church as the ruler and superior of the whole world, and the high priest called Pope, and in his name the king and queen [of Spain]." Those aborigines who did so, the document said, would be treated well. Those who did not were assured that "with the help of God we shall forcefully . . . make war against you . . . take you and your wives and your children and shall make slaves of them . . . and shall do to you all the harm and damage that we can." This was the document Coronado read to the Zunis.[18]

Here we have, it seems to me, a classic case of a people summoning myth about the origin of their society and using myth to incite and justify action. Viewed in another way, however, it might also be said that the encounter between Coronado's Christians and Zuni theology represented a confrontation between Europeans, who saw themselves as people of history, and natives, whom the Europeans regarded as a people of myth.[19]

In a graceful and provocative essay, *Beyond Geography: The Western Spirit Against Wilderness,* Frederick Turner argues that the Spaniards' Judeo-Christian tradition had, in a sense, removed them from the world of myth. For Turner, the mythical world that Zunis and most, if not all, native Americans inhabited, teaches the interconnectedness of man and nature. In mythical religions, Turner suggests, spirits reside *in* the natural world, and the world itself has a cyclical, timeless quality. Spaniards, on the other hand, inherited a tradition in which human

17. See William A. Christian, Jr., *Local Religion in Sixteenth-Century Spain* (Princeton: Princeton University Press, 1981), pp. 3–4, 42–47, 161, and Christian, *Person and God in a Spanish Valley* (New York: Seminar Press, 1972), pp. 181–82.

18. The *requerimiento* is translated in Charles Gibson, ed., *The Spanish Tradition in America* (New York: Harper Torchbooks, 1968), pp. 59–60. Coronado mentions the reading of this document, with the attendance of a notary, in a letter to Viceroy Mendoza (August 3, 1540), quoted in George P. Hammond and Agapito Rey, ed. and trans., *Narratives of the Coronado Expedition, 1540–1542* (Albuquerque: University of New Mexico Press, 1940), pp. 167–68. See also p. 322.

19. This neat dichotomy is easy to exaggerate. For a recent scholarly articulation of this dichotomy, which juxtaposes the "biological outlook" of Indians and the "anthropological outlook" of Europeans (and, in the process, tendentiously romanticizes Indians) see Calvin Martin's Introduction to *The American Indian and the Problem of History* (New York: Oxford University Press, 1987), pp. 3–26.

existence, divorced from nature and myth, moved relentlessly forward in history—that is, forward in linear time instead of cyclical time. The Spaniards' otherworldly Christian god had created nature, but was not in nature. Christianity, Turner argues, "had effectively removed divinity from its [natural] world," leaving the world empty and devoid of spirit.[20] Thus, Turner suggests, what the Europeans ethnocentrically and wrongly called the *New* World, could be despoiled as well as subdued—its forests leveled, its grasses grazed to the ground, and even its native inhabitants destroyed in the name of progress by a people bound for glory in another world. Of course, the consequences of this legacy remain with us yet today. It has formed part of the foundation of our slowly changing attitudes toward wilderness, wildlife, and conservation, as well as toward those peoples who inhabited the wilderness of the Americas.

Coronado and his lieutenants seem to have been imbued with the sense of profound moral superiority that characterized Spain's onward moving Christian soldiers. Apparently certain that their god approved of their actions, Coronado and his companions invaded the lands of the Pueblos, permitted animals to eat the natives' crops, appropriated food and clothing as needed (no matter if Indians went hungry or cold), and destroyed those Pueblo villages that offered resistance.

Coronado, however, conducted his expedition more humanely than did many of his contemporaries. It contrasted sharply, for example, with the predatory plundering of the southeastern part of North America by Hernando de Soto, which occurred simultaneously with Coronados' *entrada* into the Southwest. An official investigation would later clear Coronado of any wrongdoing in his treatment of Indians, but this legal distinction would have brought little comfort to those Pueblos who lost their lives or loved ones as a result of Coronado's invasion. Coronado's men had committed numerous acts of violence toward the natives, but the worst had occurred during the so-called Tiguex War, when Spaniards led by García López de Cárdenas destroyed the pueblo of Arenal, set fire to the rooms to smoke out resistors, then captured fleeing Indians and burned them at the stake.[21]

20. Frederick Turner, *Beyond Geography: The Western Spirit Against Wilderness* (New York: Viking Press, 1980), p. 82.
21. Bolton, *Coronado*, pp. 210–13. As sympathetic as Bolton was to his subject, even he says of the Tiguex War that "one's sympathies are likely to be altogether in favor of the Indians, whose country had been invaded, and which they tried manfully to defend" (p. 229).

It is often said that we should not judge historical figures or events by the standards of our day, but by the standards of the age. This, of course, begs the question—which standards of an age? Clearly, several standards of conduct, some of them contradictory, may exist simultaneously. If we judge Coronado according to the standards set by rapacious thugs such as Nuño de Guzmán, the notorious slave hunter of Nueva Galicia, then Coronado looks good indeed. If, on the other hand, we judge Coronado by the standards of another of his contemporaries, the celebrated Dominican "Protector of the Indians," Bartolomé de las Casas, who questioned the morality of Spanish imperialism in the Americas, then Coronado's invasion of the lands of Cíbola and Quivira was illegal and immoral.[22]

By any standard of his day, however, Coronado's expedition failed. He discovered nothing that a sixteenth-century Spanish official would regard as treasure. Lured by myth into the unknown, Coronado lost his fortune, health, and prestige. Pedro de Castañeda, chronicler of the expedition, put the best light on this failure when he wrote: "Granted that they did not find the riches of which they had been told, [but] they found a place in which to search for them."[23] Even that place, however (what we call today the American Southwest), was soon forgotten and new myths developed about the land. Writing some two decades after Coronado's return, Castañeda lamented that new myths about New Mexico had developed—strange ideas about its geography, imaginary animals, and confusion about its natives. "People," Castañeda wrote, "very frequently magnify or belittle, without regard to reality, things which they have heard, perhaps from those who were not familiar with them."[24]

In an age in which continuity, rather than discontinuity, characterized the work of terrestrial explorers,[25] the geographical discoveries of Coronado's expedition had to be rediscovered by the next

22. For Guzmán, see Donald E. Chipman's sympathetic biography, *Nuño de Guzmán and the Province of Pánuco in New Spain, 1518–1533* (Glendale, Ca.: The Arthur H. Clark Co., 1967). There are many editions of works by Las Casas and studies of his life. See, for example, Bartolomé de las Casas, *History of the Indies*, Andrée M. Collard, ed. and trans. (New York: Harper Torchbooks, 1971).

23. Dobie, *Coronado's Children*, p. viii.

24. Castañeda's Narrative, in Hammond and Rey, ed. and trans., *Narratives of the Coronado Expedition*, p. 192.

25. See Eugene Lyon, "Continuity in the Age of Conquest: The Establishment of Spanish Sovereignty in the Sixteenth Century," in R. Reid Badger and Lawrence A. Clayton, eds. *Alabama and the Borderlands* (University: University of Alabama Press, 1985), pp. 154–61.

generation of Europeans to penetrate the northern frontier of New Spain. Forty years after Coronado's failure, in 1581, the so-called Chamuscado-Rodríguez expedition made its way up the Rio Grande to the lands of the Pueblos, naming the area San Felipe del Nuevo México. The leaders of the expedition believed themselves to be the first Spaniards to visit the Pueblos. In an apparent reference to Coronado, the chief chronicler of the Chamuscado-Rodríguez expedition, Hernán Gallegos, noted that "before this time numerous Spaniards with ample commissions from the viceroys of New Spain had entered the land in an attempt to discover this settlement, and they had not found it. Thus we concluded that our project was directed by the hand of God."[26]

The rediscovery of New Mexico gave rise, of course, to new myths, as the search for the fabulous continued. Once Juan de Oñate had planted a semblance of a permanent settlement in New Mexico in 1598, for example, he set out in all directions to make new discoveries. Following a trip from New Mexico to what he believed to be the Pacific, Oñate had sent Father Francisco de Escobar to Mexico to report in detail on how the expedition learned of "extraordinary riches and monstrosities never heard of before."[27] Along the route to the Pacific, Father Escobar explained to the viceroy in exquisite detail, Oñate's small band had learned of, but never actually saw, a variety of curious peoples: one group had ears so large that they hung on the ground; another never ate, but lived only on the odor of their food "because they lacked the natural means of discharging excrement"; and still another "whose men had virile members so long that they wound them four times around the waist, and in the act of copulation the man and woman were far apart."[28] Indians who passed these stories on to the credulous members of the Oñate party must have had a fine

26. George P. Hammond and Agapito Rey, ed. and trans., *The Rediscovery of New Mexico, 1580–1594* (Albuquerque: University of New Mexico Press, 1966), p. 83.

27. Oñate to the Viceroy, San Bartolomé, August 7, 1605, in George P. Hammond and Agapito Rey, eds. and trans., *Don Juan de Oñate: Colonizer of New Mexico, 1595–1628* (2 vols.; Albuquerque: University of New Mexico Press, 1953), 2: 1007.

28. Father Escobar's Report (mistitled a "diary"), in Hammond and Rey, eds. and trans., *Don Juan de Oñate*, 2: 1025 (see, too, p. 1029 for Escobar presenting this report to the viceroy).

time, but the viceroy was not amused. "This conquest is becoming a fairy tale," Viceroy Montesclaros wrote to the king.[29]

The fairy tales continued, and old myths endured alongside the new. Nearly a century after Coronado failed to find gold at Quivira, Fray Alonso de Benavides solemnly reported that a Portuguese pilot had sailed to Quivira from the Atlantic coast, and found the Indians of Quivira possessed of "earrings and necklaces of gold, very bulky and so soft that with the fingers they made of them whatever they wished."[30] Meanwhile, one of Fray Benavides's contemporaries, Fray Antonio de la Ascención, urged new efforts to explore the California coast, locate the Strait of Anián, and "learn in what place and locality the great city of Quivira is located."[31] Since the 1550s, when a European map-maker misread one of the early chronicles and put Quivira to the northwest of New Mexico instead of the northeast, cartographers had placed Quivira on or near the Pacific at about 40° north latitude. Some put it near the mouth of the Strait of Anián. Until the end of the eighteenth century, this bit of mythical geography continued to show up on new maps depicting the Pacific coast of North America.[32] Clearly, Coronado and his successors, including Oñate, had failed to puncture the inflated myth of Quivira, which continued to float on the horizon of the Spanish imagination from the Pacific Ocean to the prairies of Kansas.

If Coronado failed to find his dream, failed to dispell rumors of wealth to the north, and failed to situate New Mexico firmly so that it had to be rediscovered, why is he so well remembered? Why in the

29. October 28, 1605, Mexico City, in Hammond and Rey, eds. and trans., *Don Juan de Oñate*, 2: 1009.

30. *The Memorial of Fray Alonso de Benavides, 1630*, Frederick Webb Hodge and Charles Fletcher Lummis, eds., Mrs. Edward E. Ayer, trans. (Chicago: Privately printed, 1916), p. 64.

31. Antonio de la Ascención to the king, Pueblo, March 22, 1632, translated in Homer Aschmann, "A Late Recounting of the Vizcaíno Expedition and Plans for the Settlement of California," *Journal of California Anthropology* 1 (Winter 1974): 182. See, too, W. Michael Mathes, ed. and trans., *Spanish Approaches to the Island of California, 1628–1632* (San Francisco: Book Club of California, 1975), for the context of Ascención's understanding, and for a similar statement by Ascención, written in 1629 (p. 21).

32. Henry R. Wagner, "Quivira: A Mythical California City," *California Historical Society Quarterly* 3 (October 1924): 262–67; Wagner, *The Cartography of the Northwest Coast of America to the Year 1800* (2 vols.; Berkeley: University of California Press, 1937), pp. 43–45; Carl I. Wheat, *Mapping the Transmississippi West* (5 vols. in 6; Institute of Historical Cartography, 1957–63), 1: 151.

modern Southwest have we perpetuated his name in literature, in symposia, in the names of hotels, motels, and highways, in places on the land, on historic monuments and markers, and in the pageantry, festivals, and celebrations held in hundreds of communities during the Coronado Cuartocentennial of 1940? There are many reasons to remember Coronado and to judge his expedition a success, but these have more to do with the standards of our day than with his. The playwright Thomas Wood Stevens, whose drama, "The Entrada of Coronado," was written and performed for the Coronado Cuartocentennial, recognized this when he put these words in Coronado's mouth: "What we have won is a knowledge and a vision. It is not proved that we went in vain, for only the centuries to come can make this sure."[33]

In the twentieth century, we have concluded that Coronado did not go "in vain." We are fascinated with stories of those Europeans who went first into unknown lands, and Coronado did so on a grand scale, exploring an area substantially larger than the Iberian peninsula.[34] We love stories of adventure, and we admire courage. Coronado's expedition provides examples of both. His biographer, Herbert Eugene Bolton, termed him the "Knight of Pueblos and Plains." Perhaps no other figure in the Spanish exploration of North America conjures up such powerful, romantic associations. In 1955, when Hollywood director Robert D. Webb made a film about Spanish settlement of California, he entitled it *Seven Cities of Gold.* Although no Spaniards ever thought the Seven Cities were in California, and even though Spanish colonization of California got underway in 1769, 239 years after Coronado had dispelled the myth of the Seven Cities, the myth of Seven Cities proved as irresistible to Hollywood filmmakers as it had been to Coronado.[35]

On a loftier level, we treasure the records of the Coronado expedition for the unique information they provide about the early ethnology and ecology of the lands through which Coronado passed. As one archaeologist has put it, Coronado's expedition "represents a

33. Thomas Wood Stevens, *The Entrada of Coronado: A Spectacular Historic Drama* (Albuquerque: Coronado Cuarto Centennial Commission, 1940), p. 131.

34. The square miles embraced by the present-day states of Arizona and New Mexico alone (235,575) exceed those of Spain and Portugal combined (230,438).

35. See Donald C. Cutter, "With a Little Help from Their Saints," *Pacific Historical Review* 52 (May 1984): 135. In this article, Cutter recalls that Billy Wilder directed the film, but the *New York Times* review of October 8, 1955, credits Robert D. Webb as director. Letter, Cutter to Weber, December 11, 1984.

watershed that is important to us all. With Coronado came literacy in the sense that his exploits were written down. . . . So, with the coming of Coronado, the line between history and prehistory was established"[36]—or, could we say, the line between a world that we imagine is perceived through history and a world that we suppose is understood through myth?

In many communities, Coronado is remembered because he extends their recorded histories back in linear time—back to the days of the *conquistadores*. So it was in Kansas, for example, that the discovery near present-day Lyons of the site of the Wichita villages that Coronado believed to be Quivira, led the local newspaper editor to exclaim quite accurately how "visitors from Europe traveled through Kansas . . . seventy-nine years before Captain John Smith swashbuckled through the street of Jamestown and 235 years before the Declaration of Independence was signed in Philadelphia."[37]

At the most fundamental level, we honor Coronado because he honors us. In a broad sense, most of us are Coronado's children. He was one of us—a European—and we hold many of his values yet today. Lest there be any doubt of this, suppose for a moment that events had turned out differently in the sixteenth century. Suppose—as absurd as this might seem—that the conquest of America had been reversed. By 1550 the Aztecs had united under a new leader and expelled the Spaniards from Mexico. Imagine that during three decades of Spanish rule the Aztecs had learned from their conquerors how to forge steel weapons, make firearms, and construct large vessels. Instead of contenting themselves with driving the Spaniards from American shores, the Aztecs followed them across the Atlantic and invaded Europe.

Let us further imagine what an Aztec victory would have meant for the ways in which Coronado and the myth of Quivira would be remembered today. We might be living in an Indian America, where Coronado would be vilified as one of many invaders rather than respected as an explorer. Rather than the "Knight of Pueblos and Plains," our hero would certainly be a native, most likely the Plains Indian the Spaniards called El Turco. Historians have suggested that The Turk participated in a plot to lead Coronado astray on the level, treeless

36. Emil W. Haury, "The Search for Chichilticale," *Arizona Highways Magazine* (April 1984): 14.

37. Paul A. Jones, *Coronado and Quivira* (Lyons, Kansas: Lyons Publishing Company, 1937), p. 1.

plains of eastern New Mexico and West Texas, thereby removing him from the Pueblo world.[38] The scheme failed, and El Turco became a martyr, garroted by Coronado's order after the Spaniards discovered his ruse. In an Indian America, stories passed from generation to generation might have celebrated El Turco as a kind of indigenous Br'er Rabbit; instead of historical markers and place names honoring Coronado, an Indian America might have erected monuments to El Turco. But it is a truism that victors usually write history and that one society's heroes may be another's villains. As understood in this context, perhaps the line between history and myth is not as sharp as we often suppose it is, or would like it to be.[39]

In 1940, Clinton P. Anderson, serving as managing director of the United States Coronado Exposition Commission, suggested that "subsequent generations living in the Spanish Southwest have come to find the riches which Coronado missed."[40] Today, record numbers of newcomers, still in search of "riches," swell the populations of the states that Coronado explored. What will be our new Quiviras? What will be our new myths and our new realities? What will be the unintended consequences of the search?

In our search for riches, will we make the Southwest a garden that yields abundant crops, or will we deplete water resources and create a new desert? In our search for riches, will large-scale dams furnish ample water and hydroelectric power, or will the next generation view those dams as silt-filled monuments to the misuse of technology? In our search for riches, will nuclear energy provide inexpensive power, or become the vehicle for mass destruction? As Americans from the frostbelt move south to seek their fortunes, will the Sunbelt become the scene of a new America of individual self-fulfillment and social justice, or the setting for self-indulgence and narcissism? Will the Southwest be a land of opportunity for those Mexican immigrants who continue to follow Coronado's trails north from Mexico, or will many find that they have come in quest of another Quivira? Or will Mexican

38. Bolton, *Coronado*, pp. 301–2.

39. For an especially suggestive essay that looks at the value of myth, see M. I. Finley, "Myth, Memory and History," in Finley, *The Use and Abuse of History* (1st ed., 1975; New York: Penguin Books, 1987), pp. 11–33.

40. Foreword to George P. Hammond, *Coronado's Seven Cities* (Albuquerque: United States Coronado Exposition Commission, 1940), p. ii.

immigration Hispanicize this region and turn it into another Quebec, "reversing the consequences of the Mexican-American War," as some have warned? Or is that, too, a myth? Finally, in our relentless plunge toward the future, will we preserve enough of the past and understand our history well enough to remind us and our children of where we have been? Or is it a myth that we need to know where we have been if we are to know where we are going?

Clearly, it has not been given to any generation to know when it is pursuing an impossible dream or an obtainable goal, and there can be merit in either pursuit. But a study of the past should warn us to ask with frequency which is which—which is the impossible dream and which the obtainable goal? The arid southwestern landscape is dotted with the wreckage of those who, like Coronado, pushed on mindlessly toward chimeras. Abandoned cliff dwellings testify to man's puniness in the face of nature. The empty streets of ghost towns testify to the limits of resources and the uncertainties of market forces beyond our control. And the barren lives of some of the oldest residents of these lands—Indians and Mexicans—testify to the dolorous consequences of putting private gain above the public good.

It was Coronado's fortune that a fall from his horse, which knocked him senseless, brought him to his senses. The blow led him to turn away from his quest for the mythical Quivira and to return to the reality of family and friends in Mexico. In our time, the blow that may knock us senseless is one from which there will be no recovering. Let us hope that through public discourse, we may chart a safe course through the perilous myths that lie beyond 1984—even if that discourse is funded by big government. Orwell would have approved of the ends, if not the means.

2

Fray Marcos de Niza and the Historians[*]

In 1949, Southern Methodist University published *The Journey of Fray Marcos,* edited and translated by Cleve Hallenbeck. Designed by Carl Hertzog and illustrated by José Cisneros the book won the most prestigious award in American bookmaking that year. In some circles *The Journey of Fray Marcos* has been more admired for its appearance than for its contents, but among scholars it still enjoys a reputation as the definitive English edition of the account of the sixteenth-century friar who purported to travel up the Pacific slope of New Spain into the heart of what is today the American Southwest.

A meteorologist by profession, for some thirty years Cleve Hallenbeck had spent much of his non-working hours tracing the trails of Spanish-Mexican explorers in Texas, New Mexico, Arizona, and northern Mexico—"by auto, motorcycle, horse, mule and afoot."[1] Working out of Roswell, New Mexico, where he had been in charge of a regional office of the U.S. Weather Bureau, Hallenbeck had published a number of works on meteorology, and three earlier books on southwestern history, including the classic *Journey and Route of Alvar Nuñez Cabeza de Vaca* (1940). With the completion of his work on Cabeza de Vaca, Hallenbeck had begun a book-length manuscript called "Southwestern Trails," in which he intended to tell the stories

*This essay, presented at the Sixteenth Century Studies Conference, Arizona State University, October 31, 1987, derives from my introduction to a reprint edition Cleve Hallenbeck's *Journey of Fray Marcos* (1st ed., 1949; Dallas: SMU Press, 1987).

1. Hallenbeck to Maxwell, March 26, 1948, Hallenbeck File in the private collection of Allen Maxwell, Dallas, hereinafter cited as Maxwell Collection. See, too, the "Biographical Note" in Hallenbeck, *Fray Marcos,* p. 109.

of a number of famous roads, including the routes between New Mexico and California and the Santa Fe Trail. In the course of studying those trails he had become diverted by Fray Marcos. "That old boy really took my husband on a wild goose chase," his wife later recalled. "It took a book to settle [Fray Marcos]."[2]

Cleve Hallenbeck had chased Fray Marcos de Niza into one of the knottiest controversies in the annals of the exploration of North America—a controversy that has not yet been resolved. Did Fray Marcos's journey of 1539 take him to Cíbola, as he said it did, or is his account of that journey exaggerated? If Fray Marcos told the truth, then he deserves to be remembered as the first European to explore purposefully what is today the American Southwest; only the party of Alvar Núñez Cabeza de Vaca, shipwrecked and lost, appears to have preceded Fray Marcos's expedition into the region.

In the wake of Cabeza de Vaca came rumors that he had found magnificent cities, rich with gold. Viceroy Antonio de Mendoza, eager to establish the Crown's claim and to stave off rivals such as Hernán Cortés and Hernando de Soto, sought to investigate these reports quietly. Thus he assembled a small party, headed by a Franciscan friar, to reconnoiter the region from which Cabeza de Vaca had returned. Apparently an experienced traveler and champion of American Indians, Fray Marcos had served in Central America and in Peru before settling in Mexico City in 1537. To guide Fray Marcos, Mendoza sent Esteban, a black slave who had been with Cabeza de Vaca.

Within a year, Fray Marcos had returned to Mexico City. In a written *Relación*, or report, he claimed to have seen a city "bigger than the city of Mexico."[3] The city, the friar had learned, was called Cíbola[4]

2. Juanita Hallenbeck to Allen Maxwell, August 13, 1949, private collection of Pomona Hallenbeck, Roswell, New Mexico (hereinafter cited as Hallenbeck Collection). Mrs. Hallenbeck says "last winter, my husband worked frenziedly to finish a book-length [manuscript] that had been hanging fire for several years." She goes on to say that he was "diverted to investigate Alvar Nunez," but I believe that she misspoke. Had Cabeza de Vaca diverted Hallenbeck's attention from the trails manuscript, which had been "hanging fire for several years," then it would have gone back to the 1930s—more than several years—because the Cabeza de Vaca book appeared in 1940. The Hallenbecks' daughter, Pomona, also recalls that Fray Marcos, not Cabeza de Vaca, was the diversion. The "Southwestern Trails" manuscript is in Hallenbeck Collection.

3. The "Narrative of Fray Marcos," in Hallenbeck, *Fray Marcos*, p. 34.

4. Some contemporaries applied the name to the Zuni province, consisting of six towns, and some applied the name to the single Zuni town that Esteban and Coronado,

and was just the smallest of seven cities in a country that appeared to be "the greatest and best of the discoveries." This was an extravagant recommendation from a man who knew firsthand the wealth of Mexico and Peru. Fray Marcos did not, however, claim to have entered Cíbola. He noted in his report that he feared that he might meet the same fate as Esteban, whom the Cibolans had killed. Thus, he said, he had viewed the rich city from a prudent distance.

On the strength of Fray Marcos's *Relación* (ably translated by Hallenbeck),[5] and of verbal reports that apparently contained even greater exaggerations,[6] Viceroy Mendoza launched one of the most elaborate

---

and perhaps Fray Marcos, visited. For a discussion of this question, see Carroll L. Riley, "The Road to Hawikuh: Trade and Trade Routes to Cibola-Zuni During Late Prehistoric and Early Historic Times," *The Kiva* 41 (Winter 1975): 140–44.

5. Hallenbeck's was by no means the first translation of the *Relación* into English, and he must have benefited from previous translations. No fresh translation has appeared in print since Hallenbeck's. His must be considered the standard work. The *Relación* first became available to the English-reading public in the final and enlarged edition of Richard Hakluyt's *Principall navigations, voiages and discoveries of the English nation*, 3 vols. (London: 1598–1600), 3: 366–73. Although the flawed Hakluyt translation had been rendered from an Italian translation rather than from the original Spanish, and even though Adolph Bandelier characterized the translation as "quite indifferent," it was reprinted in Fanny Bandelier, trans., and Adolph Bandelier, ed., *The Journey of Alvar Nuñez Cabeza de Vaca* (New York: A. S. Barnes, 1905), pp. 195, 203–31. At least three other English langauge translations appeared prior to Hallenbeck's: Percy M. Baldwin, "Fray Marcos de Niza and His Discovery of the Seven Cities of Cíbola," *New Mexico Historical Review* 1 (April 1926): 193–223; Bonaventure Oblasser, *His Own Personal Narrative of Arizona Discovered by Fray Marcos de Niza Who in 1539 First Entered These Parts on His Quest for the Seven Cities of Cibola* (Topawa, Ariz.: n.p., 1939); and George P. Hammond and Agapito Rey, eds. and trans., *Narratives of the Coronado Expedition, 1540–1542* (Albuquerque: University of New Mexico Press, 1940), pp. 58–82.

Baldwin and Hallenbeck based their translations on the printed version found in the Joaquín Pacheco and Francisco de Cárdenas, *Colección de documentos inéditos relativos al descubrimiento . . . del real Archivo de Indias*, 42 vols. (Madrid: Archivo General de Indias, 1864–1884): III: 325–51. Oblasser and Hammond and Rey made their translations from identical manuscript copies in the Archivo General de Indias, in Seville. Henry R. Wagner, "Fr. Marcos de Niza," *New Mexico Historical Review* 9 (April 1934): 202, found the differences between the printed and the manuscript versions inconsequential. Carl Sauer, "The Credibility of the Fray Marcos Account," *New Mexico Historical Review* 16 (April 1941): 233, finds the printed Pacheco and Cárdenas version "remarkably exact except for . . . three mistakes," the most important of which had to do with substituting *legua* for *jornada*—an error that Hallenbeck corrected (see Hallenbeck, *Fray Marcos*, p. 103, n. 136).

6. Wagner, "Fr. Marcos de Niza," p. 223, quotes letters of August 23 and October 9, 1539, from Bishop Zumárraga and Fray Gerónimo Ximenez, with whom Fray Marcos apparently spoke. See, too, Carl Sauer, *Sixteenth Century North America: The Land*

and significant of Spain's reconnaissances of the interior of North America, that of Francisco Vázquez de Coronado. With Fray Marcos along as a guide, Coronado reached "Cíbola" in July of 1540. Before him stood one of the modest villages of the Zuni Indians in what is today western New Mexico, near the Arizona border. The gulf between the tiny Indian pueblo, numbering perhaps 100 families, and the great city of Fray Marcos's description led Coronado to pronounce Fray Marcos a liar: "He has not told the truth in a single thing that he said, but everything is the opposite of what he related, except the name of the cities and the large stone houses."[7] Another of Fray Marcos's contemporaries, Pedro de Castañeda, a soldier who marched with Coronado in 1540, learned that when Fray Marcos had received reports of the death of Esteban he had been sixty leagues from Cíbola. Fray Marcos and his entourage, Castañeda wrote, were "seized with such fear . . . they turned back without seeing more land than what the Indians had told them of. On the contrary, they were traveling by forced marches, with their habits up to their waists."[8]

Since Coronado's day, scholars have been divided as to whether or not Fray Marcos came within sight of Cíbola on his 1539 journey, or whether fear of meeting the same fate as Esteban had led him to fabricate that entire portion of his report to the viceroy. In the 1940s, when Hallenbeck was preparing his critical edition of Fray Marcos's *Relación*, the Franciscan's own version of events appeared as fact in the writings of the most eminent historians and anthropologists of the Southwest, including Hubert Howe Bancroft, Adolph Bandelier, Woodbury Lowery, Herbert Eugene Bolton, George P. Hammond, and in an earlier work of Hallenbeck himself.[9] Only a handful of scholars

---

and the People as Seen by the Europeans (Berkeley: University of California Press, 1971), p. 128.

7. Coronado to Viceroy Mendoza, August 3, 1540, in Hammond and Rey, eds. and trans., *Narratives of the Coronado Expedition*, p. 170. For the size of Hawikuh, see Hallenbeck, *Fray Marcos*, p. 40.

8. Hammond and Rey, eds. and trans., *Narratives of the Coronado Expedition*, p. 199. Cortés also believed Fray Marcos a liar; see Wagner, "Fr. Marcos de Niza," pp. 218–20.

9. Bancroft, *History of Arizona and New Mexico, 1530–1888* (San Francisco: History Company, 1889), p. 34; Rodack, trans. and ed., *Adolph F. Bandelier's The Discovery of New Mexico*, cites Bandelier's writings on this subject; Lowery, *The Spanish Settlements Within the Present Limits of the United States, 1513–1561* (New York: Putnam, 1901), pp. 260–78, 467–68; Bolton, *Spanish Borderlands: A Chronicle of Old Florida and the Southwest* (New Haven: Yale University Press, 1921), pp. 86–87 (Bolton later

doubted Fray Marcos. Among the skeptics were two nineteenth-century writers, Henri Ternaux-Compans and Henry Haynes.[10] In the twentieth century, bibliophile Henry R. Wagner, historical geographer Carl Sauer, and Coronado's biographer A. Grove Day unequivocally challenged Fray Marcos's veracity and led some other writers to take an equivocal stance.[11]

Both Henry Wagner and Carl Sauer wrote extended essays on Fray Marcos and both influenced Grove Day and Cleve Hallenbeck. Wagner put his doubts in writing at least as early as 1926, arguing that Fray Marcos failed to get north of the Gila River, "all the rest being imagination."[12] Wagner elaborated upon this theme in subsequent writing, by which time he seems to have been influenced by Carl Sauer.[13] Sauer knew the terrain over which Fray Marcos had traveled, and argued that the Franciscan explorer could not have made the journey in the length of time that he said he did. Sauer pointed out

---

modified his views—see below, n. 50); George P. Hammond and Agapito Rey, eds. and trans., *New Mexico in 1602: Juan de Montoya's Relation of the Discovery of New Mexico* (Albuquerque: Quivira Society, 1938), p. 16; and Hammond and Rey, eds. and trans., *Narratives of the Coronado Expedition*, p. 5. For Hallenbeck's own earlier endorsement of Fray Marcos's story, see his *Legends of the Spanish Southwest*, written with Juanita H. Williams (Glendale: Arthur H. Clark Co., 1938), p. 20: "a careful perusal of his [Fray Marcos's] written report convinces us that Fray Marcos did not intentionally fabricate his evidence."

10. Ternaux-Compans, *Voyages, relations et mémoires originaux, pour servir a l'histoire de la découverte de l'Amérique*, 21 vols. (Paris: Arthus Bertan, 1837–41), 9: vi; Haynes, "Early Exploration of New Mexico," in Justin Winsor, ed., *Narrative and Critical History of America*, 8 vols. (Boston: Houghton, Mifflin & Co., 1884–1889), 2: 473–504. Vol. 2 was copyrighted in 1886; Hallenbeck's 1889 date is incorrect.

11. Wagner and Sauer are discussed below. For Day, see his *Coronado's Quest: The Discovery of the Southwestern United States* (Berkeley: University of California Press, 1940), pp. 59 and n. 22, pp. 331–33, which provides a fine summary of the arguments against Fray Marcos. Wagner and Sauer apparently also influenced Frederick Webb Hodge, *History of Hawikuh, New Mexico: One of the So-Called Cities of Cíbola* (Los Angeles: Ward Ritchie Press, 1937), pp. 26–27, and Herbert Eugene Bolton, *Coronado: Knight of Pueblos and Plains* (Albuquerque: University of New Mexico Press, 1949), pp. 35–36, both of whom judiciously provide their readers with both interpretations (Bolton's biography appeared in the same year as Hallenbeck's *Fray Marcos*, and could not have influenced Hallenbeck or been influenced by him).

12. H. R. Wagner, letter to the editor of the *New Mexico Historical Review* 1, 3 (July 1926): 371, taking issue with Baldwin, "Fray Marcos de Niza," p. 193, who credited Fray Marcos with being the first European to "indisputably set foot on the soil of New Mexico."

13. Wagner, "Fr. Marcos de Niza," pp. 184–227, and Wagner, *The Spanish Southwest, 1542–1794: An Annotated Bibliography*, 2 vols. (1st ed., 1937; reprint New York: Arno Press, 1967), I: 89–103.

serious inconsistencies in Fray Marcos's story, which he labeled "a tissue of fraud, perhaps without equal in the history of New World explorations."[14] Whereas Wagner had termed Fray Marcos a "liar," but excused his exaggerations because he regarded Fray Marcos as a victim of an "overheated imagination" warped by the "overcharged atmosphere" of early sixteenth-century gold rushes, Sauer took a less charitable view of Fray Marcos's motives.[15] Sauer explained Fray Marcos's *Relación* as a calculated lie—"a political instrument" designed to block the claims of Cortés and others to the north country. In the 1940s, Hallenbeck embraced Sauer's conspiratorial view.[16]

Refining and elaborating upon the Wagner-Sauer position, Hallenbeck became the first to devote a book to the question of Fray Marcos. In *The Journey of Fray Marcos*, Hallenbeck termed Fray Marcos a "plain liar."[17] Like Sauer, with whom he corresponded, Hallenbeck argued that the friar could not have maintained the pace of travel that would have taken him to Zuni and back to Compostela as quickly as his official report suggests, and concluded that Fray Marcos traveled no farther than the upper Sonora Valley, only two-thirds of the way to Cíbola and *below* the present-day boundary between Arizona and Mexico. Hallenbeck found no evidence in Fray Marcos's *Relación* that the priest had seen any of the topographic features or peoples of present-day Arizona. Hallenbeck offered additional negative evidence that Fray Marcos had not seen Arizona, observing that when Fray Marcos returned to the Far North with Coronado, he was unable to provide Coronado with "any idea how far it was to Cíbola," and that on the one occasion when he offered an estimate of distance, Fray Marcos was extraordinarily far from the mark.[18]

14. Between 1932 and 1940, Sauer advanced his arguments in at least three publications, all noted in Hallenbeck's bibliography, and summarized those arguments in *Sixteenth Century North America*, pp. 127–29. The quote is from Sauer, "The Credibility of the Fray Marcos Account," p. 243.

15. Wagner, "Fr. Marcos de Niza," pp. 216, 226–27.

16. Hallenbeck, *Fray Marcos*, pp. 90–95, who also summarizes the views of Sauer and a number of historians on this question of motivation (pp. 70–73).

17. *Fray Marcos*, p. 73. Hallenbeck also summarized his views on Fray Marcos in another book published after his death: *Land of the Conquistadores* (Caldwell, Idaho: Caxton Printers, 1950), pp. 21–27.

18. "At the Gila River, Marcos told Coronado that the coast was only five leagues (fifteen miles) away, and that he had seen it; but Coronado learned from the Indians that it was ten *jornadas* (about three hundred miles) distant, as in fact it was." Hallenbeck, *Fray Marcos*, p. 76. Following Hallenbeck's death, Hertzog and Maxwell

Taken together, the arguments of Sauer and Hallenbeck seemed to make an overwhelming case against Fray Marcos's assertion that he had seen Cíbola. As Hallenbeck put it, "there can be no question as to what would be the ruling of any civilized court of today on this case."[19] Reviewers of Hallenbeck's *Fray Marcos*, with the exception of the Franciscan historian Angélico Chávez, agreed. They expressed sentiments much like those of Hubert Herring, Professor of History at Pomona College, who wrote in the *New York Herald Tribune* that "Hallenbeck disposes of whatever reputation for veracity the monk had." Hallenbeck's conclusions, another review noted, "appear to be inescapable."[20]

Appearances, of course, can be deceiving. A substantial number of writers and southwestern specialists have found Hallenbeck's conclusions eminently escapable. Nearly forty years after the publication of *Fray Marcos*, the Wagner-Sauer-Hallenbeck school has made some impact on the region's historiography, but most writers have ignored the controversy and continue to take Fray Marcos at his word. Among general overviews of the history of the Southwest written since Hallenbeck's day, only those by Paul Wellman and David Lavender retell Fray Marcos's story with skepticism.[21] Most of the general histories of the Southwest (including those by Paul Horgan, W. Eugene Hollon, Lynn Perrigo, and Odie Faulk) not only take Fray Marcos all the way to Cíbola, but also fail to give their readers a hint that the Franciscan

discussed the possibility of getting Carl Sauer to write an introduction to *Fray Marcos*, an idea that Mrs. Hallenbeck endorsed, indicating that "the two men conducted a lively correspondence . . . and there seemed to be a good deal of mutual admiration." Maxwell to Hertzog, August 15, 1949, quoting Juanita Hallenbeck, Maxwell Collection, Journey File.

19. Hallenbeck, *Fray Marcos*, p. 76.

20. Herring's review appeared in the *New York Herald Tribune Book Review*, October 29, 1950. The second quote is from John T. Winterich, *Saturday Review*, May 6, 1950. See, too, Joseph Henry Jackson, *San Francisco Chronicle*, July 9, 1950; Gerald Ashford, "'Journey of Fray Marcos' Explodes Historic Lie," *San Antonio Express*, March 26, 1950; and E. DeGolyer, *Dallas Morning News Book Supplement*, December 4, 1949, who also find Hallenbeck convincing. Exceptions include Fray Angélico Chávez, in the *New Mexico Historical Review* 25 (July 1950): 255–59, and perhaps Arthur Aiton, whose confused statement appeared in the *American Historical Review* 55 (July 1950): 1006.

21. Paul I. Wellman, *Glory, God and Gold: A Narrative History* (Garden City, N.J.: Doubleday, 1954), pp. 16–17 and David Lavender, *The Southwest* (New York: Harper & Row, 1980), p. 39.

might have fabricated his account.[22] The same pattern prevails among general works on the Spanish era in the Southwest,[23] and among histories of the individual southwestern states of California, Arizona, New Mexico, and Texas.[24] The authors of most of these works take Fray Marcos to the edge of Cíbola; a minority suggest that he might

22. Paul Horgan, *Great River: The Rio Grande in North American History*, 2 vols. (New York: Rinehart & Co., 1954): I, 106–7; Lynn Perrigo, *Texas and Our Spanish Southwest* (Dallas: Banks Upshaw & Co., 1960), pp. 18–20; W. Eugene Hollon, *The Southwest: Old and New* (New York: Alfred A. Knopf, 1967), pp. 54–55; Odie B. Faulk, *Land of Many Frontiers: A History of the American Southwest* (New York: Oxford University Press, 1968), p. 10; Lynn Perrigo, *The American Southwest: Its People and Cultures* (New York: Holt, Rinehart & Winston, 1971), p. 22.

23. Olga Hall-Quest, *Conquistadores and Pueblos: The Story of the American Southwest, 1540–1848* (New York: E. P. Dutton, 1969), p. 37 and Elizabeth A. H. John, *Storms Brewed in Other Men's Worlds: The Confrontation of Indians, Spanish, and French in the Southwest, 1540–1795* (College Station: Texas A&M University Press, 1975), p. 14, accept Fray Marcos's story without a hint to their readers that a controversy exists. John Francis Bannon, *The Spanish Borderlands Frontier, 1513–1821* (New York: Holt, Rinehart & Winston, 1970), p. 16, mentions the controversy, cites the sources, and concludes that Fray Marcos "probably" saw Cíbola. David B. Quinn, *North America from Earliest Discovery to First Settlements: The Norse Voyages to 1612* (New York: Harper & Row, 1977), p. 195, questions whether Fray Marcos "saw the pueblo of Háwikuh," but does not take a position in the controversy. Mexican scholars also take Fray Marcos at his word. See, for example, Alfonso Trueba, *Las 7 Ciudades: Expedición de Francisco Vázquez de Coronado* (Mexico: Editorial Campeador, 1955), pp. 16–17.

24. This discussion of sources is not meant to be exhaustive, but merely indicative of the pattern. Among contemporary histories of individual states that suggest Fray Marcos reached Cíbola are: John Caughey, *California* (2nd edition; Englewood Cliffs, N.J.: Prentice-Hall, 1963), pp. 46–47; Walton Bean, *California: An Interpretive History* (New York: McGraw-Hill, 1968), pp. 14–15; Robert Glass Cleland, *From Wilderness to Empire: A History of California*, Glenn S. Dumke, ed. (New York: Alfred A. Knopf, 1969), p. 5; Warren A. Beck and David A. Williams, *California: A History of the Golden State* (Garden City, N.J.: Doubleday, 1972), p. 34; Jay J. Wagoner, *Early Arizona: Prehistory to Civil War* (Tucson: University of Arizona Press, 1975), p. 50 (who takes Fray Marcos all the way to Zuni, giving his readers only a hint of the controversy when he writes that Fray Marcos's account "is yet to be verified"); Marc Simmons, *New Mexico: A History* (New York: W. W. Norton, 1977), p. 18; and T. R. Fehrenbach, *Lone Star: A History of Texas and the Texans* (New York: Macmillan, 1968), pp. 23–25. Some writers of state histories tell the story of Fray Marcos without taking a clear position on how far he got. A good example is Seymour V. Connor, *Texas: A History* (New York: Thomas Y. Crowell, 1971), p. 14, who says that the friar "crossed into the present United States somewhere in eastern Arizona. Estevanico was murdered by Indians, and the padre scampered back to the safety of Mexico." It is the exceptional state history that states explicitly the Hallenbeck position that "the imaginative clergyman never got beyond the present international boundary," as does Warren Beck

have failed to cross the international boundary into what is today Arizona or New Mexico.

Carl Sauer once suggested a simple reason for the failure of the Wagner-Sauer-Hallenbeck position to win widespread acceptance. Because "we three . . . are not professors of History," he wrote, "[we] remain voices in the wilderness."[25] Perhaps that argument has some merit, but less conspiratorial explanations also suggest themselves. It is possible, for example, to imagine that historians have considered the Wagner-Sauer-Hallenbeck argument and found it unconvincing. It is also possible that many historians have overlooked these critiques of Fray Marcos's *Relación.* Historians do not always read one another's work; through inadvertence historians have perpetuated many a previously demolished argument and hoary myth.[26] In any event, specialists themselves have remained divided. Thus, the inconsistent interpretations offered by writers of general histories may reflect the contradictory conclusions of scholars who specialize in the history of northern New Spain in the sixteenth century.[27]

Part of the confusion in the historiography surrounding Fray Marcos has arisen because the few specialists who represent each side of the argument have not engaged one another in direct, sustained debate in the last few decades. Since World War II, the most ambitious effort to refute Fray Marcos's critics was that made by George Undreiner.

---

in his *New Mexico: A History of Four Centuries* (Norman: University of Oklahoma Press, 1962), p. 44. More venturesome than most writers of state histories, historical novelist James A. Michener, *Texas* (New York: Random House, 1985), pp. 34–35, accuses Fray Marcos of concocting a "massive" lie.

Some state histories do not, of course, mention Fray Marcos at all. For example: Andrew F. Rolle, *California: A History* (New York: Thomas Y. Crowell, 1963), and Lawrence Clark Powell, *Arizona* (New York: W. W. Norton, 1976).

25. Sauer, "Credibility of the Fray Marcos Account," p. 233. Writing prior to the appearance of *Fray Marcos,* Sauer included Hallenbeck in his triumvirate because of Hallenbeck's book on the route of Cabeza de Vaca, but the same charge certainly applied to the work of these three on Fray Marcos.

26. For examples, see Thomas A. Bailey, "The Mythmakers of American History," *Journal of American History* 55 (June 1968): 5–21.

27. See, for example, Fr. Angélico Chávez, *Coronado's Friars* (Washington, D.C.: Academy of American Franciscan History, 1968), p. 11 and n. 4, p. 76, who accepts Fray Marcos's story at face value and who does not cite the work of Sauer or Hallenbeck. On the other hand, Jack D. Forbes, *Apache, Navajo, and Spaniard* (Norman: University of Oklahoma Press, 1960), p. 6, expresses skepticism and cites the work of Sauer.

His valuable essay appeared in 1947, prior to the publication of Hallenbeck's work, and so Undreiner could not challenge Hallenbeck's arguments directly. Conversely, Hallenbeck did not respond to Undreiner's position. Hallenbeck had apparently completed the manuscript for *Fray Marcos* by the time that Undreiner's article appeared. Indeed, seriously ill and isolated from the scholarly community at his home in Roswell, New Mexico, Hallenbeck probably did not know of Undreiner's work. [28]

Since the publication of *Fray Marcos* in 1949, scholars have jabbed at Hallenbeck's position, but they have not tried to land a direct hit. Instead, most historians and anthropologists currently interested in Fray Marcos have turned to another arena. They have lightly dismissed the Wagner-Sauer-Hallenbeck school and have shifted the focus of the debate. Instead of asking *if* Fray Marcos saw Cíbola, ethnohistorian Madeleine Rodack has assumed that he did and asks *which* of the six Zuni villages Fray Marcos saw—Hawikuh, as Hallenbeck and others have argued, or Kiakima, for which Rodack makes a case. [29] Instead of asking *if* Fray Marcos entered present-day Arizona and New Mexico, scholars such as Albert Schroeder and Charles Di Peso have asked *which* route he took through the present Southwest. [30] There now exist

28. George J. Undreiner, "Fray Marcos de Niza and His Journey to Cibola," *The Americas* 3 (April 1947): 415–86. Assuming that the April issue of *The Americas* appeared on schedule, there would have been little time for Hallenbeck to see it. His manuscript was at SMU Press by the autumn of 1947, if not before (Everette DeGolyer had completed his reader's report of the ms by December 4—letter, DeGolyer to Mrs. Elizabeth M. Stover, Dallas, December 4, 1947, preserved in E. DeGolyer's copy of *Fray Marcos* in the DeGolyer Library, SMU). Carl Sauer did have the opportunity to address Undreiner's argument in his *Sixteenth Century North America*, pp. 127–29, but apparently declined to do so.

29. Madeleine Turrell Rodack, "Cibola Revisited," in Charles H. Lange, ed., *Southwestern Culture History: Papers in Honor of Albert H. Schroeder. Papers of the Archaeological Society of New Mexico*, no. 10 (Santa Fe: Ancient City Press, 1985), pp. 163–85. In making a case for Kiakima, Rodack revives an argument made by Adolph Bandelier. See her introduction to *Adolph F. Bandelier's The Discovery of New Mexico*, p. 35 (where *Kiakima* is rendered *Qaqima*), and ibid., p. 38, in which she dismisses Wagner and Hallenbeck thus: "They have written detailed analyses of his travels in order to show that the timing could not have allowed him to reach Cíbola and return when he did. It is true that there are several inconsistencies in the schedule of his journey, but, since his exact route is still unknown, it seems presumptuous to say that he could not have done it without being certain of just what he did."

30. Ethnohistorian Albert Schroeder, "Fray Marcos de Niza, Coronado, and the Yavapai," *New Mexico Historical Review* 30, 31 (October 1955, January 1956): 265–96, 24–37, did not cite Hallenbeck. Rather, he accepted uncritically Undreiner's

at least three hypothetical routes Fray Marcos might have taken to Zuni.[31]

Since the appearance of Hallenbeck's *Journey of Fray Marcos* in 1949, the most detailed effort to reconstruct Fray Marcos's route was that published by Charles Di Peso in 1974. Di Peso took Fray Marcos across the present-day international boundary near the New Mexico–Arizona line, much to the east of the routes of other writers. He dismissed the arguments of Carl Sauer and Cleve Hallenbeck with the offhand remark that they had "maligned" Fray Marcos "primarily because the padre did not travel where the historian would have him travel."[32] Di Peso did not, however, try to refute the Wagner-Sauer-Hallenbeck position; he simply offered an alternative. For example, Di Peso asserted that Fray Marcos returned to Culiacán on July 22, 1539, thus ignoring completely Hallenbeck's evidence that the padre had already made it to Compostela, three hundred miles to the south, a month earlier. The question is important, for it goes to the heart of whether or not Fray Marcos had time to cover the distance that he said he did.[33]

---

projection of Fray Marcos's route up to the international boundary. From that point, Schroeder attempted his own reconstruction of Fray Marcos's route through Arizona. Schroeder trivialized the arguments of Fray Marcos's critics with the statement that they "have ignored the fact that he [Fray Marcos] guided Coronado to Cíbola" (p. 266). Schroeder fails, however, to provide evidence that Fray Marcos knew the way or guided Coronado well (see Hallenbeck, *Fray Marcos*, p. 76). Certainly Coronado did not think Fray Marcos had done well. Charles Di Peso, *Casas Grandes: A Fallen Trading Center of the Gran Chichimeca*, 8 vols. (Flagstaff, Ariz.: Northland Press, 1974), 3: 806–8; 4: 75–89.

31. For brief summaries of the literature on what might be termed the western, central, and eastern routes to Cíbola, see Rodack, trans. and ed., *Adolph F. Bandelier's The Discovery of New Mexico*, pp. 35–37, and Riley, "The Road to Hawikuh," pp. 137–59. Riley has been careful not to take a stand on the Fray Marcos question. See ibid., p. 140; Riley, *The Frontier People: The Greater Southwest in the Prehistoric Period. Occasional Paper no. 1* (Carbondale, Ill.: Center for Archaeological Investigations, Southern Illinois University, 1982, p. 9); and Riley, "The Location of Chichilticale," in Lange, ed., *Southwestern Culture History*, p. 157, in which he says "I am . . . uncertain as to whether Marcos actually made the final leg of the journey to Cíbola."

32. Di Peso, *Casas Grandes*, 3: 981, n. 58.

33. Di Peso, *Casas Grandes*, 4: 88. Hallenbeck, *Fray Marcos*, pp. 63–64. If Di Peso accepted Hallenbeck's date of June 25 for return to Compostela, he would have to subtract thirty-seven days from the round trip from Culiacán to Cíbola and back, thereby having Fray Marcos average 18.8 miles per day, without resting (and Fray Marcos himself tells us of many days of rest). By ignoring Hallenbeck, Di Peso provides Fray Marcos with enough time to average 13.6 miles per day, again without resting. I am using Di Peso's own mileage estimates in making these calculations. For comparison, it is worth noting that Hallenbeck estimates that if Fray Marcos made the

But even if scholars engage one another's work more directly, it seems likely that debate about whether or not Fray Marcos made it to Zuni will never end. The question may be unanswerable. A study that incorporates recent scholarship and examines divergent viewpoints would be of great use, but no one is likely to write a definitive analysis of Fray Marcos's journey unless fresh documentation appears.[34] For the moment, the only document available to modern scholars is Fray Marcos's own *Relación,* and that is so sketchy that it lends itself to multiple interpretation. Hallenbeck, for example, observed that Fray Marcos's account "does not give us one identifiable point anywhere on or near his route. . . . Nevertheless, I think we can trace his course in some detail with a measure of confidence."[35]

Statements of such intellectual bravado notwithstanding, it must be remembered that Fray Marcos's *Relación* is sufficiently vague that even those scholars who agree that he made it to Zuni cannot agree on the route that he took, or on the location of key places, such as Vacapa and Chichilticale, that would help establish his route. Fray Marcos's narrative carries liabilities much like those that one writer has attributed to Cabeza de Vaca's account: "A reconciliation of all the data is impossible," Morris Bishop has written. "We must believe that Cabeza de Vaca was, naturally enough, occasionally forgetful, confused, or mistaken."[36] As this quote suggests, students of exploration often take comfort in explaining discrepancies between their theories and the texts by criticizing those parts of the texts that do not square with their hypotheses. Hence, we find historians referring to parts of sixteenth-century narratives that "must be in error," or that contain "puzzlingly inaccurate distances and directions," or lamenting, as one study does, "the hardest part of the narrative to adjust to facts."[37]

round trip journey from Culiacán to Compostela by way of Cíbola, that he would have traveled 2,350 miles, or 21.9 miles per day, without resting a single day. (I am using the mileages in Hallenbeck, *Fray Marcos,* p. 46, and the dates March 7 to June 25.)

34. At least one study of the route of Fray Marcos is presently in progress, that of Donald Juneau of Hammond, Louisiana. Juneau to Weber, March 10, 1986.

35. Hallenbeck, *Fray Marcos,* p. 45.

36. Morris Bishop, reviewing Hallenbeck's *Cabeza de Vaca* in the *Hispanic American Historical Review* 20 (February 1940): 141. See, too, Riley, "The Location of Chichilticale," pp. 153–62.

37. The first two quotes are from Charles B. DePratter, Charles Hudson, and Marvin T. Smith, "The Route of Juan Pardo's Explorations in the Interior of the

Scholars' use of this elastic methodology explains in part how one student of the Hernando de Soto expedition could conclude that "we quickly found that when we used the De Soto narratives alone, it was possible to take the expedition almost anywhere."[38]

The fact that participants in the Soto *entrada* left vague narratives is understandable—they were looting, not exploring. And Cabeza de Vaca's confusion is easily understood—he had been shipwrecked and was lost. In contrast, Fray Marcos set out with instructions to explore and to report on what he found, and Viceroy Mendoza chose Fray Marcos in part because he believed that the friar had sufficient competence and experience to carry out that task. Thus, it is more difficult to explain the errors in Fray Marcos's account—errors that nearly every writer including Hallenbeck must attempt to reconcile if Fray Marcos's *Relación* is to make sense.

Fray Marcos's journey, then, raises more questions than it answers. Among those questions, we should ask if Fray Marcos's spare account has become a kind of Rorschach test, allowing scholars to read into it that which they wish to see. Could it be that Catholic historians who are of the cloth, such as the Franciscans Bonaventure Oblasser and Angélico Chávez, and Rt. Rev. Msgr. George Undreiner, have found Fray Marcos truthful because they are reluctant to brand a confrére a liar?[39] Or is it that writers who have questioned Fray Marcos's veracity are "anti-friar"? Angélico Chávez leveled this charge against Hallenbeck, whose prose suggested to Chávez, "the almost pathological hate which Hallenbeck harbored against a friar four hundred years dead."[40] Could it be that anthropologists, eager for bits and pieces to reconstruct the protohistorical Southwest, have been reluctant to admit

Southeast, 1566–68," *Florida Historical Quarterly* 62 (October 1983): 152, 151, and the third quote is from Clifford M. Lewis and Albert J. Loomie, *The Spanish Jesuit Mission in Virginia, 1570–1572* (Chapel Hill: University of North Carolina Press for the Virginia Historical Society, 1953), p. 35.

38. Charles Hudson, "Research on the Eastern Spanish Borderlands," paper presented at the Columbus Quincentennial Conference on Archives and Records for Studying the Hispanic Experience in the United States, 1492–1850, September 23, 1987, p. 6.

39. In addition to translating Fray Marcos's account without reference to other authorities, Bonaventure Oblasser summarized Fray Marcos's journey with references to other scholars in "The Franciscans in the Spanish Southwest," *Franciscan Educational Conference Report* 18 (1936): 99–101.

40. Chávez, review of *The Journey of Fray Marcos* in the *New Mexico Historical Review* 25 (July 1950): 258.

that Fray Marcos might not be a useful source? Could it be that historians from the United States have found Fray Marcos "the first white man who indisputably set foot on the soil of New Mexico" or "the discoverer of Arizona . . . and *the first European to set foot on Arizona soil*" because they have been eager to push the history of their nation and region back in time?[41] Have American historians been guilty of the kind of ethnocentric reading of evidence that some scholars believe have led us to place much of the route of Cabeza de Vaca erroneously in the United States instead of in Mexico?[42] Finally, could it be that twentieth-century scholars have constructed their own Cíbolas? Happily, the author of the introduction to a book enjoys the luxury of raising questions about the coincidence of interest and interpretation without having to answer them.

41. Quotes are, respectively, from Baldwin, "Fray Marcos de Niza," p. 193, and Oblasser, "Franciscans in the Spanish Southwest," p. 101. Italics in original.
42. Alex D. Krieger, "Travels of Alvar Núñez Cabeza de Vaca," in *Homenaje a Pablo Martínez del Rio en el XXV aniversario de la edición de Los Orígenes Americanos* (Mexico: Instituto Nacional de Antropología e Historia, 1961), pp. 460, 465; Donald E. Chipman, "In Search of Cabeza de Vaca's Route Across Texas: An Historiographical Survey," *Southwestern Historical Quarterly* 91 (October 1987): 127–48.

3

Turner, the Boltonians, and the Borderlands *

For much of this century, Frederick Jackson Turner's frontier thesis has been regarded as a most useful, if not the most useful, concept for understanding the distinctive features of American civilization. The existence of a frontier, Turner argued, explained much of the difference between Europe and the New World. As he put it in the famous paper that he delivered to the American Historical Association in 1893, "The peculiarity of American institutions is the fact that they have been compelled to adapt themselves to the changes of an expanding people—to the changes involved in crossing a continent, in winning a wilderness, and in developing . . . the primitive economic and political conditions of the frontier into the complexity of city life."[1] Turner suggested that circumstances peculiar to the American frontier, such as free land, opportunity, and common danger from Indians, shaped American character and institutions in specific ways: the frontier quickened assimilation of immigrants, had a "consolidating" and "nationalizing" effect on young America, and promoted democracy.[2] Moreover, Turner wrote, "to the frontier the American intellect owes

*I wish to thank Allan G. Bogue, William Cronan, Donald C. Cutter, Lawrence Kinnaird, Patricia Nelson Limerick, and Donald Worcester for commenting on an earlier draft of this manuscript. This article first appeared in the *American Historical Review* 91 (January 1986): 66–81 and is reprinted with the permission of the editors.

1. Turner, "The Significance of the Frontier in American History," in George Rogers Taylor, ed., *The Turner Thesis Concerning the Role of the Frontier in American History* (3d ed., Lexington, Mass., 1972), 3. Turner's essay is available in a number of sources.
2. Ibid., 12, 17, 22.

its striking characteristics": inventiveness, practicality, inquisitiveness, restlessness, optimism, and individualism.[3]

This overarching explanation of American history rejected the conventional wisdom that American institutions and character had been transplanted unchanged from Europe. As Ray Allen Billington, the foremost explicator of Turner's ideas, once wrote, Turner "shook the academic world to its foundations."[4] Radical as it was, Turner's frontier thesis came to enjoy widespread acceptance, spawning a remarkable series of books and articles before coming under attack in the 1930s and 1940s. Much of the criticism was well-founded. Turner had overstated his case and failed to define terms carefully. He even used the term "frontier" imprecisely, sometimes to represent a place, sometimes a process, and sometimes a condition (a looseness of expression that I myself have failed to avoid in this essay). By the 1950s, however, Turner's defenders had clarified and refined his thesis in a convincing fashion. In modified form, it remains yet today a useful model for many historians.[5]

Since Turner offered a convincing explanation of how the New World came to differ from the Old,[6] it might be supposed that the thesis would have been embraced by scholars who have studied the northward advance of the Mexican frontier into the area of the present-day United States, as well as by those who have interested themselves in the Anglo-American westward movement. In general, that has not been the case. Nearly all of Turner's students ignored racial and ethnic minorities in the West, Hispanics and the Hispanic frontier not excepted.[7]

3. Ibid., 27.

4. Billington, *The Genesis of the Frontier Thesis: A Study in Historical Creativity* (San Marino, Calif., 1971), 3.

5. The best study of the reception of Turner's ideas is by Billington. See his *The American Frontier Thesis: Attack and Defense* (Washington, D.C., 1971). The most sophisticated defense of Turner is Billington's *America's Frontier Heritage* (New York, 1966). For recent assertions of the general validity of Turner's thesis, see Margaret Walsh, *The American Frontier Revisited* (Atlantic Highlands, N.J., 1981), 15, 71; and John Barker, *The Super Historians: Makers of Our Past* (New York, 1982), 346.

6. As Turner put it, "The advance of the frontier has meant a steady movement away from Europe"; "Significance of the Frontier," 5.

7. For a discussion of how Turner and his students ignored ethnic minorities, see Frederick C. Luebke, "Ethnic Minorities in the American West," in Michael P. Malone, ed., *Historians and the American West* (Lincoln, Nebr., 1983), 387–404. Luebke wrote, "Turner provided the key to ethnic history in his methodology, but

Moreover, scholars who specialize in the Hispanic frontiers of North America—the shifting region that has come to be called the Spanish Borderlands—have largely ignored Turner.[8] Some of his ideas have been fruitfully applied to the Borderlands by scholars working out of traditions unrelated to the Borderlands "school," but his thesis has made little impact on the historiography of the Borderlands or of Mexico itself. Yet Herbert Eugene Bolton, the founder of the Borderlands school, recognized at an early date the wisdom of applying Turner's thesis to Spanish-American frontiers.

Bolton received his doctorate in medieval history from the University of Pennsylvania but earlier studied American history under Turner at Wisconsin. As an undergraduate, Bolton took a course from Turner in 1895, less than two years after Turner delivered his famous address. Bolton stayed on at Wisconsin to do a master's degree under Turner and for the rest of his career was proud to have been, as he put it, one of Turner's "boys."[9] In 1911 Bolton took a position at the University of California—a job that he obtained with Turner's help. That year Bolton told Berkeley's president, Benjamin Ide Wheeler, that, although Turner had directed the attention of researchers toward the West, he had "not thus far reached beyond the Mississippi Valley." Historians at Berkeley, Bolton suggested to Wheeler, should extend Turner's work by studying the Southwest and the Far West, particularly Spanish activities in the area that is now the United States.[10] Bolton did not simply want to study what Turner and his disciples had neglected;

---

his students fumbled at the door"; ibid., 403. An important exception was Arthur Preston Whitaker, who worked under Turner at Harvard. See Whitaker, *The Spanish-American Frontier, 1783–1795: The Westward Movement and the Spanish Retreat in the Mississippi Valley* (1927; reprint ed., Lincoln, Nebr., 1969). Whitaker dedicated his book to Turner. He did not, however, attempt to apply the Turner thesis to the Spanish frontier but focused instead on diplomacy and politics.

8. Although the area examined by the scholars of the Bolton school of Spanish Borderlands historiography extends from California to Florida, this essay focuses on the western Borderlands, from California to Texas, and on the area that lies above the present U.S.-Mexican border. This region was Bolton's major interest and is the area that has attracted the most attention from Borderlands scholars. Moreover, to treat both the eastern and western Borderlands in a single brief essay would be unwieldy. See Donald C. Cutter, "The Western Spanish Borderlands," in Malone, *Historians and the American West*, 40–41.

9. John Francis Bannon, *Herbert Eugene Bolton: The Historian and the Man, 1870–1953* (Tucson, Ariz., 1978), 14–15, 21.

10. Report from Bolton to Wheeler, December 18, 1911, in John Francis Bannon, ed., *Bolton and the Spanish Borderlands* (Norman, Okla., 1964), 25.

he also saw the need to analyze the Hispanic frontier as Turner had the Anglo-American frontier. "For him who interprets, with Turner's insight, the methods and the significance of the Spanish-American frontier," Bolton wrote in 1917, "there awaits a recognition not less marked or less deserved."[11]

Bolton continued to play this refrain. In 1932, in his own address to the American Historical Association, "The Epic of Greater America," he harkened back to the Turner thesis. Bolton asked, "Who has tried to state the significance of the frontier in terms of the Americas?"[12] In a seminar in Mexico City in 1946, Bolton sang the praises of Turner's "epic" essay to his students and then urged them to consider "to what extent his thesis is applicable or inapplicable to Mexico. . . . Perhaps the scholar who some day will discover and formulate such a thesis sits before me. Who can tell?"[13] No such student sat before Bolton that day or any other day. Bolton pointed the way, but he did not lead by example. In his own writing, he rarely attempted to apply to the Hispanic frontier the questions raised by Turner.[14]

Bolton's published work suggests that he was far more interested in the impact of Spaniards on the frontier than in the influence of the frontier on Spaniards. Heroic figures and the high drama of exploration and international rivalry captivated him, and the establishment of Spanish institutions in the Borderlands interested him intensely. Bolton clearly saw the mission and the presidio as "characteristically and designedly frontier institutions," but he saw them as extending,

11. Bolton, "The Mission as a Frontier Institution in the Spanish American Colonies," in Bannon, *Bolton and the Spanish Borderlands*, 189. Bolton presented this essay as a faculty research lecture at the University of California in March 1917; it was reprinted widely.

12. Bolton, "The Epic of Greater America," in Bannon, *Bolton and the Spanish Borderlands*, 332. This essay was first published in the *American Historical Review*; *AHR* 38 (1932–33): 448–74.

13. Bolton, "The Northward Movement in New Spain," in Bannon, *Bolton and the Spanish Borderlands*, 68. Also see ibid., 78. This essay began as an outline for the seminar in Mexico City.

14. For a recent analysis of Bolton's work and that of his followers, see Cutter, "Western Spanish Borderlands," 39–56. For recent historiographical essays on more specific topics, see Ellwyn R. Stoddard et al., eds., *Borderlands Sourcebook: A Guide to the Literature on Northern Mexico and the American Southwest* (Norman, Okla., 1983). Included are two essays by Ralph H. Vigil, "Exploration and Conquest" and "Colonial Institutions." The index to this large reference work cites Turner only twice, although the volume does include an interesting review of theoretical literature by anthropologist Paul Kutsche, entitled "Borders and Frontiers."

holding, and "civilizing" the frontier.[15] How frontier conditions might have altered these institutions or their inhabitants seldom concerned him.

In his engaging survey, *The Spanish Borderlands*, published in the Chronicles of America series in 1921, Bolton denied by implication that the frontier influenced Hispanic institutions and character. In Bolton's view, Spanish absolutism reached to all corners of the New World under the Habsburgs and stifled initiative, individual liberty, and self-government.[16] Because of the pervasive influence of their government, Bolton wrote, Spaniards "attained to little greater degree of personal freedom and little larger share in their own government in a frontier presidio than in the City of Mexico or in Seville."[17] One exception was the remote province of Alta California. On that frontier, Bolton explained, a peculiar set of conditions—the benign climate, unusually fertile soil, the abundance of Indian labor, the paternalism of the Spanish monarchy, and the area's distance from markets—conspired to dull initiative and produce an "idle" group of Hispanic frontiersmen.[18] Idle they may have been, but, Bolton suggested, the *californios* were superior to other Mexicans because they were isolated from the rest of Mexico and had "the greater degree of independence, social at least if not political," that distance afforded them. Even at that early date, Bolton thought that he detected a "mellower spirit" in California.[19]

Bolton's students followed his example rather than his admonitions. None explicitly applied the Turner thesis to Spanish-American frontiers. Of course, some of the 104 Ph.D.'s whom Bolton trained employed the term "frontier" in the titles of their books, and many made notable contributions to our knowledge of the Hispanic frontier in North America. In the process, the Bolton school offered a valuable balance to the chauvinism of the Turnerians, who had come to see the term "frontier" as synonymous with the Anglo-American frontier. Some second-generation Boltonians recognized that frontiers had two

15. Bolton, "Mission as a Frontier Institution," 192, 199.
16. Bolton, *The Spanish Borderlands: A Chronicle of Old Florida and the Southwest* (New Haven, Conn., 1921), 233–34.
17. Ibid., 289.
18. Ibid., 290–91, 293.
19. Ibid., 294.

sides and looked searchingly at interactions along Euro-Indian frontiers.[20] But Bolton's extraordinary academic progeny concerned itself more with archival research and the reconstruction of the particulars of the past than with theory in general or with the impact of the frontier on Mexican society or institutions in particular.[21]

Nowhere was the scanty interest of the Borderlands school in the Turner thesis better illustrated than in John Francis Bannon's *The Spanish Borderlands Frontier*. Published in 1970, Bannon's study was the first effort to synthesize the burgeoning literature on the Spanish-American frontier in what is today the United States. Bannon's survey appeared in the Histories of the American Frontier series, edited by Ray Allen Billington, Turner's most distinguished disciple. Nonetheless, Bannon's *Spanish Borderlands Frontier* contains no mention of Turner or his thesis.

Like Bolton, Bannon implicitly rejected the idea that the frontier democratized Hispanic institutions. "The shadow of Spanish absolutism," he wrote, "allowed the Spanish frontiersman little chance to develop a sense of self-expression or a feeling of self-reliance."[22] Although

20. See Jack D. Forbes, "Frontiers in American History," *Journal of the West* 1 (1962): 63–73.
21. Bannon listed all of the recipient of M.A.'s and Ph.D.'s whom Bolton directed; *Herbert Eugene Bolton*, 283–90. Bolton himself used the term "frontier" in his famous essay "Mission as a Frontier Institution" and in his *Athanase de Mezières and the Louisiana-Texas Frontier, 1768–1780* (Cleveland, Ohio, 1914). Also see Lawrence Kinnaird, ed., *The Frontiers of New Spain: Nicolás de Lafora's Description, 1766–1768* (Berkeley and Los Angeles, 1958); Alfred Barnaby Thomas, ed. and trans., *Forgotten Frontiers: A Study of the Spanish Indian Policy of Don Juan Bautista de Anza, Governor of New Mexico, 1777–1787; From Original Documents in the Archives of Spain, Mexico, and New Mexico* (Norman, Okla., 1932); and Max L. Moorhead, *The Apache Frontier: Jacobo de Ugarte and Spanish-Indian Relations in Northern New Spain, 1769–1791* (Norman, Okla., 1968). A sample of the scholarship of some of Bolton's students, characterized by works that are highly particular and consist in many cases of edited documents, appears in a Festschrift published in 1932, by which time Bolton had trained over fifty Ph.D.'s. See *New Spain and the Anglo-American West: Historical Contributions Presented to Herbert Eugene Bolton*, 2 vols. (Los Angeles, 1932). Also see *Greater America: Essays in Honor of Herbert Eugene Bolton* (Berkeley, 1945). This collection is another Festschrift and contains "A Bibliography of the Historical Writings of the Students of Herbert Eugene Bolton." I do not mean to suggest that all of the Boltonians did narrow work based on archival research. Many of them also wrote wide-ranging, interpretive essays. See, for example, Norris Hundley, Jr. and John A. Schutz, eds., *The American West: Frontier and Region; Interpretations by John Walton Caughey* (Los Angeles, 1969).
22. Bannon, *The Spanish Borderlands Frontier, 1513–1821* (New York, 1970), 5.

a small body of scholarship suggested other possibilities, Bannon concluded that Hispanic, in contrast to Anglo-American, frontiersmen lacked self-determination and the personal liberty to move freely over space. "Rugged individualism was foreign to the Borderlands," he concluded.[23] Bannon did suggest, however, that the physical environment on the frontier shaped Spanish economic life and institutions. The "rugged, arid, and often sterile" terrain encouraged ranching and mining rather than agriculture.[24] Moreover, hostile Indians (along what Turner called "the meeting point between savagery and civilization") provided the reason for the existence of two major Spanish frontier institutions—the presidio and the mission.[25]

In the decade and a half since Bannon's synthesis appeared, Borderlands historians of the Bolton school have continued to investigate many of the themes that were of interest to Bolton and, with few exceptions, to ignore Turner. Borderlands specialists have written fine books examining such traditional subjects as international rivalries, Spanish-Indian relations, the lives of prominent persons, and the presidio and the mission. If Turner's ideas influenced these scholars, their work does not reveal it.[26] Historians following two other modes of inquiry, however, have used Turner's ideas in ways that have deepened our understanding of the Borderlands.

One group consists of those who have attempted comparative analyses. Some of these scholars began in the 1920s, if not before, to

23. Ibid., 6, 237–38.
24. Ibid., 233–34.
25. Ibid., 234; and Turner, "Significance of the Frontier," 4.
26. See, for example, Warren L. Cook, *Flood Tide of Empire: Spain and the Pacific Northwest, 1543–1819* (New Haven, Conn., 1973); Abraham P. Nasatir, *Borderland in Retreat: From Spanish Louisiana to the Far Southwest* (Albuquerque, N.Mex., 1976); Elizabeth A. H. John, *Storms Brewed in Other Men's Worlds: The Confrontation of Indians, Spanish, and French in the Southwest, 1540–1795* (College Station, Tex., 1975). For biography, see, for example, Felix D. Almaraz, Jr., *Tragic Cavalier: Governor Manuel de Salcedo of Texas, 1808–1813* (Austin, Tex., 1971); Edwin A Beilharz, *Felipe de Neve: First Governor of California* (San Francisco, 1971); and Francis F. Guest, *Fermín Francisco de Lasuén (1736–1803): A Biography* (Washington, D.C., 1973). On institutions, see Max L. Moorhead, *The Presidio: Bastion of the Spanish Borderlands* (Norman, Okla., 1975); John L. Kessell, *Mission of Sorrows: Jesuit Guevavi and the Pimas, 1691–1767* (Tucson, Ariz., 1970), *Friars, Soldiers, and Reformers: Hispanic Arizona and the Sonora Mission Frontier, 1767–1856* (Tucson, Ariz., 1976), and *Kiva, Cross, and Crown: The Pecos Indians and New Mexico, 1540–1840* (Washington, D.C., 1979).

apply the Turner thesis to frontiers throughout Spanish America.[27] Although these writers would disagree among themselves on many points, their collective effort suggests several conclusions that apply to the Spanish-American frontiers that pushed into areas now in the American West.

First, these historians noted that the physical environments of frontiers differ, so the impacts of frontier environments on cultures also differ. The distinguished Peruvian historian Victor Andrés Belaúnde pointed out, in an essay published in English in 1923, that the mere existence of plentiful free land, the key ingredient on the American frontier according to Turner, was not sufficient in itself to shape institutions and culture. Quality of land was more important than quantity. Land had to be accessible and capable of productivity, but much of Latin America is tropical rain forest or marginal sierra or altiplano, possessing little of what Belaúnde called "human value." Because they could not effectively exploit these marginal frontier lands, he argued, some Latin American nations "lack . . . the characteristics of frontier

---

27. I refer here deliberately to Spanish America rather than to Latin America in order not to confuse Portuguese America with Spanish America and to exempt the considerable literature on Brazilian frontiers from the discussion. For a bibliography on this subject and an often insightful if disjointed essay comparing Latin American and Anglo-American frontiers, see Alistair Hennessy, *The Frontier in Latin American History* (Albuquerque, N.Mex., 1978). Some of the most sophisticated works in frontier history have been writen on Brazilian frontiers. See, especially, Martin T. Katzman, "The Brazilian Frontier in Comparative Perspective," *Comparative Studies in Society and History* 17 (1975): 266–85. Since Hennessy's work appeared, students of Latin America have continued to probe the question of comparative frontiers. William Frederick Sharp concluded that "the classic waves of frontier development described by Frederick Jackson Turner did not occur in the Chocó." See his *Slavery on the Spanish Frontier: The Colombian Chocó, 1680–1810* (Norman, Okla., 1976), 3. Jane M. Rausch reached a similar but more guarded conclusion. See Rausch, *A Tropical Plains Frontier: The Llanos of Colombia, 1531–1831* (Albuquerque, N.Mex., 1984), 230, 245. The works of other scholars who have attempted to make broad comparisons of Anglo-American and Spanish-American frontiers are cited below. In addition, see Seymour Martin Lipsett, "The Newness of the New Nation," in C. Vann Woodward, ed., *The Comparative Approach to American History* (New York, 1968), 70–71; and C. H. Haring, *The Spanish Empire in America* (New York, 1947), 30–41. Haring employed an implicitly Turnerian approach to an analysis of the impact of the New World environment in the English, Portuguese, and Spanish frontiers. Also see Dietrich Gerhard, "The Frontier in Comparative View," *Comparative Studies in Society and History* 1 (1959): 205–29. Gerhard, in this landmark essay, noted that "Latin America would be another appropriate area for comparison. I do not feel, however, competent to deal with it" (p. 206).

countries."[28] Turner, who claimed that the American frontier was unique, might not have disagreed. After all, he had argued that "Western democracy . . . came stark and strong and full of life, from the American forest" and would hardly have expected the Amazon jungle or the arid frontiers of northern Mexico to make the same impact on society that the more hospitable woodlands of the Old Northwest did.[29]

Second, in their comparative studies these scholars have moved well beyond the simple notion of the frontier as a line between "savagery and civilization" to remind us that a variety of indigenous societies can exist in a frontier zone and that different host societies have different impacts on the cultures and institutions of intruders. Hence, an understanding of the frontier process must take into account peoples and their motives on both sides of a frontier. Spanish Americans, comparative historians tell us, attempted to assimilate indigenous Americans rather than push them back or annihilate them as the English generally did. Moreover, Spaniards often encountered indigenous peoples whose culture rendered them easily assimilable. The Spanish-American frontier, in the words of geographer Marvin Mikesell, was a "frontier of inclusion" in contrast to the Anglo-American "frontier of exclusion."[30]

Third, these historians have also moved beyond the simple environmentalism expressed in Turner's famous essay.[31] Several of those

28. Belaúnde, *The Frontier in Hispanic America*, Rice Institute Pamphlets, no. 10 (Houston, Tex., 1923), 208. Other writers would agree with Belaúnde. See, for example, Donald J. Lehmer, "The Second Frontier: The Spanish," in Robert G. Ferris, ed., *The American West: An Appraisal* (Santa Fe, N.Mex., 1963), 143–44.

29. Turner, as quoted in Rex W. Strickland, *The Turner Thesis and the Dry World* (El Paso, Tex., 1964), 16. Strickland saw the Turner thesis as inapplicable to the Rio Grande Valley of New Mexico and West Texas.

30. Mikesell, "Comparative Studies in Frontier History," *Annals of the Association of American Geographers* 50 (1960): 65. Also see Hennessy, *Frontiers in Latin American History*, 19–20; and Forbes, "Frontiers in American History," 65, and "Frontiers in American History and the Role of the Frontier Historian," *Ethnohistory* 15 (1968): 205; T. M. Pearce, "The 'Other' Frontiers of the American West," *Arizona and the West* 4 (1962): 105–12; and Owen Lattimore, "The Frontier in History," in Robert A. Manners and David Kaplan, eds., *Theory in Anthropology* (Chicago, 1968), 375. For a recent summation, see Howard Lamar and Leonard Thompson, eds., *The Frontier in History: North America and Southern Africa Compared* (New Haven, Conn., 1981).

31. Billington made a convincing case that Turner was not simply an environmentalist or a monocausationist, but that is not apparent in Turner's famous and influential essay. See Billington, *The American Frontier Thesis*, 13–15.

who have compared Latin American and Anglo-American frontiers
have concluded that the culture pioneers brought to the frontier was
far more important than the impact of the frontier on that culture.[32]
In advancing this argument, Billington has nearly turned Turner's
thesis on its head. He has suggested that Turner did not intend to
explain all of American history as shaped by a single force. Notwithstanding Turner's unequivocal assertion that "free land, its continuous
recession, and the advance of American settlement westward, explain
American development,"[33] Billington concluded that the frontier could
not "affect *major* changes in either the personalities or the behavioral
patterns of frontiersmen. . . . The bulk of the customs and beliefs of
the pioneers were transmitted, and were only slightly modified by the
changing culture in which they lived. . . . Men, not geography, explain
the differences between the Anglo-American and Latin-American
frontiers, for individuals of different backgrounds will respond in different ways to identical physical environments."[34] Ironically, those
historians of comparative frontiers who have modified and reinter-
preted Turner's thesis have moved closer to Bolton's position. In his
own work, and in that of many of his students, Bolton focused on the
interplay of cultures on both sides of the frontier, be it Spanish and
Indian or Spanish and French. Bolton also stressed the importance of
the institutions and the culture of the individuals that the invading
country brought to a frontier. Nonetheless, with only a few excpetions,
historians working in the Bolton tradition have paid scant attention
to how comparative studies of frontiers might shed light on our understanding of the Borderlands.[35] There is additional irony here in that

32. Even Belaúnde, who made a strong case for environmental differences, used
politics and culture to explain why the frontier failed to provide opportunity in those
areas where Latin America's geography resembled that of the United States; *The
Frontier in Hispanic America*, 212–13. Also see Lehmer, "The Second Frontier," 144–
50; and William H. Lyon, "The Third Generation and the Frontier Hypothesis,"
Arizona and the West 4 (1962): 48.
33. Turner, "Significance of the Frontier," 3.
34. Billington, *America's Frontier Heritage*, 54. (Emphasis added.) Billington
expressed similar sentiments in three other essays: "The Frontier in American Thought
and Character," in Archibald B. Lewis and Thomas F. McGann, eds., *The New World
Looks at Its History* (Austin, Tex., 1963), 78–79; "Frontiers," in Woodward, *The
Comparative Approach to American History*, 77–78; and "Turner and Webb," in Harold
M. Hollingsworth and Sandra L. Myres, eds., *Essays on the American West* (Austin,
Tex., 1969), 89.
35. Bannon, for example, relied solely on Lehmer's "The Second Frontier" in his

Bolton was an early and passionate advocate of comparative analysis in the study of hemispheric history.

A few other scholars, however, whose training was not in the Bolton tradition, have taken up the challenge of applying Turner's ideas explicitly to Mexico's far northern frontiers. Their conclusions have varied. The least sophisticated inquiry is a study by Rex Strickland, who argued unequivocally that the Spanish-American frontier "did not produce even a semblance of democracy."[36] Silvio Zavala, the eminent Mexican historian, offered a more measured assessment.[37]

---

study of the Spanish Borderlands. For other exceptions, see Forbes, "Frontiers in American History"; Oakah L. Jones, Jr., *Los Paisanos: Spanish Settlers on the Northern Frontier of New Spain* (Norman, Okla., 1979); and David J. Weber, *The Mexican Frontier, 1821–1846: The American Southwest under Mexico* (Albuquerque, N.Mex., 1982). Also see Sandra L. Myres, "The Ranching Frontier," in Hollingsworth and Myres, *Essays on the American West*, 33; and David J. Weber, ed., *Foreigners in Their Native Land: Historical Roots of the Mexican Americans* (Albuquerque, N.Mex., 1973), 19–21. Jones is a second-generation Bolton student, having studied with Max L. Moorhead, a student of Bolton's. Forbes and I are third-generation Boltonians, having studied with Donald C. Cutter, who studied with Bolton but finished his work under Lawrence Kinnaird, another student of Bolton's. Myres studied under Donald Worcester, who completed his M.A. under Bolton's supervision and his Ph.D. under Kinnaird. In speaking of a third generation of Boltonians, however, I may be pushing the idea of Bolton's influence and "school" too far.

36. Strickland, *Turner Thesis*, 8. Strickland received his Ph.D. from the University of Texas, where he worked under Walter Prescott Webb. Webb argued that Spanish institutions did not adapt to the environmental challenge of the Great Plains. Although Spaniards succeeded as explorers on the high plains, they failed as colonists. Unlike Strickland, Webb did not mention Turner or the frontier thesis and instead denied the direct influence of Turner on his thinking. It is clear, however, that Webb had read Turner's essay before writing his book. See Webb, *The Great Plains* (Boston, 1931), 85–139; and Gregory M. Tobin, *The Making of a History: Walter Prescott Webb and the Great Plains* (Austin, Tex., 1976), 110–11. Also see Necah Stewart Furman, *Walter Prescott Webb: His Life and Impact* (Albuquerque, N.Mex., 1976), 122. Two decades after the appearance of *The Great Plains*, Webb urged historians to examine the frontiers of Latin America in light of Turner's thesis; Webb, *The Great Frontier* (Austin, Tex., 1951), 411–12.

37. In this respect, Zavala stands apart from his Mexican counterparts who, like American historians, have made little attempt to apply Turner's thesis to Mexico's frontiers. See, for example, María del Carmen Velázquez, *Colotlán: Doble frontera contra los bárbaros* (Mexico City, 1961), *Establecimiento y pérdida del septentrión de Nueva España* (Mexico City, 1974), and *El Marqués de Altamira y las Provincias Internas de Nueva España*. Also see César Sepúlveda, *La frontera norte de México: Historia, conflictos, 1672–1975* (Mexico City, 1976), and *Tres ensayos sobre la frontera septentrional de la Nueva España* (Mexico City, 1977). Spanish historians who have examined the Mexican frontier, such as Luis Navarro García and Mario Hernández Sánchez-Barba, have also ignored the Turner thesis. An important exception is Mexican

Turner's thesis, Zavala believed, might apply to the northern frontier of Mexico—part of which now lies in the present United States. Citing Alexander von Humboldt approvingly, Zavala suggested that the insecurity of life in the Mexican north and the unavailability of a docile Indian labor force "stamped the character of the northern people with a certain temper and energy."[38] Zavala also quoted a contemporary of von Humboldt, Miguel Ramos de Arizpe, who claimed that, compared to other Mexicans, northerners were more energetic, hard working, liberty loving, and "devoted to the liberal and mechanical arts." Mexico's northern frontier, Zavala concluded, "seemed to be the guardian of liberty," but he also recognized that the isolated region could become a refuge for political despots, whose power could not be curbed easily by the distant central government.[39]

Zavala's idea that distance could encourage despotism seems to apply especially well to Alta California, the most isolated province on the Mexican frontier. The point has been made forcibly by C. Alan Hutchinson, who explicitly tested Turner's thesis in Mexican California. An Englishman trained outside of the Bolton tradition, Hutchinson found that the region lacked two ingredients that were essential to Turner's interpretation: land and liberty. Missions or large estates occupied the choicest land in California, Hutchinson argued, and distance alone discouraged Mexicans from moving there. To explain

historian Vito Alessio Robles. Although he did not cite Turner, Alessio Robles briefly made some of the same points on which Zavala later elaborated. Alessio Robles, "Las condiciones sociales en el norte de la Nueva España," *Memorias de la Academia Mexicana de la Historia* 4 (1945): 156–57. American historians, not of the Bolton school, who have explicitly applied the Turner thesis to the Mexican frontier include Strickland and C. Alan Hutchinson.

38. Zavala, "The Frontiers of Hispanic America," in Walker D. Wyman and Clifton B. Kroeber, *The Frontier in Perspective* (Madison, Wis., 1965), 48. For the larger essay in Spanish of which "Frontier of Hispanic America" is a part, see *Cuadernos Americanos* 17 (1958): 374–84. For the original Spanish version of "Frontiers of Hispanic America" with more extensive documentation, see David J. Weber, ed., *El México perdido* (Mexico City, 1976), 150–66.

39. Zavala, "Frontiers of Hispanic America," 49–50. Discussing frontiers generally in the period before 1750, William H. McNeill recently came to a similar conclusion. "Compulsion and legally reinforced forms of social hierarchy were more generally characteristic of frontier society than were equality and freedom"; McNeill, *The Great Frontier: Freedom and Hierarchy in Modern Times* (Princeton, N.J., 1983), 26. McNeill's explanation, however, differs from Zavala's yet also applies to some Hispanic frontiers. McNeill saw egalitarianism diminished by the need of frontier elites to control scarce labor and resources, the need to sustain armies for protection on frontiers, and dependency on outside markets.

why the California frontier failed to promote democracy and instead became a refuge for petty tyrants, Hutchinson spun Turner's argument around. "The frontier," he wrote, "reproduces, in somewhat more visible fashion, what is already present in the homeland from which the settlers came."[40] In this sense, the Turner thesis applies. Whereas the American frontier promoted democracy, the Mexican frontier promoted caudillismo, or petty despotism. Finally, Hutchinson argued that frontier California's abundant and exploitable supply of Indian laborers discouraged the californios from working with their own hands. Thus, they failed to develop "such frontier virtues as independence or resourcefulness."[41] Perhaps because he based his conclusions on an examination of the neglected Mexican period (1821–46) rather than the preceding Spanish era, which has held greater interest for historians, Hutchinson's conclusions regarding the relationship between the frontier and political democracy have been largely ignored by Borderlands scholars.

At the same time that a number of scholars tested the frontier thesis in comparative studies, a group of social historians found some of Turner's ideas applicable to the Borderlands. In the main, the Bolton school demonstrated little interest in social history.[42] The few scholars who have concerned themselves with the nature of Borderlands society have generally come out of other traditions, and, with few exceptions, the most sophisticated studies have been written in the last two decades by historians who have adopted the quantitative methods and interdisciplinary modes of inquiry of the "new" social history. Many who have used these fresh approaches have focused on urban history, where Turner's thesis has little explanatory value.[43] Others, however, have

40. Hutchinson, *Frontier Settlement in Mexican California: The Híjar-Padrés Colony and Its Origins, 1769–1835* (New Haven, Conn., 1969), 398. For a reprint of Hutchinson's commentary on the Turner thesis, see David J. Weber, ed., *New Spain's Far Northern Frontier: Essays on Spain in the American West, 1540–1821* (Albuquerque, N.Mex., 1979), 173–77, and *El México perdido*, 140–49. Hutchinson received his Ph.D. from the University of Texas.

41. Hutchinson, *Frontier Settlement*, 399.

42. See, for example, Antonio José Ríos-Bustamante, "A Contribution to the Historiography of the Greater Mexican North in the Eighteenth Century," *Aztlán* 7 (1976): 350.

43. For a discussion of some of this literature, see Roger W. Lotchin and David J. Weber, "The New Chicano Urban History," *History Teacher* 16 (1983): 219–47.

written about the era of the shifting Spanish-American colonial frontier and have posed questions that would have intrigued Turner, who
was himself a pioneer in interdisciplinary research and in the use of
quantitative techniques.[44] Yet it seems clear that Turner's ideas have
influenced these scholars only slightly; they seldom mention him
explicitly. Instead, they acknowledge an intellectual debt to the Berkeley school of demography, to American social historians such as John
Demos and Stephen Thernstrom, or to the French Annales school
and focus on questions involving infant mortality, longevity, household size and composition, sex ratios, illegitimacy, and migration.[45]

Several practitioners of the new social history, however, have also
commented on the impact of the frontier on Hispanic society. They
have implicitly embraced Turner's notion that the frontier altered the
character of Mexican frontiersmen in a variety of ways, such as promoting individualism and egalitarianism and providing what Turner
called "conditions of social mobility."[46] The new social historians were
not the first to make such suggestions, but they examined frontier
society in greater detail and with more sophistication than their predecessors did.[47]

44. Billington, *The American Frontier Thesis*, 15–16.

45. See, for example, James Michael McReynolds, "Family Life in a Borderland
Community: Nacogdoches, Texas, 1779–1861" (Ph.D. dissertation, Texas Tech Uni-
versity, 1978). McReynolds modeled his dissertation after studies by John Demos.
See Demos, *A Little Commonwealth: Family Life in Plymouth Colony* (New York, 1970).
Also see Janie Louise Aragón, "The People of Santa Fe in the 1790s," *Aztlán* 7 (1976):
391–417. Aragón did not look at frontier society in a broad context but probed census
data to answer questions about population growth, occupations, and ethnic structure.
For an examination of some of this literature in a broader context than I am able to
provide in this brief essay, see Richard Griswold del Castillo, "Quantitative History
in the American Southwest: A Survey and Critique," *Western Historical Quarterly* 15
(1984): 407–26.

46. Turner, "Contributions of the West to Democracy," in Ray Allen Billington,
ed., *Selected Essays of Frederick Jackson Turner: Frontier and Section* (Englewood Cliffs,
N.J., 1961), 95. Also see Gilberto Miguel Hinojosa, *A Borderlands Town in Transition:
Laredo, 1755–1870* (College Station, Tex., 1983), 17–18, 43. Hinojosa found a high
level of social stratification by ethnic group in Laredo, but he did not attempt to
compare the frontier with the metropolis.

47. See, for example, France V. Scholes, "Civil Government and Society in New
Mexico in the Seventeenth Century," *New Mexico Historical Review* 10 (1935): 97–
98. Scholes argued that the frontier lessened social distinctions. (Scholes was not a
Bolton student but studied with Turner at Harvard.) Alessio Robles suggested that
the struggle against Indians, the physical environment, and the lack of Indian labor
strengthened the character of colonists in the north, making them more energetic,

Alicia Tjarks has written the most ambitious and searching of these new studies. In an article entitled the "Urban Evolution of Texas," she explicitly mentioned the Turner thesis and argued that similarities existed between the American frontier and the proto-urban communities of early eighteenth-century Hispanic Texas. Tjarks found that the Hispanic pioneers in Texas exhibited "all of the features typical of the frontier." They were future-oriented, stoic, strong, lovers of the wild, and reluctant to accept official control.[48] Tjarks's study of late eighteenth-century census reports in Texas, in which she did not mention Turner, reveals an open society, less stratified than the society of central Mexico. Frontier Texas, she argued, represented a land of opportunity of Mexican immigrants in the late eighteenth century. Although political democracy did not flourish, upward social mobility occurred easily in this "melting pot of races."[49]

Tjarks also studied census returns from late eighteenth-century New Mexico. There, too, she found a racial melting pot but concluded that the process of racial blending occurred more slowly in New Mexico than in Texas. In the case of New Mexico, a considerable amount of racial amalgamation had occurred among Mexican immigrants even before they reached the province. Compared to her work on Texas, Tjarks's study of New Mexico is much narrower chronologically and less suggestive about the impact of the frontier on that society.[50] But another scholar, Antonio José Ríos-Bustamante, studied census data

farsighted, and tenacious; "Las condiciones sociales en el norte de la Nueva España," 156–57. François Chevalier described the Mexican north (sixteenth- and seventeenth-century Nueva Galicia and Nueva Vizcaya in particular) as an area that allowed greater individual initiative and enterprise than did central Mexico, but he attributed this to distance from central authority rather than to frontier conditions; Chevalier, Land and Society in Colonial Mexico: The Great Hacienda, ed. Lesley Byrd Simpson and trans. Alvin Eustis (1951; reprint ed., Berkeley and Los Angeles, 1970), 148–51. For more recent assessments of the frontier as an area of relatively high social mobility, see Manuel Patricio Servín, "California's Hispanic Heritage: A View into the Spanish Myth," in Weber, New Spain's Far Northern Frontier, 117–33; and Ralph Vigil, "The Hispanic Heritage and the Borderlands," Journal of San Diego History 19 (1973): 33, 38–39. For frontier individualism in New Mexico, see Marc Simmons, "Settlement Patterns and Village Plans in Colonial New Mexico," in Weber, New Spain's Far Northern Frontier, 97–115.

48. Tjarks, "Evolución urbana de Texas durante el siglo XVIII," Revista de Indias 131–38 (1973–74): 609.

49. Tjarks, "Comparative Demographic Analysis of Texas, 1777–1793," Southwestern Historical Quarterly 77 (1974): 322, 293–94.

50. Tjarks, "Demographic, Ethnic, and Occupational Structure of New Mexico, 1790: The Census Report of 1790," The Americas 35 (1978): 80.

from late eighteenth-century Albuquerque and found that its frontier community possessed some of the characteristics that Turner noted on the American frontier (although neither Ríos-Bustamante nor Tjarks mentioned Turner in their studies of New Mexico). Albuquerque's citizens, according to Ríos-Bustamante, exhibited a higher degree of social mobility, a more rapidly growing rate of miscegenation, and greater egalitarianism than did the people who lived in central Mexico.[51]

Similarly, Leon Campbell did not mention Turner explicitly, but he explained the nature of society at the small military posts in Hispanic Alta California in Turnerian terms. Campbell concluded that in frontier garrisons "social distances between officers and enlisted men were greatly reduced" and upward social mobility was easily achieved.[52] He saw California as a land of opportunity where "the widespread distribution of *land* . . . meant that California society was markedly less rigid than that of the metropolitan regions."[53] Isolated and enjoying a salutary neglect by Spanish officials, californios "shared in the optimistic dream of the future largely associated only with the Anglo-Saxon culture."[54] Some of Campbell's conclusions stand in opposition to those of C. Alan Hutchinson, with whose work Campbell was apparently unfamiliar.[55]

In a major study of frontier society published at the end of the 1970s, Oakah L. Jones also took a Turnerian view of the frontier— without mentioning Turner. In *Los Paisanos: Spanish Settlers on the Northern Frontier of New Spain,* Jones examined the culture and institutions of Hispanic civilian settlers in the provinces along both sides of what became the U.S.-Mexican border. Frontier conditions, Jones concluded, altered Hispanic society dramatically. Although Hispanic frontiersmen depended on the government in the early stages of settlement, with the passage of time they "became more self-reliant, more individualistic, less class conscious, and more conservative in

51. Ríos-Bustamente, "New Mexico in the Eighteenth Century: Life, Labor, and Trade in la Villa de San Felipe de Albuquerque, 1706–1790," *Aztlán* 7 (1976): 379.
52. Campbell, "The First Californios: Presidial Society in Spanish California," *Journal of the West* 11 (1972), reprinted in Oakah L. Jones, Jr., *The Spanish Borderlands: A First Reader* (Los Angeles, 1974), 112, 115.
53. Ibid., 116. (Emphasis added.)
54. Ibid. Campbell's article ranges across both the Spanish and Mexican periods without taking into account changes that might have occurred in California's institutions or economy with the advent of Mexico's independence from Spain in 1821.
55. See Hutchinson, *Frontier Settlement.*

their political outlook than the people of central New Spain."[56] In general, Jones found that the harshness of frontier life had a leveling effect. In a phrase aimed perhaps at cliometricians, Jones noted that on the frontier "class rivalry and distinction had little place except for statistical purposes."[57]

Thus, although they have rarely cited Turner, Borderlands historians with an interest in social history have suggested in their recent works that Hispanic frontiersmen enjoyed greater opportunity for upward social mobility and lived in a more egalitarian society than their countrymen in the more settled areas of Mexico. Anthropologists, most notably Miguel León-Portilla and Frances León Swadesh, have come to similar conclusions.[58]

Ironically, although many of these studies have used quantitative techniques, the idea that frontier society was relatively open is based on impressionistic evidence. No scholar has made a statistical comparison between frontier societies and societies in more settled areas of central Mexico. Hence, claims to "relative" openness have only been asserted, not empirically demonstrated. Conventional wisdom—

56. Jones, Los Paisanos, 238, 252–53.
57. Ibid., 247.
58. León-Portilla described the distinctive "ethos" of the residents of the present-day Mexican north, which he ascribed in part to the frontier. See León-Portilla, "The Norteño Variety of Mexican Culture: An Ethnohistorical Approach," in Edward H. Spicer and Raymond H. Thompson, eds., Plural Society in the Southwest (New York, 1972), 109–14. Swadesh examined a group of settlers in the Chama Valley of New Mexico and found that frontier conditions made them hard working, self-reliant, and independent. Their society was more fluid and egalitarian than the societies in more settled areas of New Mexico or Mexico, and land and trade with Indians provided opportunities for advancement. See Swadesh, Los primeros pobladores: Hispanic Americans of the Ute Frontier (South Bend, Ind., 1974), 17, 46, 60, 156–57, 159, 173. Henry F. Dobyns argued that the Hispanic frontier in Arizona did not promote individualism as Turner found on the American frontier. Instead, Dobyns suggested that Hispanics brought their own sense of individualism with them, and he surmised that "Hispanic individualism probably survived intact." Dobyns seemed to believe that the Hispanic frontier in Arizona promoted social mobility. He acknowledged that some soldiers achieved upward mobility at the Tucson presidio. His conclusion that "the population of this frontier post remained socially stratified along ethnic lines" must be tempered by his statement that miscegenation was well advanced in the presidio and that "army service function[ed] as one of those institutions of cultural contact between Spaniards and friendly Native American tribesmen which facilitated the acquisition of Hispanic traits by the latter." Dominated by the church and the military, Tucson's society failed to develop a middle class, much less democracy. See Dobyns, Spanish Colonial Tucson: A Demographic History (Tucson, Ariz., 1976), 62, 65, 111–12. Neither Dobyns, León-Portilla, nor Swadesh cited Turner directly.

a wisdom that Turner helped render conventional—suggests, however, that this assertion is probably correct. Nonetheless, it is interesting to note that by the late eighteenth century racial and class distinctions had begun to break down throughout Mexico; for this period we have the most detailed census records and the largest number of studies on the northern frontier.[59]

If most social historians and anthropologists agree that the frontier altered the character of Mexican frontiersmen in ways that resemble Turner's description of changes among American frontiersmen, why has Turner's thesis failed to exert greater influence on Borderlands historiography or, for that matter, on Mexican historiography? Much of the explanation lies in understanding that the frontier never developed mythic importance in Mexican letters and popular culture and that Mexico's far northern frontier made little impact on Mexico's national culture and institutions. For Turner, "the *most important* effect of the frontier" was "the promotion of democracy here and in Europe."[60] But is there any evidence that the Mexican frontier was a cradle of Mexican democracy or the crucible of a Mexican national character? Some historians have answered that question affirmatively for the northern frontier of sixteenth-century Mexico. Commenting on Spanish expansion northward from Mexico City into the area of Zacatecas, Woodrow Borah characterized that region as a "melting pot" in which different races and ethnic groups "merged into a hybrid culture, clearly Hispanic but equally clearly a subtype—in other words, Mexican. The frontier rather than the center was the creator of Mexican culture and Mexican allegiance."[61]

Other writers have argued convincingly that residents of the present-day northern states of Mexico—Sonora, Sinaloa, Chihuahua,

59. See L. N. McAlister, "Social Structure and Social Change in New Spain," *Hispanic American Historical Review* 43 (1963): 349–70.

60. Turner, "Significance of the Frontier," 22. (Emphasis added.) Turner wrote a separate essay on "Contributions of the West to Democracy," published in the *Atlantic Monthly* in 1903. For a reprint, see Turner, *The Frontier in American History* (New York, 1920), 243–68; and Billington, *Selected Essays*, 77–97.

61. Borah, "Discontinuity and Continuity in Mexican History," *Pacific Historical Review* 48 (1979): 15. Philip Wayne Powell advanced a similar argument. See Powell, *Mexico's Miguel Caldera: The Taming of America's First Frontier, 1548–1597* (Tucson, Ariz., 1977), 262, and "North America's First Frontier, 1546–1603," in George Wolfskill and Stanley Palmer, eds., *Essays on Frontiers in World History* (Austin, Tex., 1981), 26. Zavala took the opposite view; "Frontiers of Hispanic America," 51.

Durango, Coahuila, Nuevo León, and Tamaulipas—possess a unique character that has altered Mexican national life and politics.[62] No one, however, has made a case that the shifting Mexican-American frontier—those parts that are now within the United States (the border states from California to Texas)—ever made an impact on Mexican character and institutions. Some Mexicans hoped that it might liberate Mexico from its "semifeudal routine," as one writer put it in 1831, but Mexico's far northern frontier never exercised such influence. So long as it belonged to Spain or to Mexico, the region was too under-populated, too peripheral, and too underdeveloped to influence activities in the nation's core.[63] Indeed, in the years before the Mexican-American War, the cutting edge of Mexico's northern frontier was not the area of most rapid and effective "Mexicanization," to para-phrase Turner. Nor did Mexicans generally regard the arid, hostile, and remote world of the shifting frontier as a "garden" that would lead to the constant rebirth or regeneration of Mexican culture—an idea that Henry Nash Smith has shown was central to the Anglo-American ethos. The Anglo-American frontier may or may not have promoted democracy, as Turner argued, but, because Americans widely believe that it did, the idea itself is of considerable importance. In Mexico, however, there has been no counterpart to American idealization of frontier life. No myth about the salubrious impact of the frontier exists on which a Mexican Turner might construct a credible intellectual edifice.[64]

Silvio Zavala appears to have been correct in arguing that the far northern frontier was not "the source of the Mexican national type." In Mexico, the greatest blending of Indian and Mexican cultures took place in the nation's center, Zavala explained, making that region the

62. See, for example, Barry Carr, "The Peculiarities of the Mexican North, 1880–1928: An Essay in Interpretation," *Institute of Latin American Studies Occasional Papers*, no. 4 (Glasgow, 1971); and León-Portilla, "The Norteño Variety," 104–7.
63. Zavala, as quoted in Weber, *Mexican Frontier*, 283. I discussed this point further. Also see Hennessy, *The Frontier in Latin American History*, 13, 14, 26.
64. Turner, "Significance of the Frontier," 5; and Smith, *Virgin Land: The American West as Symbol and Myth* (1950; reprint ed., Cambridge, 1970), 4, 250–60. Also see Powell, *Mexico's Miguel Caldera*, 226. Powell has lamented that the American "western" of fiction and film has had no counterpart in a Mexican "northern," and he characterized the Mexican north as "an almost forgotten historical world" in Mexican popular culture. Also see Hennessy, *The Frontier in Latin American History*, 3, 13, 21.

cradle of Mexican civilization. In contrast, he wrote, the northern frontier "can be considered only a source of social peculiarities."[65]

One of the sources of those peculiarities was the United States, with which Mexico has shared a shifting frontier. Contact with North Americans, which increased dramatically in the first half of the nineteenth century, began to "Americanize" Mexican culture even before the United States invaded northern Mexico in 1846.[66] Following the conquest and acquisition by the United States of the Mexican frontier in 1846–48, zones of interaction between Hispanics and Anglos continued to exist. By some definitions, these zones of intercultural contact represent frontiers, but not in the sense that Turner meant when he defined the Anglo-American frontier.[67] Hispanics seldom found opportunity in frontier California, Arizona, New Mexico, and Texas. To the contrary, Hispanics found opportunity denied them as they became victims of racial discrimination and xenophobia. Although some individuals managed to make their way up the socioeconomic ladder, Hispanics as a group were pushed to the bottom rungs by biased individuals and institutions—forced to become foreigners in what had been their native land. Hence, Turner's thesis has held no interest for historians studying Hispanic-American frontiers in the United States in the last half of the nineteenth century,[68] although this period has been especially fertile for applications of the Turner thesis to the Anglo-American westering experience, aspects of which Turnerians have named the cattlemen's frontier, the transportation frontier, the miners' frontier, the farmers' frontier, and the Indian frontier.[69] It should not be surprising, however, that there has been no corollary

65. Zavala, "Frontiers of Hispanic America," 51.

66. Weber, *Mexican Frontier*, 283.

67. Forbes, "Frontiers in American History," 65, 68–69.

68. See, for example, Weber, *Foreigners in Their Native Land*; Leonard Pitt, *The Decline of the Californios: A Social History of the Spanish-Speaking Californians, 1846–1890* (Berkeley and Los Angeles, 1968); Arnoldo de León, *The Tejano Community, 1836–1900* (Albuquerque, N.Mex., 1982); and Robert J. Rosenbaum, *Mexicano Resistance in the Southwest: "The Sacred Right of Self-Preservation"* (Austin, Tex., 1981).

69. These terms are taken from titles of books in the Histories of the American Frontier series, conceived and first edited by Ray Allen Billington and now edited by Howard R. Lamar, Martin Ridge, and David J. Weber and published by the University of New Mexico Press.

study of the "Hispanic frontier" following that group's subjugation at mid-century.

The Turner thesis, then, has had little direct influence on Borderlands scholarship. Although Bolton endorsed Turner's mode of analysis, neither he nor his disciples attempted to apply it. Only a few historians have explicitly tested Turner's ideas in studies of Hispanic frontiers in what is now the United States, and these scholars have not been of the Bolton school. Turner's interpretations, however, have probably influenced some Borderlands scholars who do not explicitly refer to him. His remarkable success in challenging the idea that the "germs" of European institutions planted themselves in North America and spread westward unchecked has led to a new conventional wisdom. It appears that most Borderlands scholars see no need to cite Turner's works or to carry on a running dialogue with him when they assert that the frontier altered the society and institutions of Hispanics.

If the Turner thesis has had little influence on Borderlands scholars in the past, it seems even less likely to gain their interest in the future. The thesis has been modified to the point that historians have difficulty either embracing it as an explanatory device or using it as a foil. Turner's original statement in 1892 was clear: "The existence of an area of free land, its continuous recession, and the advance of American settlement westward, explain American development." Turner and his defenders, however, subsequently refined the thesis so that it has gained sophistication but lost the elegant simplicity and force with which Turner's rhetorical excesses originally endowed it.[70]

Meanwhile, new and more satisfying explanations about frontier interactions have arisen on the foundation that Turner built, and historians have turned increasingly to them. The work of scholars such as geographer Marvin Mikesell, anthropologist Owen Lattimore, and ethnohistorian Jack Forbes have proved especially useful, for they remind us that a frontier represents a human as well as a geographical environment. We no longer think of the frontier as a line between "civilization and savagery" but as an interaction between two different cultures. The natures of these interactive cultures—both the culture

70. Turner, "Significance of the Frontier," 3. For Turner's rhetoric, see Ronald H. Carpenter, *The Eloquence of Frederick Jackson Turner* (San Marino, Calif., 1983).

of the invader and that of the invaded—combine with the physical environment to produce a dynamic that is unique to time and place. Finally, it seems clear that Borderlands historians, like their counterparts in the history of the American West, have found other avenues of inquiry that take them beyond the Turner thesis, even if they have not yet found a substitute for it.[71]

71. On the history of the American West, see Malone, Historians and the American West, 8; and Gene M. Gressley, "Whither Western American History? Speculations on a Direction," Pacific Historical Review 53 (1984): 493–94. No other overarching explanatory device has replaced Turner's thesis in Borderlands history, but sociologist Emmanuel Wallerstein's world systems theory has found growing acceptance among social scientists who work in the border region, even if historians are embracing it timidly. See, for example, the special issue of Review, vol. 4 (1981). Also see Timothy G. Baugh, "Southern Plains Societies and Eastern Frontier Pueblo Exchange during the Protohistoric Period," Papers of the Archaeological Society of New Mexico 9 (1984): 157–67; and Thomas D. Hall, "Varieties of Ethnic Persistence in the American Southwest" (Ph.D. dissertation, University of Washington, 1981). In Mexican Frontier, I applied Wallerstein's model to the Southwest when it belonged to Mexico.

4

John Francis Bannon
and the Historiography
of the Spanish Borderlands
*Retrospect and Prospect**

To the uninitiated, the term *Spanish Borderlands* might seem to point to an area of the Pyrenees where Spain borders on France, or the western fringes of Estremadura where Spain meets Portugal. For over a half century, however, most American scholars have understood this term to mean the shifting frontiers of the Spanish empire in North America, from the Floridas through Virginia and across the continent to California and the Pacific Northwest. The name of the great his-

*I am grateful to Joseph Wilder, editor of the *Journal of the Southwest*, who prompted me to write this essay. Upon learning of the death of John Francis Bannon in June 1986, Wilder suggested that I write a short piece that would represent "an intellectual testimony and critique of Bannon's scholarly importance." As my essay grew longer than either of us initially imagined, Wilder never lost patience. And when I asked that I might use the essay as one of the Horn Lectures at the University of New Mexico in the fall of 1987, and publish it with the other lectures that I gave on that occasion, Wilder graciously agreed. Thus, the conception and form of this essay owe much to Joseph Wilder.

I also appreciate the help of an excessive number of people who read preliminary versions of the manuscript: representing the eastern Borderlands, Amy Bushnell and William Coker; the western Borderlands, Donald Cutter, Elizabeth John, and Oakah Jones; representing Chicano history, Albert Camarillo and Richard Griswold del Castillo; and representing the next generation of Borderlands historians, two graduate students who have already produced important work: Charles R. Cutter, who is completing his Ph.D. in history at the University of New Mexico, and Jack S. Williams, who is finishing his Ph.D. in anthropology at the University of Arizona. Although I have adopted many of their suggestions, I could not incorporate them all. Limitations of the essay remain my own.

Finally, I owe thanks to several institutions, for I wrote this essay while a Fellow at the Center for Advanced Study in the Behaviorial Sciences at Stanford, where I received financial support from the Andrew W. Mellon Foundation and from my own university. I especially appreciate the help of the Center's remarkable staff.

torian Herbert Eugene Bolton, who gave shape and direction to this field of study, remains inextricably linked to the Spanish Borderlands. For those scholars whose intellectual formation took place since the 1960s, however, John Francis Bannon came to be associated as closely with the Borderlands as Bolton had been for an earlier generation.

Bannon wrote the books that the last generation of Borderlands historians read in their student years or, if they taught Borderlands history, assigned to their own students as required texts. In 1964 the University of Oklahoma Press published Bannon's anthology of Bolton's essential essays, *Bolton and the Spanish Borderlands*, which found its way onto required reading lists in some college courses.[1] Six years later, in 1970, Bannon's *The Spanish Borderlands Frontier, 1513–1821*, appeared in Ray Allen Billington's distinguished Histories of the American Frontier Series. This extraordinary overview of the entire field made Bannon's name synonymous with the Borderlands. Published by the University of New Mexico Press, which acquired the Billington series from Holt, Rinehart and Winston in 1972, *The Spanish Borderlands Frontier* went into its fifth printing in 1987.[2] Notable for its fine bibliography as well as for its broad synthesis, it remains the standard text and general reference work in the field. Indeed, it is the only synthesis. Bolton's brief, episodic narration of some of the more colorful themes, *The Spanish Borderlands: A Chronicle of Old Florida and the Southwest*, published in 1921, did not represent a true attempt at an overview. Until Bannon's book appeared, then, no one had summarized the burgeoning scholarship on the entire Borderlands. Since 1970 no one else has succeeded (although I myself have been foolish enough to begin to write such a book).

John Francis Bannon wrote prodigiously. By the mid-1980s he had written or edited, according to one count, fourteen books, eight chapters in five other books, ten scholarly articles, sixty-seven book reviews, and thirty-three encyclopedia articles. He also wrote introductions

1. In hardcover, the book went through two editions, selling nearly 5,000 copies before going out of print. A paperback edition, printed in 1974, has had more modest sales: 1,670 copies through 1985. John N. Drayton, Editor-in-Chief, University of Oklahoma Press, to Weber, November 13, 1986.

2. Holt, Rinehart and Winston brought the book out simultaneously in paperback and hardcover editions. It appears that Holt issued a single printing before New Mexico acquired the series. The University of New Mexico Press has issued four printings, representing more than 12,000 copies. David Holtby, Editor, University of New Mexico Press, to Weber, November 17, 1986.

and forewords to a number of books and served as editor of two journals and on the editorial boards of eight others.[3] It seems no exaggeration to say that for the last generation, scholars of the Spanish Borderlands have looked to Bannon as the leading representative of their field. Bannon, for example, was the first Borderlands scholar elected to the presidency of the Westery History Association, an office that he held in 1965–66, five years after the association's founding.

Jack Bannon towered over the field literally as well as figuratively. One of his colleagues described him as "tall and handsome as his movie-actor brother Jim, star of the 'Red Ryder' Hollywood series."[4] Over six feet tall and garbed in the traditional black of his Jesuit Order, Jack stood out at scholarly meetings. Gregarious and unassuming, he could usually be found in animated conversation. I saw him for the last time in 1982 in Phoenix, at the Western History Association's annual meeting. We slipped into a coffee shop for a quiet conversation; when we parted ways, I walked away heavy hearted. Jack had retired in 1973 from Saint Louis University, where he had taught since 1939 and where he chaired the history department for nearly thirty years (1943–71)! A popular teacher and genial colleague, he had accepted visiting professorships at several universities after his retirement, but his eyesight had been failing for several years and decades of smoking had worsened his emphysema. He had done his life's work, he told me, and was waiting to die. We exchanged an occasional letter after that, but I never saw Jack again. In June of 1986 his last doctoral student, Helen Canada, kindly sent me the sad news. Emphysema had taken Jack's life on June 5, 1986, in his eighty-first year.

The death of John Francis Bannon may mark the end of an era in the study of the Spanish Borderlands. In some ways, it was his era, but in a larger sense Bannon's work represented an extension of the era of the field's founder, Herbert E. Bolton. Jack was a thoroughgoing Boltonian. Indeed, his very entry into the field occurred as a result of Bolton's intervention. Bannon had taken early historical training

3. William Barnaby Faherty, S.J., Professor Emeritus, Saint Louis University, to Weber, October 23, 1986, who graciously sent biographical information to me. Also, see below, n. 8.
4. Typescript obituary written by William Barnaby Faherty, S.J., Professor Emeritus of History, Saint Louis University.

in medieval history (as, coincidentally, had Bolton). He had studied
for three years in France, had earned an M.A. in medieval history
from Saint Louis University (1929), and had taught at a small college
for several years when the Society of Jesus sent him to Berkeley to
study with Bolton, about 1936. At that time Bannon had never heard
of Herbert Bolton or the Borderlands but, as he would later recall,
Bolton had been "badgering" Father Gilbert J. Garraghan "to intercede
with Jesuit superiors to send him some 'bright young men' who might
help him to exploit the Jesuit treasures collected from the archives of
Mexico and Spain and elsewhere and get themselves a Ph.D. in the
process."[5]

At Berkeley, Bolton found a niche for Bannon in his research
program. Several Jesuits had preceded Bannon around Bolton's famous
"Round Table" seminar, and two of them, W. Eugene Shiels and Peter
Masten Dunne, had examined the expansion of the Jesuit missions
up the west coast and central plateau of New Spain. It remained for
Bannon to carry the story still farther north, covering the years prior
to the arrival in Sonora of one of Bolton's favorite historical figures,
Father Eusebio Francisco Kino. Thus the Jesuit missions in Sonora,
from their beginnings in 1621 to Kino's arrival in 1687, became the
subject of his doctoral dissertation. With a fresh Ph.D. degree in hand,
Bannon returned to Saint Louis University in 1939 to fill a position
in the history department (sixteen years later the dissertation became
a book: *The Mission Frontier in Sonora, 1621–1687*).[6]

At Berkeley, then, Bannon followed Bolton not only into the
Borderlands, but into close examination of a favorite topic of Bolton's,
the missions, in one of Bolton's favorite areas, Sonora. During his
long career as a professor in Saint Louis, Bannon would also emulate
Bolton by promoting an understanding of the Borderlands as essential
to a fully realized picture of early American history and by touting the
virtues of comparative studies of America's past. Bannon accomplished
these larger ends mainly through the writing of textbooks and edited
volumes for classroom use. Writing a textbook can be much like a
childhood disease; a single episode is unpleasant, but usually provides
lifetime immunity. Immunization never took on Bannon. He wrote

5. Bannon, "A Western Historian—How He Got That Way," *Western Historical Quarterly* 1 (July 1970): 244.
6. New York: United States Catholic Historical Society, 1955.

several college-level texts whose subjects ranged over three continents.[7] These included *Colonial North America: A Short Survey* (1946),
in which he argued for a multiethnic approach to understanding America's colonial past; a massive single-volume history, *Latin America: An
Historical Survey* (1947, 1958, 1963, 1977), written with fellow Jesuit
Peter Masten Dunne and brought up to date by Robert Ryal Miller;
and a two-volume history of the Western Hemisphere, *The History of
the Americas* (1952, 1963). Bolton had published a modest outline of
his own course, *History of the Americas: A Syllabus with Maps* (1928,
1935). Bannon's two-volume work put considerable flesh on Bolton's
outline. In addition, Bannon edited two anthologies designed to expose
students to conflicting viewpoints among historians: *The Spanish Conquistadores: Men or Devils?* (1960) and *Indian Labor in the Spanish Indies:
Was There Another Solution?* (1966).[8]

Both Bannon and Bolton unabashedly promoted the study of the
Borderlands and colonial Latin America, but each adopted a style
suited to his temperament and circumstances. Bolton enjoyed the
resources of a major research university to which he could attract
doctoral students with low tuition and the premier library in the field—
the Bancroft Library. Much of his energies went into building the field
through training an astounding 104 Ph.D.'s and 323 M.A.'s, many
of whom he sent out to other institutions to spread the message.
Bannon, on the other hand, taught at a small private university with
more limited resources and a costly Ph.D. program. Nonetheless, twenty
historians earned doctorates under his direction and fifty earned M.A.'s—
numbers that most mentors would find satisfying.[9] New technologies,

7. His first textbook, an interpretive essay on European history, *The Epitome of
Western Civilization* (Milwaukee: Bruce Publishing Co., 1942), "was used as a text-
book in a number of mid-western colleges." William Barnaby Faherty, S.J., Professor
Emeritus, Saint Louis University, to Weber, November 21, 1986.

8. For a bibliography of Bannon's writings, see the festschrift prepared by some
of his former students: Russell M. Magnaghi, ed., *From the Mississippi to the Pacific:
Essays in Honor of John Francis Bannon, S.J.* (Marquette: Northern Michigan University
Press, 1982), pp. 124–32. This bibliography is not, however, complete. Among the
missing items are Bannon's foreword to Paul M. Roca, *Paths of the Padres Through
Sonora: An Illustrated History and Guide to Its Spanish Churches* (Tucson: Arizona
Pioneers Historical Society, 1967), pp. ix–xiii, and "In Memorium: Peter Masten
Dunne," in Juan Antonio Balthasar, *Juan Antonio Balthasar: Padre Visitador to the
Sonora Frontier*, Peter Masten Dunne, ed. (Tucson: Arizona Pioneers Historical Soci-
ety, 1957), pp. i–iii.

9. Bannon's Ph.D. students are listed in Magnaghi, ed., *From the Mississippi to*

however, enabled Bannon to reach a wider audience than Bannon could. In the mid-1950s Bannon wrote and narrated several series of weekly programs for public and commercial television: "Before There Was a U.S.A.," "The Great American West," and "This Was St. Louis." For American Airlines he wrote two booklets, *History Below the Jet Trails* (*Saint Louis to Los Angeles*) (1959) and *West to the River* (*New York to Saint Louis*) (1960).

As if it were not enough that Bannon emulated his mentor as a scholar of the Borderlands, a proponent of the history of the Americas, and a popularizer and promoter of history, he paid Bolton the supreme compliment of writing his biography: *Herbert Eugene Bolton: The Historian and the Man, 1870–1953* (1978).

Finally, Bannon's interpretation of Spain's expansion into the Borderlands resembled Bolton's in that it emphasized its positive aspects. Eager to counter what they saw as an Anglophile explanation of early American history, Bolton and Bannon slighted the negative impact of Spanish colonization on native peoples although they did not completely overlook it. Bannon's work fitted comfortably into what historian Benjamin Keen has characterized as the "romantic" and "Hispanophile tone of the Bolton tradition."[10]

Bannon wrote his earliest work on the Borderlands, *The Mission Frontier in Sonora*, almost entirely from the point of view of the Jesuits. "The tale of the Black Robes' first century on the Western Slope," he enthusiastically proclaimed, "is a glorious one. Great names dot its pages."[11] All of these names were Spanish, and no hint appears in Bannon's early work that the Jesuits' "success" might have represented another people's loss. Bannon dismissed the religion of Sonora Indians with the comment that they possessed "practically no religion, at least in the European sense," and he explained Indian resistance to white encroachment as a character defect: "Belligerent and marauding Apaches . . . and unruly Seris . . . were to retard for long years the normal

---

the Pacific, p. 133, and a biographical essay in that same volume gives the total of his M.A. recipients: Clifford J. Reutter, "John Francis Bannon: Ethnographer, Padre of the Peoples," p. 3. Graduate students who completed their degrees under Bolton's direction are identified by name in John Francis Bannon, *Herbert Eugene Bolton: The Historian and the Man* (Tucson: University of Arizona Press, 1978), pp. 283–90.

10. Benjamin Keen, "Main Currents in United States Writings on Colonial Spanish America, 1884–1984," *Hispanic American Historical Review* 65 (November 1985): 670. Keen elaborates on p. 662.

11. *The Mission Frontier in Sonora*, p. 142.

civilian development of Sonora."[12] He saw Sonora Indians largely through the eyes of his Jesuit sources and repeated the Jesuits' ethnocentric observations freely. Only after offering his reader a long description of Sonora Indians by Father Ignaz Pfefferkorn, which included such terms as "mean and despicable . . . feels no compassion, whom no disgrace shames . . . whose motives are those of the animal," was Bannon moved to ask, "One wonders if Padre Ignaz did not let his love of rhetoric run a little freely."[13]

Bannon's *Spanish Borderlands Frontier* also displayed the pro-Spanish tendency of the Bolton school. The book, he explained, told the story of "the advance of civilization into wilderness." The natives who inhabited the "wilderness" represented little more than a "challenge."[14] Ironically, Bannon took a more sympathetic view of invaded peoples when he wrote about Anglo-American expansion into areas occupied by Spaniards.

Meanwhile, other scholars had revealed less flattering aspects of the Spanish colonial experience. Homer Aschmann, Sherburne Cook, Henry Dobyns, and Peveril Meigs, for example, portrayed missionaries as unwitting contributors to the deaths of appalling numbers of mission Indians in Baja California, Alta California, and Pimería Alta.[15] Cook argued that by confining Indians in close quarters and by keeping them forcibly in mission compounds, Franciscans in Alta California both sapped the Indians' will to live and placed them in an environment where European diseases spread more quickly. These criticisms of the mission system appeared well before 1970, but did not find their way into Bannon's *Spanish Borderlands Frontier*. Nor did the works of Aschmann, Cook, and Dobyns merit notice in Bannon's extensive bibliography (Bannon did cite Meigs's book on the Dominican missions of Baja California, although he ignored its dreary conclusions).

12. Ibid., pp. 48, 139.
13. Ibid., p. 14.
14. Ibid., pp. 3–4.
15. Homer Aschmann, *The Central Desert of Baja California*. Ibero-America no. 42 (Berkeley: University of California Press, 1949); Sherburne F. Cook, *The Indian Versus the Spanish Mission* and *The Physical and Demographic Reaction of the Nonmission Indians in Colonial and Provincial California*, both first published in 1943 as volumes 21 and 22 of *Ibero-Americana*, and conveniently reprinted in Cook, *The Conflict Between the California Indian and White Civilization* (Berkeley: University of California Press, 1976); Henry F. Dobyns, "Indian Extinction in the Middle Santa Cruz Valley, Arizona," *New Mexico Historical Review* 38 (April 1963): 163–81; and Peveril Meigs, *The Dominican Mission Frontier of Lower California* (Berkeley: University of California Press, 1935).

In the 1970s, scholars who took a dim view of the missionaries' achievements became more vocal.[16] At the end of the decade, Bannon acknowledged that they had raised compelling questions about the mission's "place as a beneficient [sic] force."[17] Bannon recognized the work of anthropologists Edward Spicer and Henry Dobyns as fair,[18] but others, he observed, had rushed to judgment and put "preconceived conviction" ahead of research. Although Bannon declined to name the latter group, it appears that he had in mind Sherburne Cook, Bernard Fontana, and Daniel S. Matson. At the hands of these scholars, Bannon wrote: "good things are minimized; obvious less favorable aspects and the actual failings of the mission experiment are magnified."[19] Bannon's own Christophilic, triumphalist bias had run in the opposite direction. By the late 1970s he offered a more measured defense of the missions, urging sympathy for the missionaries as products of their time who intended no malevolence.[20]

In studying the Borderlands, then, Bannon followed Bolton's lead

16. See, for example, Robert Archibald, "Indian Labor at the California Missions: Slavery or Salvation?" *Journal of San Diego History* 24 (Spring 1978): 172–82; and Robert Heizer, "Impact of Colonization on the Native California Societies," *Journal of San Diego History* 24 (Winter 1978): 121–39. John Kessell also notes epidemics among Indians, although he does not comment on them, and shows the Franciscans in an unromantic light, right to their quarrels and hemorrhoids. See, for example, his *Friars, Soldiers, and Reformers: Hispanic Arizona and the Sonora Mission Frontier, 1767–1856* (Tucson: University of Arizona Press, 1976). For further sources, see W. R. Swagerty, "Spanish-Indian Relations, 1513–1821," in Swagerty, ed., *Scholars and the Indian Experience: Critical Reviews of Recent Writing in the Social Sciences* (Bloomington: Indiana University Press, 1984), p. 54.

17. "The Mission as a Frontier Institution: Sixty Years of Interest and Research," *Western Historical Quarterly* 10 (July 1979): 305.

18. Bannon's bibliography cited Edward H. Spicer's *Cycles of Conquest: The Impact of Spain, Mexico, and the United States on the Indians of the Southwest, 1533–1960* (Tucson: University of Arizona Press, 1962) and Henry F. Dobyns's *Spanish Colonial Tucson: A Demographic Study* (Tucson: University of Arizona Press, 1976).

19. Bannon, "The Mission as a Frontier Institution," p. 319. Bannon's bibliography included an anthology of Cook's earlier work, *The Conflict Between the California Indian and White Civilization* (Berkeley: University of California Press, 1976), and the introduction to Daniel S. Matson and Bernard L. Fontana, trans. and eds., *Friar Bringas Reports to the King: Methods of Indoctrination on the Frontier of New Spain, 1796–97* (Tucson: University of Arizona Press, 1977), a portion of which he paraphrased.

20. Bannon, "The Mission as a Frontier Institution," pp. 308, 318–20. For a more detailed response, see two articles by Francis F. Guest, "An Examination of the Thesis of S. F. Cook on the Forced Conversion of Indians in the California Missions," *Southern California Quarterly* 41 (Spring 1979): 1–77, and "Cultural Perspectives on California Mission Life," *Southern California Quarterly* 65 (Spring 1985): 1–65.

both in choice of subject and in approach. Whereas Bolton's manifold contributions emphasized publication of the results of archival research in monographs and scholarly articles, Bannon's major contribution took the form of synthesis—whether in textbooks, television, or encyclopedia articles. The integration and dissemination of historical knowledge were Bannon's forte.

Jack taught or encouraged some of us directly, and through his books and articles he indirectly continues to teach and to influence the field. As he wrote of Alfred B. Thomas, good teachers "live on in the memories of their students and the work they do."[21]

Bannon perpetuated Bolton's approach to the Borderlands even as the field began to move away from Bolton's framework and to fragment—as so many areas of history have done since the 1950s.[22] Bannon's *Spanish Borderlands Frontier* gave the field an outward appearance of unity, even as it broke into parts that began to lose connection with one another.

One massive crack in the Bolton framework ran down the middle of the continent, dividing students of the eastern Borderlands from those who study the western Borderlands. Books, articles, and bibliographies have come to focus on *either* the Southwest or the Southeast. Few writers have worked comfortably in both areas, or sought to explain continuities or variations among the Hispanic communities that once occupied the entire southern tier of North America, as Bolton did so successfully in his famous essays on the "Mission as a Frontier Institution" and "Defensive Spanish Expansion and the Significance of the Borderlands."[23] Writers in the Southeast and Southwest generally acknowledge that "the Borderlands" embraces both areas,

21. Introduction to *Militarists, Merchants and Missionaries: United States Expansion in Middle America: Essays Written in Honor of Alfred Barnaby Thomas*, Eugene R. Huck and Edward H. Moseley, eds. (University, Ala.: University of Alabama Press, 1970), p. ix.

22. See for example the repetition of this theme in the essays in Michael G. Kammen, ed., *The Past Before Us* (Ithaca, N.Y.: Cornell University Press, 1980).

23. Bolton's essays, first published in 1917 and 1930, have been reprinted in Bannon, ed., *Bolton and the Spanish Borderlands*, pp. 187–211 and 32–64. Exceptions to my generalization include the recent dissertation by William R. Swagerty, "Beyond Bimini: Indian Responses to European Incursions in the Spanish Borderlands, 1513–1600" (Ph.D. dissertation, University of California, Santa Barbara, 1981), and Henry F. Dobyns, ed., *Spanish Colonial Frontier Research*, Spanish Borderlands Research Series, no. 1 (Albuquerque: Center for Anthropological Research, 1980), both of which cover the Borderlands from Atlantic to Pacific.

but limit their studies to one region or the other even while using the broader term *Spanish Borderlands*. [24]

Although Bannon more than any other Boltonian helped keep the eastern and western Borderlands united, his heart was in the Southwest and his definition of the Borderlands lacked consistency. In 1964, Bannon accepted the Bolton framework of a Spanish Borderlands that swept across North America from sea to sea. [25] In an essay published three years later, however, Bannon retreated far from the Atlantic. He limited the Spanish Borderlands to "that sweep of territory extending from Texas through the Southwest, on both sides of the border, and swinging up the Pacific side of the continent to include California." [26]

Three years later, in *The Spanish Borderlands Frontier* (1970) Bannon again included the Southeast in his definition of the Borderlands but expressed a preference for the West because "it was in the western Borderlands that the Spanish expansionist movement worked itself out most effectively." [27] To the dismay of one historian of the eastern Borderlands, William Coker, Bannon "seemed reluctant to include this area as a rightful part of the Spanish Borderlands," and his bibliography on the Southeast was woefully out of date. [28] Indeed, in *The Spanish Borderlands Frontier* Bannon termed Louisiana a "quasi-Borderland" on the grounds that it was never part of the Provincias Internas of New Spain, and in a subsequent article, he dismissed the Floridas somewhat offhandedly, remarking that "from several points of view [they] are listed as a borderland largely out of courtesy." [29] Here

24. See, for example, Oakah L. Jones, *The Spanish Borderlands—A First Reader* (Los Angeles: Lorrin L. Morrison, 1974), p. xi, which confines itself to the western half of the continent, and William S. Coker and Jack D. L. Holmes, "Sources for the History of the Spanish Borderlands," *Florida Historical Quarterly* 49 (August 1971): 380–93, which confines itself almost entirely to the eastern Borderlands. Seldom have writers defined their spatial limits in the titles of their work on the Borderlands, as does Donald C. Cutter, "The Western Spanish Borderlands," in Michael P. Malone, ed., *Historians and the American West* (Lincoln: University of Nebraska Press, 1983), pp. 39–56. Cutter also discusses the split between east and west (pp. 40–41).

25. "Introduction," *Bolton and the Spanish Borderlands*, pp. 5, 12, 19.

26. Foreword to Roca, *Paths of the Padres Through Sonora*, p. x.

27. *Spanish Borderlands Frontier*, p. 3.

28. Coker's review appeared in the *Florida Historical Quarterly* 50 (July 1971): 71–72. I am grateful to him for calling it to my attention.

29. *Spanish Borderlands Frontier*, p. 191. Bannon, "The Mission as a Frontier Institution: Sixty Years of Interest and Research," *Western Historical Quarterly* 10 (July 1979): 309.

Bannon seems to have diverged from Bolton's path. In so doing, he exemplified a trend; he did not start one.

Historically and ecologically, the eastern and western Borderlands might have óccupied separate continents. Administratively, they were united only in the broadest sense as part of the viceroyalty of New Spain (although regarding this question, too, some Borderlands historians disagree). At a more immediate bureaucratic level, however, officials in the eastern Borderlands often answered directly to higher authorities in the Caribbean, be it the captaincy general of Cuba or the *audiencia* of Santo Domingo, or even the Council of the Indies in Spain. In day-to-day affairs, then, the eastern and western borderlands fell under separate administrative structures, and significant communication did not exist between them. What has held those areas together as an intellectual construct in the twentieth century has been their presence within the boundaries of the United States.[30]

Bolton recognized this North American framework explicitly. In 1921 he began his brief overview of *The Spanish Borderlands*, which introduced both the term and the concept, with a clear definition: "This book is to tell of Spanish pathfinders and pioneers in the regions between Florida and California, now belonging *to the United States*, over which Spain held sway for centuries."[31] But the United States, of course, did not exist during those centuries that "Spain held sway" over much of North America. Moreover, the boundaries of the United States as we know them today are not ample enough to contain the historic Spanish Borderlands, which spilled over into what is today northern Mexico.

This predicament points to another split in the field: the present international border divides some historians. For obvious reasons, this division applies to the western Borderlands more than the eastern. Whereas some Borderlands historians confine their study to the area

30. Cutter, "The Western Spanish Borderlands," pp. 40–41. For a contrary view, see Engel Sluiter, *The Florida Situado: Quantifying the First Eighty Years, 1571–1651* (Gainesville, Fla.: University of Florida Libraries, 1985), p. 9, who argues that "Spanish Florida was a child of Mexico, and its fortunes and vicissitudes can best be understood in the context of Mexican historical development."

31. Bolton, *The Spanish Borderlands*, p. vii, italics added. See, too, Bolton, ed., *Arredondo's Historical Proof of Spain's Title to Georgia: A Contribution to the History of One of the Spanish Borderlands* (Berkeley: University of California Press, 1925), p. xi, which he regarded as "a token of the unity of the story of all Spanish North America."

of the present-day United States, others look southward to what is today northern Mexico.[32] As Bannon put it, "there are not a few historians who broaden the concept of the Borderlands so as to encompass the north Mexican provinces—Nuevo Santander, Nuevo León, Coahuila, Chihuahua . . . Sinaloa, Sonora, and Baja California."[33] By this definition Borderlands history spilled out of the area "now belonging to the United States," as Bolton defined the idea in his *Spanish Borderlands* some fifty years earlier.

Neither Bolton nor his students, however, felt constrained by the present United States border. Indeed, in 1921 Bolton probably limited the scope of his *Spanish Borderlands* to the United States in order to fit the requirements of the series in which it appeared. As his other work makes clear, he knew that Arizona could only be explained as part of the larger entity of Pimería Alta and that Spanish administrative units such as the Provincias Internas defied understanding unless scholars crossed present-day boundaries.[34] For Bolton, then, as for many other historians, the Borderlands did not fit neatly into the conceptual box of the present United States. Indeed, historians Howard F. Cline and Donald C. Cutter have urged vastly expanded definitions. Cline suggested that the "Greater Borderlands" included "the Central American, Caribbean, and Gulf peripheries, together with the vast area of Aridamérica," and Cutter once argued that "the Borderlands can extend as far as Hawaii, Guam, and the Philippine Islands."[35]

The more expansive definitions by Cline and Cutter have not been widely accepted, but historians who work in the western Borderlands commonly extend their inquiry into northern Mexico. Here, of course, they invade the domain of historians of Mexico and here, too, division

32. See, for example, the difference in emphasis in two anthologies: Jones, "Introduction," *The Spanish Borderlands—A First Reader*, which includes northern Mexico, and Weber, *New Spain's Far Northern Frontier, 1540–1821: Essays on Spain in the American West* (Albuquerque: University of New Mexico Press, 1979), confined largely to the present-day United States.

33. *Spanish Borderlands Frontier*, p. 3.

34. See Allen Johnson, editor of the *Chronicles of America* series, to Bolton, March 7, 1920, quoted in Bannon, *Herbert Eugene Bolton*, p. 135. Bolton's own proclivities toward a more panoramic sweep are probably more accurately reflected in a textbook that he wrote with Thomas Maitland Marshall, *The Colonization of North America, 1492–1783* (New York: Macmillan, 1920).

35. Cline, "Imperial Perspectives on the Borderlands," in K. Ross Toole et al., eds., *Probing the American West* (Santa Fe: Museum of New Mexico, 1962), p. 173, and Cutter, "The Western Spanish Borderlands," p. 42.

exists among historians. Is the history of the Spanish Borderlands part of the history of Mexico? Historians of Mexico do not agree among themselves on an answer. Some include the area north of the present-day border in their considerations of northern Mexico in the colonial era, but most American historians who study Mexico suggest implicitly that northern Mexico ends historically somewhere along the present-day border.[36] In a provocative essay, published in 1982, José Cuello made the latter assumption explicit.[37]

Cuello found considerable disparity between the historiography of colonial Mexico, which has made great advances in methodology and conceptualization since World War II, and the study of the colonial Mexican North, which in his view had languished. The disparity occurred in large part, Cuello argued, because many historians have understood northern Mexico to be a part of the Borderlands. This categorization, in Cuello's view, linked northern Mexico to a field that "has mysteriously lagged behind the thematic and methodological advances that have characterized the study of colonial Mexico's central

36. Many American historians of Mexico see the western Borderlands as part of their subject. See, for example, Susan M. Deeds, "Land Tenure Patterns in Northern New Spain," *The Americas* 41 (April 1985): 446–61. One often looks in vain, however, for the northern frontier of New Spain in general histories of Mexico, such as Colin M. MacLachlan and Jaime E. Rodríguez O., *The Forging of the Cosmic Race: A Reinterpretation of Colonial Mexico* (Berkeley: University of California Press, 1980), or in more specialized studies, such as Ida Altman and James Lockhart, eds., *Provinces of Early Mexico: Variants of Spanish American Regional Evolution* (Los Angeles: UCLA, 1976). When authors do treat the Borderlands in a general history of Mexico, their treatment is limited to several major themes: the initial exploration of the area, the establishment of settlements in the western Borderlands, and the impact of the Bourbon reforms on administrative structure in the late eighteenth century (in all cases, the area is touched upon lightly, with the greatest attention given to exploration, as is the case with United States history texts). See Michael C. Meyer and William L. Sherman, *The Course of Mexican History* (New York: Oxford University Press, 1979), and Robert Ryal Miller, *Mexico: A History* (Norman: University of Oklahoma Press, 1985).

I have confined this discussion to historians from the United States, although the point would apply to Mexicans who have written about Mexican history, with Vito Alessio Robles, María del Carmen Velázquez, and Silvio Zavala among the few exceptions. See, also, no. 100, below.

37. The quotes in the next two paragraphs may be found in José Cuello, "Beyond the 'Borderlands' is the North of Colonial Mexico: A Latin-Americanist Perspective to the Study of the Mexican North and the United States Southwest," in *Proceedings of the Pacific Coast Council on Latin American Studies*, vol. 9, Kristyna P. Demaree, ed. (San Diego: San Diego State University Press, 1982), pp. 1–3.

regions." Including northern Mexico within the Borderlands has prevented historians of Mexico "from seeing the many thematic continuities that the North shares with . . . the parent field."

Cuello, whose own research has been in colonial Saltillo, apparently felt chagrined to be identified with a field lost in "the boundless
desert of adventure stories, missionary chronicles, and institutional
narratives." Rather than stand by and watch "the cession of even more
of the study of colonial Mexico's North to historians of the Hispanic
heritage of the United States," Cuello suggested a counterattack. Mexican historians, he urged, ought to embrace northern Mexico, which
they have traditionally neglected, but stop at the area of the present-
day border and leave the Borderlands to American history. The Borderlands field, he suggested, was a disreputable partner from whom
historians of Mexico should seek a divorce. Borderlands history, he
argued, is not "an integral part of the Latin American historical field
because the conceptual structure which organizes Borderlands history
and selects its methodologies and themes belongs to the field of United
States history."

Many historians would agree with Cuello that United States history
has provided *a* conceptual structure for the field, just as the boundaries
of the United States have shaped (and restricted) the way in which
historians look at British North America.[38] But United States history
has not provided the only conceptual framework for the field. As
Donald Cutter has put it, the study of the Spanish Borderlands "aims
in great measure to enrich the comprehension of American national
heritage rather than to illumine Spanish colonial history, though it
may do both."[39] And in doing both well, historians of the Borderlands
have relied upon the same methodologies and explored many of the
same themes as their counterparts in colonial Latin America.

Historians working in the Borderlands, then, have not agreed on
the spatial boundaries of their field. Does it include both the southwestern and southeastern part of what is today the United States?
Should historians who work in north Mexican states such as Baja
California, Chihuahua, or Nuevo León be regarded as Borderlands

38. See Jack P. Greene and J. R. Pole, *Colonial British America: Essays in the New History of the Early Modern Era* (Baltimore and London: Johns Hopkins University Press, 1984), p. 9.
39. Cutter, "The Western Spanish Borderlands," p. 53.

historians, Mexican historians, or both? Answers to those questions were not clear prior to, or subsequent to, the publication of Bannon's *Spanish Borderlands Frontier* in 1970.

As Bannon was putting the finishing touches on his manuscript, a new division arose. Growing scholarly interest in Chicano history and in studies of the U.S.-Mexico border region blurred the outer edges of the traditional time-frame of the Spanish Borderlands—a chronological limit previously marked by the demise of the Spanish empire in North America in 1821.

Beginning in the late 1960s, historians began to look seriously at how Hispanic peoples fared in North America in the nineteenth and twentieth centuries. In the western half of America, some historians did more intensive work in the years 1821–1846, when the western half of North America belonged to independent Mexico—an area that might be regarded as Mexico's northern Borderlands.[40] Other historians in the southwestern United States moved still further ahead in time, looking at Mexicans and Mexican Americans in the border region of the United States in the decades since the Mexican-American War and the Treaty of Guadalupe Hidalgo abruptly pushed the border much farther south.

Members of this latter group have identified themselves as Chicano historians or historians of Chicanos. Here, too, division exists. As Richard Griswold del Castillo explained, those "who study the recent history of this area from the perspective of the United States have since become identified as students of the American Southwest, while those who have maintained a Mexican perspective have seen themselves as historians of the Chicano experience."[41] The interests of many Chicano historians stretch back to the Spanish colonial era, but their published scholarship focuses on the years since 1846.[42]

40. For this literature, see Weber, *The Mexican Frontier, 1821–1846: The American Southwest Under Mexico* (Albuquerque: University of New Mexico Press, 1982).
41. Richard Griswold del Castillo, "New Perspectives on the Mexican and American Borderlands," *Latin American Research Review* 19 (1984): 200.
42. See, for example, Albert Camarillo, *Chicanos in a Changing Society: From Mexican Pueblos to American Barrios in Santa Barbara and Southern California, 1848–1930* (Cambridge: Harvard University Press, 1979), Mario T. García, *Desert Immigrants: The Mexicans of El Paso, 1880–1920* (New Haven: Yale University Press, 1981), and Arnoldo de León, *The Tejano Community, 1836–1900* (Albuquerque: University of New Mexico Press, 1982). Among the few exceptions are Juan Gómez-Quiñones, "The Origins and Development of the Mexican Working Class in the United States:

That Chicano historians have found little in common with members of the Spanish Borderlands school is not surprising. The Borderlands tradition, with its emphasis on institutions and on *Spanish* activity seemed elitist and irrelevant to a generation increasingly interested in the social history of the mixed-blood population that comprised the vast majority of Mexicans and Mexican Americans.[43] Moreover, the Mexican Americans as an ethnic group did not exist until after the United States acquired northern Mexico. Indeed, some historians have doubted the existence of any meaningful continuities between the experiences of Spanish colonials in North America and the wave of immigrants that entered the United States from Mexico in the twentieth century.[44] Thus, Chicano historians trained since the early 1970s have tended to identify themselves more closely with the history of the United States or one of its subfields—urban history, social history, labor history, or women's history—rather than with the history of the Spanish empire in North America.[45] A case can be made, as Juan

Laborers and Artisans North of the Río Bravo, 1600–1900," in Elsa Cecilia Frost, Michael C. Meyer, and Josefina Zoraida Vázquez, comps., *El trabajo y los trabajadores en la historia de México* (Mexico and Tucson: El Colegio de México and the University of Arizona Press, 1979), pp. 463–517, and Gilberto Miguel Hinojosa, *A Borderlands Town in Transition: Laredo, 1755–1870* (College Station: Texas A&M University Press, 1983). Textbooks and anthologies in Chicano history either touch on the colonial period lightly, as do Matt S. Meier and Feliciano Rivera, *The Chicanos: A History of Mexican Americans* (New York: Hill and Wang, 1972), or ignore it, as does Rodolfo Acuña, *Occupied America: A History of Chicanos*, 2nd ed. (New York: Harper & Row, 1981). Matt S. Meier, *Bibliography of Mexican American History* (Westport, Conn.: Greenwood Press, 1984), includes a heading for the "Colonial Period."

43. See, for example, Manuel Patricio Servín, "California's Hispanic Heritage: A View into the Spanish Myth," in Weber, ed., *New Spain's Far Northern Frontier,* pp. 117–33.

44. Moses Rischin, "Continuities and Discontinuities in Spanish-Speaking California," in *Ethnic Conflict in California History,* Charles Wollenberg, ed. (Los Angeles: Tinnon-Brown, 1970), pp. 45–60, has argued that the Spanish period has little relevance to the present: "if there is a continuity it is primarily sentimental" (p. 55). See, too, Arthur F. Corwin, "Mexican American History: An Assessment," *Pacific Historical Review* 42 (August 1973): 270–73.

45. This was not true of the first generation of Chicano historians, such as Rudy Acuña, Juan Gómez-Quiñones, Matt S. Meier, Jesús Chavarría, or Carlos Cortés, who moved from Latin American history into Chicano history in the late 1960s to meet the growing demand for scholarly work and teaching in that area. The current generation, including Al Camarillo, Pedro Castillo, Juan García, Mario García, Richard Griswold del Castillo, Gilberto Hinojosa, Ricardo Romo, Arturo Rosales, and Vicki Ruiz, has tended to receive its training in United States history rather than Latin American history. A minority, Arnoldo de León and Oscar Martínez chief among them, have received their training in Latin American history.

Gómez-Quiñones and Luis Leobardo Arroyo have done, that "Chicano history is a new pursuit, a break in the previous tradition."[46]

But no sharp line marks a clear boundary between Chicano history and Borderlands history. Although some Chicano writers have sought to replace the Spanish Borderlands with the romanticized indigenous concept of "Aztlán," others have seen Chicano history as part of a "new" Borderlands history, with its origins in the years of Spanish control—in the "Colonial Borderlands."[47] Indeed, substantial evidence supports the assertion of historian Carlos Cortés that

the Chicano movement of the 1960s and '70s has had a major quantitative and qualitative impact on the course of Borderlands historiography . . . it has increased interest in and led to expanded research and writing about Borderlands history, particularly the period since . . . 1846.[48]

Viewed from one angle, Chicano history has subsumed and invigorated the study of the old Spanish Borderlands. From another angle, Chicano history might be seen as a logical extension of Borderlands history. One of the most respected members of our small cadre, Donald Worcester, has taken that position by challenging the notion that "Spanish Borderlands history ended when Spanish officials left the scene." Worcester has criticized his fellow Borderlands historians whose "horizons . . . have remained limited to the colonial era."[49] In his

46. "On the State of Chicano History: Observations on Its Development, Interpretations, and Theory, 1970–1974," *Western Historical Quarterly* 7 (April 1976): 155.

47. The term *Colonial Borderlands* was recently used by Ralph Vigil, "Historical Overview," in Ellwyn R. Stoddard, Richard L. Nostrand, and Jonathan P. West, eds., *Borderlands Sourcebook: A Guide to the Literature on Northern Mexico and the American Southwest* (Norman: University of Oklahoma Press, 1983), p. 28. John R. Chávez, *The Lost Land: The Chicano Image of the Southwest* (Albuquerque: University of New Mexico Press, 1984), pp. 8, 147–48. Ralph H. Vigil, "The New Borderlands History: A Critique," *New Mexico Historical Review* 48 (July 1973): 189–208, argues the need for greater historical dimension to Chicano history. See, too, Griswold del Castillo, "New Perspectives," p. 200.

48. "The New Chicano Historiography," in Stoddard et al., eds., *Borderlands Sourcebook*, p. 60.

49. Donald E. Worcester, "The Significance of the Spanish Borderlands to the United States," *Western Historical Quarterly* 7 (January 1976): 5–18. The quotation is from the reprint of this article in Weber, ed., *New Spain's Far Northern Frontier*, p. 10. Worcester prepared this essay as his 1975 presidential address to the Western History Association.

view, "the Spanish Borderlands remain, still expanding and more important than ever."[50]

Worcester's efforts to expand the field of the Spanish Borderlands beyond its traditional chronological limits to include the study of Mexicans, Cubans, and Puerto Ricans in contemporary America has been implicitly endorsed by some writers, judging from the titles of their works, and by the major journal in Western history, the *Western Historical Quarterly*.[51] The *Quarterly* biennially bestows the "Herbert Eugene Bolton Award in Spanish Borderlands History" on the best article on "any phase of the history of the Spanish Borderlands, from the Floridas to the Californias, from the sixteenth century *to the present*."[52] The *Quarterly* apparently applies the same definition in its listings of "Recent Articles," where pieces devoted to Mexican-Americans fall under the rubric of "Spanish Borderlands."[53]

From the perspective of Donald Worcester or the editors of the *Western Historical Quarterly*, the old Spanish Borderlands represents a region or a fixed place with an ongoing history. Bolton and Bannon, on the other hand, saw the Borderlands as a process as well as a place—a shifting frontier on the edges of the Spanish empire in North America. In the main, they conceptualized that process in terms of the nation state and its institutions, and so for them the process stopped in 1821 with the end of Spanish hegemony on the continent.

Efforts to move out of the Bolton-Bannon construct and to apply the term *Spanish Borderlands* to the years beyond the Spanish era, however, seem destined to fail. Reasons are many, but not least among them is that new and more readily comprehensible names have replaced it—the American South, the Southwest, the Sunbelt, and the Borderlands (minus the adjective *Spanish*).

In the southwestern United States in recent years, the term *Spanish Borderlands* has not won general acceptance to describe the region after 1821, but the word *Borderlands* has come into vogue. Social scientists as well as historians increasingly understand the Borderlands as the region along both sides of the present-day United States–Mexico

50. Ibid., p. 13.
51. Some of that work is discussed below. See notes 54–57.
52. Emphasis is mine. The guidelines for the award elaborate by expressing interest in studies of "the northward movement of Spanish-speaking peoples into the United States in recent times."
53. Some articles on Chicanos necessarily find their way into the category "Immigration, Ethnicity, and Race." See, for example, vol. 17 (July 1986), pp. 376, 381.

border. Those social scientists who engage primarily in policy-oriented research often ignore historical dimensions prior to our own century,[54] but many social scientists and historians use the term *Borderlands* to refer to the present U.S.-Mexico border region thoughout its history, embracing even those eras before the border existed.[55] Such scholars seem less influenced by the nationalist perspective that informed Bolton and Bannon, and more interested in supranational questions of ecology, culture, and the impact of nations on colonized peoples. The term *Borderlands* is sufficiently vague, however, that some scholars have sensibly become more precise, referring to the "United States–Mexico Borderlands, rather than using Borderlands" without a modifier.[56] The geographical and interdisciplinary scope of this new Borderlands scholarship is evident in a massive bibliographical guide published in 1983, *Borderlands Sourcebook,* and in the *Journal of Borderlands Studies,* inaugurated in 1986. The Association of Borderlands Scholars sponsored both publications.[57]

Clearly, the term *Borderlands* has come to hold different meanings for different constituencies. In the southeastern United States, the *Borderlands,* with or without an adjective, still refers almost exclusively to the period when the Spanish empire extended into that region.[58] In the Southwest, on the other hand, the mention of *Borderlands*

54. See, for example, Richard R. Fagan, "How Should We Think About the Borderlands? An Afterword," *The New Scholar* 9 (1984): 271–73.

55. Referring to historical sources for the years before 1846, for example, sociologist Ellwyn Stoddard, "Border Studies as an Emergent Field of Scientific Inquiry: Scholarly Contributions of U.S.-Mexico Borderlands Studies," *Journal of Borderlands Studies* 1 (Spring 1986): 7, has noted that "although no U.S.-Mexico Borderlands existed during this period, these records describe the milieu from which it was created." See, too, the scope of Michael C. Meyer's essay, "The Borderlands: An Historical Survey for the Non-Historian," in ibid., pp. 133–41.

56. See, for example, Niles Hansen, *Border Region Development and Cooperation: Western Europe and the U.S.-Mexico Borderlands in Comparative Perspective* (El Paso: Center for Inter-American and Border Studies, 1985), and *Statistical Abstract of the United States–Mexico Borderlands* (Los Angeles: UCLA Latin America Center, 1984).

57. Stoddard et al., eds., *Borderlands Sourcebook.*

58. See, for example, William S. Coker and Thomas D. Watson, *Indian Traders of the Southeastern Spanish Borderlands: Panton, Leslie & Company and John Forbes and Company, 1783–1847* (Pensacola: University of West Florida Press, 1986); R. Reid Badger and Lawrence A. Clayton, eds., *Alabama and the Borderlands: From Prehistory to Statehood* (University, Ala.: University of Alabama Press, 1985); and *Calendars of the Spanish Florida Borderlands Collection* (Gainesville: University of Florida Press, 1985). Michael C. Scardaville, "Approaches to the Study of the Southeastern Borderlands," in Badger and Clayton, eds., *Alabama and the Borderlands,* pp. 184–96.

would seldom bring to mind the area from Louisana to Florida. Historians of the Southwest follow an inconsistent and bewildering variety of practices, at times contradicting even themselves.[59] For some historians of the Southwest the *Spanish Borderlands* refers only to the years before 1821; others use the term to embrace the period both before and after 1821. Still others employ *Borderlands* without the "Spanish" designation to mean the eras before and after 1821.[60]

Several historians who write about the Spanish empire in what are today the north Mexican states and/or the southwestern United States have tried to avoid the confusion surrounding the term *Borderlands* by substituting for it the "Hispanic Southwest," the "Greater Southwest," "the northern frontier of New Spain," or "the far northern frontier of New Spain"—depending upon the geography encompassed.

59. Historian Félix D. Almaraz, for example, has used "Mexican Borderlands" as an umbrella term to cover a group of essays ranging from the late eighteenth century to the present, even as he contradicts his implicit definition with an explicit definition of the "Mexican Borderlands" as "encompassing less than three decades," from Mexican independence in 1821 to the Treaty of Guadalupe Hidalgo in 1848. Almaraz, ed., "The Mexican Borderlands," a special issue of the *Journal of the West* 24 (April 1985): 5.

60. A sample of titles of books, articles, and dissertations that have appeared since 1975 and that treat the history of the western Borderlands, primarily the years before 1821, suggests the variety of practices: Janet Fireman, *The Spanish Royal Corps of Enginers in the Western Borderlands, 1764–1815* (Glendale, Calif.: Arthur H. Clark Co., 1977); Ronald Ives, *José Velásquez: Saga of a Borderland Soldier* (Tucson: Southwestern Mission Research Center, 1984); Max L. Moorhead, *The Presidio: Bastion of the Spanish Borderlands* (Norman: University of Oklahoma Press, 1975); Abraham P. Nasatir, *Borderland in Retreat: From Spanish Louisiana to the Far Southwest* (Albuquerque: University of New Mexico Press, 1976); Arnoldo De León, "The Mixedbloods and the Missions: Unsung Heroes in the Spanish Borderlands," in *Contemporary Perspectives on the Old Spanish Missions of San Antonio*, Felipe de Ortego y Gasca, ed. (San Antonio: The Old Spanish Missions and Our Lady of the Lake University of San Antonio, 1979), pp. 23–30; Ralph E. Vigil, "Bartolomé de las Casas, Judge Alonso de Zorita, and the Franciscans: A Collaborative Effort for the Spiritual Conquest of the Borderlands," *The Americas* 38 (July 1981): 45–57; and Austin Nelson Leiby, "Borderland Pathfinders: The 1765 Diaries of Juan María Antonio de Rivera" (Ph.D. dissertation, Northern Arizona University, 1985).

Some works use the term *Spanish Borderlands* to embrace an area that extends chronologically beyond the Spanish colonial period. See, for example, José Cisneros, *Riders Across the Centuries: Horsemen of the Spanish Borderlands* (El Paso: Texas Western Press, 1984) and Duane Kendall Hale, "Mineral Exploration in the Spanish Borderlands, 1513–1846," *Journal of the West* 20 (April 1981), pp. 5–20. Jacinto Quirarte has an interesting variation: "The Borderlands: New Spaniards and Mexicans (1593–1848)" in *Chicano Art History: A Book of Selected Readings*, Jacinto Quirarte, ed. (San Antonio: Research Center for the Arts and Humanities, University of Texas at San Antonio, 1984): 27–39.

The two latter terms seem most descriptive for the years prior to 1821, but whatever term we use seems fraught with some difficulty, as the editors of a recent volume noted as they agonized over a title for their book:

We chose to limit our investigations to the Spanish colonial period— which immediately made the name "Southwest" anachronistic! Simultaneously many Mexican colleagues pointed out the "imperialist" overtones in blanketing their "North" with a name like the "Greater Southwest." While most North Americans immediately grasp the meaning of the Southwest, they are quite puzzled by the term "northern New Spain." Rarely do they recall that part of the United States from California to Florida was once all a part of colonial New Spain.[61]

In its post-Bannon era, then, the field of the Spanish Borderlands faces unresolved problems of self-definition. As I have sought to emphasize, those definitional problems are spatial and temporal more than methodological or interpretive. The Spanish Borderlands, however defined, are a place in time, and they are spacious enough to accommodate a variety of methods, interpretations, and theories. Moreover, approaches to understanding the Borderlands have themselves changed, just as they have for other historic regions, from English colonial America to the American West.[62] It seems overly facile, then, to identify the Borderlands with a single school of thought or methodology. Bolton himself, for example, used Spanish docu-

61. Thomas H. Naylor and Charles W. Polzer, eds., *The Presidio and Militia on the Northern Frontier of New Spain* (Tucson: University of Arizona Press, 1986), p. 4, whose work is a product of a remarkable project entitled "Documentary Relations of the Southwest" which studies an area extending southward to the twenty-second parallel. Notwithstanding the fact that Florida was part of the Viceroyalty of New Spain, a trend toward using northern New Spain to indicate the western Borderlands seems to have emerged. See, for example, Peter Gerhard, *The North Frontier of New Spain* (Princeton: Princeton University Press, 1982); Oakah L. Jones, Jr., *Los Paisanos: Spanish Settlers on the Northern Frontier of New Spain* (Norman: University of Oklahoma Press, 1979); Weber, ed., *New Spain's Far Northern Frontier*. Those whose work extends over time from New Spain into the years of Mexican independence need a different term. Some writers may wish to follow Michael C. Meyer: *Water in the Hispanic Southwest: A Social and Legal History, 1550-1850* (Tucson: University of Arizona Press, 1984).
62. Even the once-despised narrative style, at which Bolton excelled and for which he was once admired, has regained respectability. Lawrence Stone, "The Revival of Narrative: Reflections on a New Old History," *Past and Present* 85 (November 1979): 3–24.

ments to write ethnology of native Americans, and to illuminate historical geography and social and cultural history. (One of his remarks, however, suggests that he believed that the detail of social history could descend into triviality: "The 'new historians,'" Bolton wrote with apparent sarcasm in 1930, "will thrill to learn that [Juan Bautista de] Anza's soldiers could not eat frijoles on the trail because they carried no pots in which to cook them."[63]

To my mind, then, the problem of self-definition that historians of the Borderlands face in the post-Bannon era have less to do with method or with the field as a school of thought than the way in which borderlands, by their very nature, do not fit squarely into categories. Indeed, the problem of "fit" has become so acute that academic history departments no longer seem to have room for practitioners of the field. History departments in major doctorate-granting institutions in both the eastern and western Borderlands have given the field a low priority, and that represents a departure from recent practice.

For several generations Bolton's progeny, Bannon among them, dominated the teaching of colonial Latin America, especially in the South and Southwest. To those of us in the field, names of Bolton-trained Ph.D.'s come readily to mind, many of them associated with doctorate-granting departments at major universities: John Tate Lanning at Duke, William Binkley at Vanderbilt, Alfred Barnaby Thomas at the University of Alabama, Max Moorhead at the University of Oklahoma, Charles Wilson Hackett and J. Lloyd Mecham at the University of Texas, George Hammond at the University of New Mexico and the University of California, Berkeley, Rufus Wyllys at Arizona State University, Russell Ewing at the University of Arizona, Gregory Crampton at the University of Utah, Lawrence Kinnaird and Woodrow Borah at Berkeley, Owen Coy at the University of Southern California, and John Caughey at the University of California, Los Angeles.

Among the Borderlands historians who once held key positions in

---

63. The quote is from Bolton's introduction to *Anza's California Expeditions* in Bannon, ed., *Bolton and the Spanish Borderlands*, p. 286. For Bolton's interest in ethnology of Indians, see, for example, ibid., pp. 286–87, and Bolton, *The Hasinais: Southern Caddoans as Seen by the Earliest Europeans*, Russell M. Magnaghi, ed. (Norman: University of Oklahoma Press, 1987), a previously unpublished work that Bolton wrote between 1906–1908. Ethnohistory, of course, need not be defined as the history of native Americans; the study of Hispanics represents a venture into the history of an ethnic group.

doctorate-granting departments, we should also include "second generation Boltonians," including Donald Cutter, presently at St. Mary's University in San Antonio but associated through most of his career with the University of Southern California and the University of New Mexico; Philip Wayne Powell of the University of California at Santa Barbara; and Donald Worcester, who taught at the University of Florida and at Texas Christian University. Then, too, the list should embrace historians trained out of the Bolton tradition, such as France Scholes and Arthur Whitaker, who also studied the Borderlands and held positions at the University of New Mexico and the University of Pennsylvania, respectively.

In the minds and work of Bolton-trained Ph.D.'s and their confrères, the Borderlands and Colonial Latin America were inextricably bound. By the 1980s, however, all of these distinguished historians had either long since retired or taken positions where they do little teaching of graduate students. Today, although the number of historians has grown, the number of doctorate-granting history departments with specialists in the Borderlands has diminished. History departments at major universities did not replace the Boltonians as they retired.

I have not taken a survey and I may very well have overlooked some institutions and individuals, but my impression is that only one major university on the West Coast employs a historian with doctoral training in the Borderlands—the University of California at San Diego, where Ramón Gutiérrez teaches. In the Southwest, from Arizona through Texas and including Nevada, Utah, and Colorado, perhaps only two historians of the Spanish Borderlands teach at doctorate-granting institutions—John Kessell at the University of New Mexico and Ted Warner at Brigham Young University. In the Southeast, from Louisiana to Florida and up to the Carolinas, the picture is also bleak, with perhaps only four doctorate-granting departments employing historians trained in the Spanish Borderlands—Louisana State University with Paul Hoffman, Tulane with Richard Greenleaf, Duke University with John TePaske, and the University of Florida, where Michael Gannon and Eugene Lyon hold joint appointments in the history department. North of the Mason-Dixon Line a few Borderlands historians ply their trade in doctorate-granting departments. Oakah Jones at Purdue University and William Swagerty at the University of Idaho come to mind.

I can only speculate on why so few historians trained in the Borderlands are represented in major departments. To some departments the field has come to be regarded as stodgy and uninteresting, as José Cuello suggested.[64] That, however, may be as much effect as cause, and perhaps even a question of changing academic fashions. Putting aside the question of the quality of the work in the field, several practical reasons for its decline in major departments suggest themselves.

First, growing interest in Latin American history in the post-Castro era and increased financial support for fieldwork in Latin America have led to the proliferation of scholars whose research has taken them deeper into Latin America, beyond the present United States–Mexico border. Thus, scholars who previously might have limited their work to the Borderlands due to financial exigency can now work farther afield.

Second, many departments have chosen to hire a "main-line" Latin Americanist rather than a person who specializes on the periphery of the Spanish empire. Bolton once reminded us not to mistake the tail for the dog and draw conclusions about all of Latin America based on what we know about the Borderlands; many history departments apparently decided to find specialists who focused on the dog.[65] Indeed, some historians of Latin America, as José Cuello has so clearly stated, ask if Borderlands history constitutes even the tail of Latin America, or if it is not merely United States history.

Third, at the same time that some historians of Latin America wonder if the Borderlands is a subfield of American history, most historians of the United States either dismiss it as part of Latin American history or as a regional aberration of mainstream American history. The story of American history has been told from the perspective of the winners—the descendants of the English—and the lives and activities of progeny of the losing Spanish side have not been woven into the fabric of American history. American history itself is usually seen as a process—as the story of the expansion of English America rather than the stories of the diverse cultures that comprise our national heritage. Hence, specialists in the history of English colonial Virginia

64. See, too, Guillermo Lux's description of Chávez, *The Lost Land*, as "a study which comfortably fits within the staid "Borderlands" framework." *El Palacio* 91 (Spring 1985): 63.

65. Bolton, "Defensive Spanish Expansion and the Significance of the Borderlands," in Bannon, ed., *Bolton and the Spanish Borderlands*, p. 34.

or colonial New York are understood to write *American* history; specialists in Spanish colonial Florida or California write *regional* history. One looks in vain through books on early America, with titles such as *The Formative Years, 1607–1763, The Urban Idea in Colonial America,* or *The Colonial Revival in America,* for some mention of Hispanics.[66] In this intellectual milieu, it is no wonder that academic departments do not look to specialists in the Spanish Borderlands to fill positions in colonial America.

Finally, in the southwestern United States those departments with sufficient size to hire a specialist in the Hispanic history of their region have looked increasingly, since the late 1960s, to the recent history of Mexican Americans. Research and teaching in the history of this ethnic group has meshed neatly with the stylish concerns of social and urban history. Moreover, in some areas of the Sunbelt, Mexican-American history seemed in many ways more vibrant and relevant to students' interests than did Spain's long dead North American empire.

Historians of the Spanish Borderlands do, of course, teach at colleges and universities that do not offer a Ph.D. in history (I myself teach at such a school). But it is history departments at major universities that play a key role in shaping a field through setting agendas for research and through training new Ph.D.'s. Thus, a downward spiral seems set in motion that will continue to diminish the number of historians of the Spanish Borderlands. The decline of professors who teach in this field has, not surprisingly, been accompanied by a corresponding diminution in the number of courses on the Spanish Borderlands and the enrollments in those that remain. As one measure,

66. These three titles are respectively by Clarence L. Ver Steeg (New York: Hill & Wang, 1964); Sylvia Doughty Fries (Philadelphia: Temple University Press, 1977); and Alan Axelrod, ed. (New York: W. W. Norton, 1985). For American history textbooks, see Scardaville, "Approaches to the Study of the Southeastern Borderlands," in Badger and Clayton, eds., *Alabama and the Borderlands,* pp. 188–90. Two recent volumes show greater awareness of their geographical limits: Jack P. Greene and J. R. Pole, eds., *Colonial British America: Essays in the New History of the Early Modern Era* (Baltimore: Johns Hopkins University Press, 1984), and D. W. Meinig, *The Shaping of America: A Geographical Perspective on 500 Years of History.* Volume One: *Atlantic America, 1492–1800* (New Haven: Yale University Press, 1986). Pauline Maier, among others, has urged "abandoning the confines of British colonial America. Less needs to be learned about the British West Indies than about the Indians of the mainland, and about the Spanish borderlands, French Canada, and Louisiana, whose development played so critical a role in the dynamics of imperial conflict." "Colonial History: Is It All Mined Out," *Reviews in American History* 13 (March 1985): 6.

sales of two of Bannon's books, *The Spanish Borderlands Frontier* and *Bolton and the Spanish Borderlands,* have dropped markedly.[67]

This view from the academy, then, suggests that the field of the Spanish Borderlands in the post-Bannon era is moribund. Indeed, even those few historians in the United States who work in the field generally fail to identify themselves as Borderlands specialists. Instead, they designate their specialties as America, Latin America, Mexico, or the American West. They identify, that is, with core areas rather than with peripheries.[68]

By a more important measure, however, the study of the Spanish Borderlands is alive, if not entirely well. By whatever name, scholarly works on the Borderlands continue to appear at a remarkable rate. The 1980s alone saw the publication of numerous monographs, articles, edited or translated documents, and doctoral dissertations that illuminate the history of the Spanish empire in what is now the United States (I am using, here, the narrowest definition of the Spanish Borderlands).

The range and quality of current work on Spanish colonial North America is impressive. Between 1980 and 1986 American scholars have produced an astonishing number of studies of such traditional themes as exploration,[69] administration and politics,[70] economics and

67. *The Spanish Borderlands Frontier* sold some 1,500 copies a year in the mid-1970s; by the mid-1980s (1985 and 1986) it sold fewer than 500 copies a year (David Holtby, Editor, University of New Mexico Press, to Weber, November 17, 1986). The paperback edition of *Bolton and the Spanish Borderlands,* which averaged sales of 150 copies a year between 1974 and 1984, sold 75 copies in fiscal year 1984–85 and 93 copies in 1985–86 (John N. Drayton, Editor-in-Chief, University of Oklahoma Press, to Weber, November 13, 1985). My impression of declining numbers of courses and enrollments is not based on sales of Bannon's books alone (other books may well have replaced it), but also from conversations with colleagues at different institutions where the Borderlands history courses once were taught and well attended.

68. See, for example, the following entries in Jaques Catell Press, ed., *Directory of American Scholars,* 4 vols., 8th ed. (New York and London: R. R. Bowker, 1982): William Coker, Donald Cutter, Michael Gannon, Jack D. L. Holmes, Oakah Jones, John Kessell, David Weber, Donald Worcester, and J. Leitch Wright. One exception is Bannon himself.

69. Adolph F. Bandelier, *The Discovery of New Mexico by the Franciscan Monk Friar Marcos de Niza in 1539,* Madeleine Rodack, ed. and trans. (Tucson: University of Arizona Press, 1981); Dan L. Flores, *Jefferson & Southwestern Exploration: The Freeman & Custis Accounts of the Red River Expedition of 1806* (Norman: University of Oklahoma Press, 1984); Robert S. Weddle, *Spanish Sea: The Gulf of Mexico in North American Discovery, 1500–1685* (College Station: Texas A&M University Press, 1985); Paul E. Hoffman, "A New Voyage of North American Discovery: Pedro

trade,[71] ranching,[72] Spanish-Indian relations,[73] the church and the missions,[74] military history and the presidio,[75] international rivalry,[76] historiography,[77] and biography.[78] Work published in the 1980s has also illuminated such relatively neglected areas as science,[79] disease and medicine,[80] material culture,[81] architecture,[82] cultural diffusion,[83]

de Salazar's Visit to the 'Island of Giants,'" *Florida Historical Quarterly* 58 (April 1980): 415–26, and Hoffman, "The Chicora Legend and Franco-Spanish Rivalry in *la florida,*" *Florida Historical Quarterly* 62 (April 1984): 419–38; Eugene Lyon, "Continuity in the Age of Conquest: The Establishment of Spanish Sovereignty in the Sixteenth Century," in Badger and Clayton, eds., *Alabama and the Borderlands*, pp. 154–61; W. Michael Mathes, "Apocryphal Tales of the Island of California and the Strait of Anián," *California History* 62 (Spring 1983): 52–59; Richard A. Weaver, "The 1776 Route of Father Francisco Garcés into the San Bernardino Valley: A Revaluation of the Evidence and Its Implications," *Journal of California and Great Basin Anthropology* 4 (Summer 1982): 142–47.

70. Janice Borton Miller, *Juan Nepomuceno de Quesada, Governor of Spanish East Florida, 1790–1795* (Washington: University Press of America, 1981); David Hart White, *Vicente Folch, Governor in Spanish Florida, 1787–1811* (Washington: University Press of America, 1981); Light T. Cummins, "Spanish Administration in the Eastern Borderlands, 1763–1800," *Proceedings of the Pacific Coast Council on Latin American Studies* 7 (1980–81): 1–9.

71. Amy Bushnell, *The King's Coffer: Proprietors of the Spanish Florida Treasury, 1565–1702* (Gainesville: University of Florida Press, 1981). Coker and Watson, *Indian Traders of the Southeastern Spanish Borderlands;* William E. Foley and C. David Rice, *The First Chouteaus: River Barons of Early St. Louis* (Urbana: University of Illinois Press, 1983); Sluiter, *The Florida Situado;* Brian E. Coutts, "Boom and Bust: The Rise and Fall of the Tobacco Industry in Spanish Louisiana, 1770–1790," *The Americas* 42 (January 1986): 299–309; Coutts, "Flax and Hemp in Spanish Louisiana, 1777–1783," *Louisiana History* 26 (Spring 1985): 129–39; Daniel H. Usner, Jr., "The Frontier Exchange Economy of the Lower Mississippi Valley in the Eighteenth Century," *William and Mary Quarterly* 44 (April 1987): 165–92.

72. Jack Jackson, *Los Mesteños: Spanish Ranching in Texas, 1721–1821* (College Station: Texas A&M University Press, 1986).

73. Charles R. Cutter, *The Protector de Indios in Colonial New Mexico, 1659–1821* (Albuquerque: University of New Mexico Press, 1986); Gilbert C. Din and Abraham P. Nasatir, *The Imperial Osages: Spanish Indian Diplomacy in the Missssippi Valley* (Norman: University of Oklahoma Press, 1983); Jack August, "Balance of Power Diplomacy in New Mexico: Governor Fernando de la Concha and the Indian Policy of Conciliation," *New Mexico Historical Review* 56 (January 1981): 71–97; Jack D. L. Holmes, "Juan de Villebeuvre and Spanish Indian Policy in West Florida, 1784–1797," *Florida Historical Quarterly* 58 (April 1980): 387–99; Elizabeth A. H. John, "Nurturing the Peace: Spanish and Comanche Cooperation in the Early Nineteenth Century," and "An Earlier Chapter of Kiowa History," *New Mexico Historical Review* 59 (October 1984): 345–69 and 60 (October 1985): 379–97; Stephen Edward Reilly, "A Marriage of Expedience: The Calusa Indians and Their Relations with Pedro Menéndez de Avilés in Southwest Florida, 1566–1569," *Florida Historical Quarterly* 59 (April 1981): 295–421; Jane C. Sánchez, "Spanish-Indian Relations During the Otermín Admin-

the ownership of land and water,[84] ecology,[85] women,[86] blacks,[87] society,[88] labor,[89] demography,[90] and urban areas.[91] In listing these overlapping categories, I do not intend to provide an inventory of all writings on the Spanish Borderlands in the 1980s, but I do wish to suggest the considerable variety of topics that has appeared in published work.

istration, 1677–1683," *New Mexico Historical Review* 58 (April 1983): 133–51; Thomas D. Watson, "Strivings for Sovereignty: Alexander McCillivray, Creek Warfare, and Diplomacy, 1783–1790," *Florida Historical Quarterly* 58 (April 1980): 400–414.

74. John L. Kessell, *The Missions of New Mexico Since 1776* (Albuquerque: University of New Mexico Press, 1980); Kieran McCarty, O.F.M., *A Spanish Frontier in the Enlightened Age: Franciscan Beginnings in Sonora and Arizona, 1767–1770* (Washington: Academy of American Franciscan History, 1981); Richard E. Greenleaf, "The Inquisition in Eighteenth-Century New Mexico," *New Mexico Historical Review* 60 (January 1985): 29–60; Francis F. Guest, "Junípero Serra and His Approach to the Indians," *Southern California Quarterly* 67 (Fall 1985): 223–61; Frank Marotti, Jr., "Juan Baptista de Segura and the Failure of the Florida Jesuit Mission, 1566–1572," *Florida Historical Quarterly* 63 (January 1985): 267–79; Fred Lamar Pearson, Jr., "Timucuan Rebellion of 1656: The Rebolledo Investigation and the Civil-Religious Controversy," *Florida Historical Quarterly* 61 (January 1983): 260–80.

75. William S. Coker and Hazel P. Coker, *The Siege of Pensacola, 1781, in Maps with Data on Troop Strength, Military Units, Ships, Casualties, and Related Statistics* (Pensacola: Perdido Bay Press, 1981); and Coker and Coker, *The Siege of Mobile, 1780, in Maps with Data on Troop Strength, Military Units, Ships, Casualties, and Prisoners of War Including a Brief History of Fort Charlotte (Condé)* (Pensacola: Perdido Bay Press, 1982); Thomas Wm. Dunlay, "Indian Allies in the Armies of New Spain and the United States: A Comparative Study," *New Mexico Historical Review* 56 (July 1981): 237–58; Richard S. Whitehead, "Alta California's Four Fortresses," *Southern California Quarterly* 65 (Spring 1983): 67–94.

76. Paul E. Hoffman, *The Spanish Crown and the Defense of the Caribbean, 1535–1585* (Baton Rouge: LSU Press, 1980); Carl A. Brasseaux and Richard E. Chandler, "The British Incident, 1769–1770: Anglo-Hispanic Tensions in the Western Gulf," *Southwestern Historical Quarterly* 87 (April 1984): 357–70; Gilbert C. Din, "War Clouds on the Mississippi: Spain's 1785 Crisis in West Florida," *Florida Historical Quarterly* 60 (July 1981): 51–76; David J. Langum, "The Caring Colony: Alta California's Participation in Spain's Foreign Affairs," *Southern California Quarterly* 62 (Fall 1980): 217–28.

77. Cutter, "The Western Spanish Borderlands"; Jack D. L. Holmes, "A New Look at Spanish Louisiana Census Accounts: The Recent Historiography of Antonio Acosta," *Louisiana History* 21 (Winter 1980): 77–86; David J. Weber, "Turner, the Boltonians, and the Borderlands," *American Historical Review* 91 (February 1986): 66–81.

78. Ronald Ives, *José Velásquez: Saga of a Borderland Soldier* (Tucson: Southwestern Mission Research Center, 1984), and Harry Kelsey, *Juan Rodríguez Cabrillo* (San

The 1980s have also seen the production of some superb reference works for Borderlands historians, such as Peter Gerhard's historical geography,[92] the multi-authored *Northern New Spain: A Research Guide*,[93] a useful collection of maps by James and Robert Martin,[94] and bibliographies and bibliographical essays, including William Swagerty's

Marino: Huntington Library, 1986); John L. Kessell, "Diego de Vargas: Another Look," *New Mexico Historical Review* 60 (January 1985): 11–28.

79. Iris H. W. Engstrand, *Spanish Scientists in the New World: The Eighteenth Century Expeditions* (Seattle: University of Washington Press, 1981).

80. Jack D. L. Holmes, "Spanish Medical Care in the Mobile District: Advanced or Retarded?" *Journal of the Florida Medical Association* 71 (July 1984): 463–68; Robert H. Jackson, "Disease and Demographic Patterns at Santa Cruz Mission, Alta California," *Journal of California and Great Basin Anthropology* 5 (1983): 33–57 (one of a series of articles by Jackson on the impact of disease in missions).

81. Cisneros, *Riders Across the Centuries*; Marc Simmons and Frank Turley, *Southwestern Colonial Ironwork: The Spanish Blacksmithing Tradition from Texas to California* (Santa Fe: Museum of New Mexico Press, 1980), and many of the essays in Marta Weigle, ed., *Hispanic Arts and Ethnohistory in the Southwest* (Santa Fe: Ancient City Press, 1983), such as Marc Simmons, "Carros y Carretas: Vehicular Traffic on the Camino Real," pp. 325–34.

82. Mardith Schuetz, "Professional Artisans in the Hispanic Southwest: The Churches of San Antonio, Texas," *The Americas* 40 (July 1983): 17–71.

83. William Mason, "Indian-Mexican Cultural Exchange in the Los Angeles Area, 1781–1834," *Aztlán* 15 (Spring 1984): 123–44; Oakah L. Jones, Jr., "Hispanic Tradition and Improvisation on the *Frontera Septentrional* of New Spain," *New Mexico Historical Review* 56 (October 1981): 333–47; L. Jill Loucks, "Acculturation Through the System: Archaeological Insights from an Early 17th Century Spanish Mission," in *Forgotten Places and Things: Archaeological Perspectives on American History*, Albert E. Ward, ed. (Albuquerque: Center for Anthropological Studies, 1983), pp. 149–56.

84. Michael C. Meyer, *Water in the Hispanic Southwest: A Social and Legal History, 1550–1850* (Tucson: University of Arizona Press, 1984); Alan V. Briceland, "Land, Law, and Politics on the Tombigbee Frontier, 1804," *Alabama Review* 33 (April 1980): 94–124; Iris H. W. Engstrand, "California Ranchos: Their Hispanic Heritage," *Southern California Quarterly* 67 (Fall 1985): 281–90.

85. Dan L. Flores, "The Ecology of the Red River in 1806: Peter Curtis and Early Southwestern Natural History," *Southwestern Historical Quarterly* 88 (July 1984): 1–42.

86. Cheryl J. Foote and Sandra K. Schackel, "Indian Women of New Mexico, 1535–1680," and Salomé Hernández, "Nueva Mexicanas as Refugees and Reconquest Settlers, 1680–1696," both in *New Mexico Women: Intercultural Perspectives*, Joan M. Jensen and Darlis A. Miller, eds. (Albuquerque: University of New Mexico Press, 1986), pp. 17–40, 41–69; Myra Ellen Jenkins, "Some Eighteenth Century New Mexico Women of Property," in Weigle, ed., *Hispanic Arts and Ethnohistory in the Southwest*, pp. 335–46; Gloria Miranda, "Gente de Razón Marriage Patterns in Spanish and Mexican California: A Case Study of Santa Barbara and Los Angeles," *Southern California Quarterly* 63 (Spring 1981): 1–21.

87. Gilbert C. Din, "Cimarrones and the San Malo Band in Spanish Louisiana,"

splendid discussion of sources on Spanish-Indian relations.[95] The tran-
scribing, translating, editing, and publication of documents also continues (this has been a hallmark of Borderlands historiography, intended,
as Donald Cutter has said, "to make the information transcend its
natural linguistic limits and permit it to become a dual heritage").[96]

Louisiana History 21 (Summer 1980): 237–61; Jane Landers, "Spanish Sanctuary:
Fugitives in Florida, 1687–1790," *Florida Historical Quarterly* 62 (January 1984): 296–
313.
    88. Janie T. Aragón, "Santa Fe de Nuevo México," *Proceedings of the Pacific Coast
Council on Latin American Studies* 7 (1980–81): 29–36; Gilbert C. Din, "The Canary
Islander Settlements of Spanish Louisiana," *Louisiana History* 27 (Fall 1986): 353–
74; Ramón A. Gutiérrez, "From Honor to Love: Transformations of the Meaning of
Sexuality in Colonial New Mexico," in *Kinship Ideology and Practice in Latin America*,
Raymond T. Smith, ed. (Chapel Hill: University of North Carolina Press, 1984),
pp. 237–63; Jack D. Forbes, "Hispano-Mexican Pioneers of the San Francisco Bay
Region: An Analysis of Racial Origins," *Aztlán* 14 (Spring 1983): 175–89; Ramón
A. Gutiérrez, "Honor Ideology, Marriage Negotiation, and Class-Gender Domination
in New Mexico, 1690–1846," *Latin American Perspectives* 12 (Winter 1985): 81–104.
    89. H. Allen Anderson, "The Encomienda in New Mexico, 1598–1680," *New
Mexico Historical Review* 60 (October 1985): 353–77; David H. Snow, "A Note on
Encomienda Economics in Seventeenth-Century New Mexico," in Weigle, ed., *His-
panic Arts and Ethnohistory in the Southwest*, pp. 347–57.
    90. William S. Coker, "Religious Censuses of Pensacola, 1796–1801," *Florida
Historical Quarterly* 61 (July 1982): 54–63; John H. Hann, "Demographic Patterns
and Changes in Mid-Seventeenth Century Timucua and Apalachee," *Florida Historical
Quarterly* 64 (April 1986): 371–92.
    91. Hinojosa, *Borderlands Town in Transition;* Marc Simmons, *Albuquerque: A
Narrative History* (Albuquerque: University of New Mexico Press, 1982); Robert B.
Lloyd, "Development of the Plan of Pensacola during the Colonial Era, 1559–1821,"
Florida Historical Quarterly 64 (January 1986): 253–92.
    92. *The North Frontier of New Spain* (Princeton: Princeton University Press, 1982).
    93. Thomas C. Barnes, Thomas H. Naylor, and Charles W. Polzer, *Northern New
Spain: A Research Guide* (Tucson: University of Arizona Press, 1981). See, too, Paul
E. Hoffman, "La documentación colonial en la Luisiana," *Archivo Hispalense* (1985):
333–52.
    94. James C. Martin and Robert S. Martin, *Maps of Texas and the Southwest,
1513–1900* (Albuquerque: University of New Mexico Press, 1984).
    95. Glenn R. Conrad and Carl A. Brasseaux, *A Selected Bibliography of Scholarly
Literature on Colonial Louisiana and New France* (Lafayette: The Center for Louisiana
Studies, 1982); James Howlett O'Donnell III, *Southeastern Frontiers: Europeans, Afri-
cans, and American Indians, 1513–1840: A Critical Bibliography* (Bloomington: University of Indiana Press, 1982); W. R. Swagerty, "Spanish-Indian Relations, 1513–
1821," in *Scholars and the Indian Experience*, W. R. Swagerty, ed. (Bloomington:
Indiana University Press, 1984), pp. 36–78.
    96. Cutter to Weber, Madrid, February 1987. See, for example, Herbert K. Beals,
ed. and trans., *For God and Country: The Diary of Buno de Hezeta* (Portland: West
Imprints, 1984); David Bushnell, comp., *La República de las Floridas: Texts and Doc-*

Then, too, microfilm editions of documents and new finding aids to archival collections have emerged in the 1980s, including one of the most sophisticated and ambitious electronic data bases of unpublished primary source materials for historians—the "Documentary Relations of the Southwest," a project housed at the University of Arizona and directed by Charles Polzer.[97]

Thus far, I have been trying to characterize recent historical literature by North American scholars on the Spanish empire in what is now the United States. If I were to extend the spatial definition of the Spanish Borderlands to include the region that has become Mexico's northern states, or to extend the temporal definition to include the nineteenth-century history of Chicanos and the United States–Mexico border region, then the quality and quantity of Borderlands scholarship becomes even more impressive.[98]

uments (Mexico: Institutio Panamericano de Geografía e Historia, 1986); Carmela Leal, ed., *Residents of Texas, 1782–1836* (San Antonio: University of Texas Institute of Texan Cultures, 1984); Juan Pantoja y Arriaga and Esteban José Martínez, *The Voyage of the Frigate Princesa to Southern California in 1782*, Richard S. Whitehead, ed., and Geraldine V. Sahyun, trans. (Santa Barbara, Calif.: Santa Barbara Mission Archive-Library, 1982); Alfred Barnaby Thomas, ed. and trans., *Alonso de Posada Report, 1686: A Description of the Area of the Present Southern United States in the Late Seventeenth Century* (Pensacola: Perdido Bay Press, 1982); James M. Daniel, ed. and trans., "Diary of Pedro José de la Fuente: Captain of the Presidio of El Paso del Norte, August–December, 1675," *Southwestern Historical Quarterly* 83 (January 1980): 259–78; John H. Hanna, ed. and trans., "Translation of the Ecija Voyages of 1605 and 1609 and the González *Derrotero* of 1609," and other documents, in *Florida Archaeology* 2 (1986): entire issue; Lawrence Kinnaird and Lucia B. Kinnaird, eds. and trans., "The Red River Valley in 1796," *Louisiana History* 24 (Spring 1983): 184–94; Marc Simmons, ed. and trans., "The Chacón Economic Report of 1803," *New Mexico Historical Review* 60 (January 1985): 81–88; and the Journal of don Diego de Vargas, being prepared for publication in a multi-volume series by John Kessell.

97. Two other recent projects are described in Michael V. Gannon, "Documents of the Spanish Borderlands: A Calendaring Project at the University of Florida," *William and Mary Quarterly* 38 (October 1981): 718–22, and "The Papers of Panton, Leslie and Company," being filmed at the University of West Florida, and discussed in Coker and Watson, *Indian Traders*, pp. 371–75.

98. For recent work on Chicano history, see, Meier, comp., *Bibliography of Mexican American History*, and for Border Studies, see Stoddard et al., eds., *Borderlands Sourcebook*. Recent work on the north Mexican states in the Spanish colonial period is not extensive, but includes such studies as Evelyn Hu-DeHart, *Missionaries, Miners, and Indians: Spanish Contact with the Yaqui Nation of Northwestern New Spain, 1533–1820* (Tucson: University of Arizona Press, 1981); Naylor and Polzer, eds., *The Presidio and Militia on the Northern Frontier of New Spain, 1570–1700*; Michael M. Swann, *Tierra Adentro: Settlement and Society in Colonial Durango* (Boulder: Westview Press, 1982); Elizabeth A. H. John, "La situación y visión de los Indios de la Frontera Norte

The vigorous production of fresh scholarship on the Spanish Borderlands seems inconsistent with the small number of historians of the Borderlands in doctorate-granting departments at major research universities in the United States. Much of this new work has been done, however, by historians teaching at small universities and colleges, by historians without university affiliations or without membership in history departments,[99] and by occasional historians not usually associated with the Spanish Borderlands, such as Michael Meyer, who have strayed into the field. In addition, important contributions have been made by foreign scholars[100] and by practitioners of other disciplines: geographers,[101] attorneys,[102] archaeologists, and cultural

---

de Nueva España (Siglos XVI–XVIII)," *América Indígena* 65 (julio–septiembre 1985): 465–83; with more work to come in this decade from historians such as José Cuello, Susan Deeds, and Oakah Jones.

99. For example: Jack D. L. Holmes, Jack Jackson, Myra Ellen Jenkins, Elizabeth John, Kieran McCarty, Marc Simmons, and Robert Weddle.

100. By definition, the Borderlands have been peripheral to Spanish and Mexican historiography, but important contributions have been made by the few scholars from Spain and Mexico who have interested themselves in *América Septentrional.* Recent works include Fernando Boneu Companys, *Gaspar de Portolá: Explorer and Founder of California,* Alan K. Brown, trans. and ed. (Lérida: Instituto Esudios Llerdenses, 1983); Rafael Cervantes, ed., *Diario del Padre Fray José Gaspar de Solís en su visita a los misiones de Texas, 1768* (Guadalajara: Editorial Font, 1981); María del Carmen Velázquez, *Notas sobre sirvientes de las Californias y proyecto de obraje en Nuevo México* (Mexico: Colegio de Mexico, 1985); Lino Gómez Canedo, *El Reformismo Misional en Nuevo México (1760–1768)* (Guadalajara: Dirección de Bibliotecas, Universidad Autónoma de Guadalajara,1981); Sylvia-Lyn Hilton, "Ocupación española de Florida: algunas repercusiones en la organización sociopolítica indígena, siglos xvi y xvii," *Revista de Indias* 42 (enero/junio 1982): 41–70; Jesús Lorente Miguel, "Commercial Relations between New Orleans and the United States, 1783–1803," in Jacques Barbier and Allan J. Kuethe, eds., *The North American Role in the Spanish Imperial Economy, 1760–1819* (Manchester; Manchester University Press, 1984), pp. 177–91; Juan Marchena Fernández, "Guarnaciones y población militar en Florida Oriental, 1700–1820," *Revista de Indias* 41 (enero/junio 1981): 9–142; Pablo Tornero Tinajero, "Canarian Immigration to America: The Civil Military Expedition to Louisiana of 1777–1779," *Louisiana History* 21 (Fall 1980): 377–86. Here, too, if I defined the Borderlands more broadly, this list could be expanded.

101. Gerhard, *The North Frontier of New Spain;* William E. Doolittle, "Cabeza de Vaca's Land of Maize: An Assessment of Its Agriculture," *Journal of Historical Geography* 10 (July 1984): 246–62.

102. Morris S. Arnold, *Unequal Laws Unto a Savage Race: European Traditions in Arkansas, 1686–1836* (Fayetteville: University of Arkansas Press, 1985); Charles T. Dumars et al., *Pueblo Indian Water Rights: Struggle for a Precious Resource* (Tucson: University of Arizona Press, 1984); G. Emlen Hall, *Four Leagues of Pecos: A Legal History of the Pecos Grant* (Albuquerque: University of New Mexico Press, 1984); Hans W. Baade, "The Law of Slavery in Spanish Louisiana, 1769–1803," in *Louisiana's*

anthropologists.[103] Some of these specialists write works that could easily be mistaken for history in an era when boundaries between disciplines have become increasingly blurred. Indeed, non-historians, whether they employ the clear language favored by most historians or the more recondite idioms of their own disciplines, have made such important contributions to our understanding that historians of the Borderlands cannot ignore their work.[104] If some social scientists have made uncritical use of sources or clumsy attempts to force evidence to fit a model, we have the dubious consolation of knowing that historians, too, have written bad history.[105]

Legal Heritage, Edward F. Haas, ed. (Pensacola: Perdido Bay Press, 1983), pp. 43–86, and Baade, "The Historical Background of Texas Water Law," *St. Mary's Law Journal* 18 (1986): 1–98.

103. T. N. and T. J. Campbell, *Indian Groups Associated with Spanish Missions of the San Antonio Missions National Historic Park. Center for Archaeological Research Special Report No. 16* (San Antonio: University of Texas at San Antonio, 1985); Kathleen Deagan, ed., *Spanish St. Augustine: The Archaeology of a Colonial Creole Community* (New York: Academic Press, 1983): Stanley South, *The Discovery of Santa Elena* (Institute of Archaeology and Anthropology, University of South Carolina, 1980); Caleb Curren, "In Search of De Soto's Trail (A Hypothesis of the Alabama Route)," *Bulletins of Discovery* 1 (October 1986): 1–15; Chester B. DePratter, Charles Hudson, and Marvin T. Smith, "The Route of Juan Pardo's Explorations in the Interior of the Southeast, 1566–1568," *Florida Historical Quarterly* 62 (October 1983): 125–58; Dobyns, ed., *Spanish Colonial Frontier Research;* Alfonso Ortiz, ed., *Southwest,* vol. 10 of the *Handbook of North American Indians,* William C. Sturtevant, ed. (Washington: Smithsonian Institution, 1983); Carroll Riley and Joni L. Manson, "The Cibola-Tiguex Route: Continuity and Change in the Southwest," *New Mexico Historical Review* 58 (October 1983): 347–68; Florence C. Shipek, "California Indian Reactions to the Franciscans," *The Americas* 41 (April 1985): 480–93; David Hurst Thomas, Grant D. Jones, Roger S. Durham, and Clark Spencer Larsen, "The Anthropology of St. Catherines Island," *Anthropological Papers of the American Museum of Natural History* 55, pt. 2 (1978): 155–248; Andrew O. Wiget, "Truth and the Hopi: An Historiographic Study of Documented Oral Tradition Concerning the Coming of the Spanish," *Ethnohistory* 29 (Summer 1982): 181–99; Jack S. Williams, "San Agustín del Tucson," and "The Presidio of Santa Cruz de Terrenate," in *The Smoke Signal,* nos. 47, 48 (Spring and Fall 1986): 113–28, 129–48; Williams, "Archaeological Evidence of Spanish Military Policy in Northern New Spain, 1700–1821," in Stephen L. Dyson, ed., *Comparative Studies in the Archaeology of Colonialism* Oxford: B. A. R., 1985), pp. 115–29.

104. On the blurring of disciplinary lines, see, for example, the remark of one distinguished anthropologist that "practice has gone beyond the theoretical differences that are supposed to divide anthropology and history." Marshall Sahlins, "Other Times, Other Customs: The Anthropology of History," *American Anthropologist* 85 (September 1983): 534; for an example of sociology informed by Borderlands history, and the potentially useful application of theory for historians, see Thomas D. Hall, "Incorporation in the World-System: Toward a Critique," *American Sociological Review* 51 (June 1986): 390–402.

105. See, for example, David Henige's admirable "If Pigs Could Fly: Timucuan

Thus, notwithstanding its ambivalent identity, or perhaps because of it, the study of the history of the old Spanish Borderlands remained vigorous in the last years of the Bannon era. But the character of the field has changed; it has expanded over time and space and become energized by new questions and interdisciplinary approaches. Not surprisingly, growth has led to what Howard Lamar has described as struggles over "turf" with scholarly neighbors, and changes in the field's character have raised new questions of self-definition.[106]

The usual insecurities of a field in ferment have been exacerbated by the simple fact that the Borderlands, poised on the margins of American and Latin American history, do not fit squarely into the core of either area. But students of the Borderlands need not become intellectually marginalized simply because they study the peripheries of empires and states. If the Borderlands do not fit entirely into the history of English America or Latin America, they do occupy great blocks of time and space in both areas. The work of historians of the Borderlands is recognized and read by both American and Latin American historians (as well as practitioners of other disciplines), and is published in scholarly journals and cited in reference works in both areas—be it the *Handbook of Latin American Studies* or the *Harvard Guide to American History.*

Rather than walking uneasily on the narrow edges of empires, historians of the Spanish Borderlands who follow Jack Bannon should recognize that they have a secure foothold in both English- and Spanish-speaking America. As the juncture of those two worlds continues to grow in population and in economic and strategic importance, the perspective of Borderlands historians seems likely to become increasingly valued. Generous of spirit, open to change, and always a promoter of the Borderlands, John Francis Bannon would have approved of the field's new directions, even as he would have hoped that presentism does not eclipse the study of Spain's colonial empire in North America.

Population and Native American Historical Demography," *Journal of Interdisciplinary History* 16 (Spring 1986): 701–20, a critique of Henry F. Dobyns, *Their Number Become Thinned: Native American Population Dynamics in Eastern North America* (Knoxville: University of Tennessee Press, 1983).

106. Howard R. Lamar, "Much to Celebrate: The Western History Association's Twenty-fifth Birthday," *Western Historical Quarterly* 17 (October 1986): 405.

5

Mexico's Far Northern Frontier, 1821–1854
*Historiography Askew**

The portion of the American West that once belonged to independent Mexico extended north to the forty-second parallel and embraced the present-day states of California, Arizona, New Mexico, Texas, Nevada, Utah, western Colorado, and small portions of Wyoming, Kansas, and Oklahoma. Upon gaining independence from Spain in 1821, Mexico inherited title to this vast area but, like Spain, it effectively occupied only small portions of the immense region. Native Americans controlled most of the area in 1821; Mexican permanent settlement was confined largely to coastal California, southernmost Arizona, the Rio Grande basin of New Mexico, and the San Antonio River valley of Texas.[1] Mexico's far northern frontier, then, included the region that we know today as the American Southwest. From 1821 to 1854 independent Mexico held the region or dwindling portions of it.

Historians have produced a substantial number of studies of this vast region during the Mexican era, but that historiography has been notably unbalanced, ethnocentric, and incomplete.

During the Mexican era, weak lines of communication spanned the immense distances separating Mexico's frontier provinces. Mexican frontiersmen lived in considerable isolation from one another,

---

*This article appeared originally in the *Western Historical Quarterly* 7 (July 1976): 279–93, and is reprinted with the permission of the editors. The last decade has seen additional scholarship on the Southwest's Mexican era, but considerable research and writing remain to be done before we can restore the imbalance described in this essay.

1. In 1821 Nacogdoches in east Texas had been nearly abandoned, leaving settlements at San Antonio and La Bahía (Goliad).

although their provinces were linked indirectly through the metropolis, Mexico City. This dispersal of relatively isolated Mexican communities in the four present-day southwestern states is mirrored in the
historical literature. Indeed, in a sense there is no historiography
pertaining to Mexico's far northern frontier. Instead, there are books
and articles dealing with portions of the Mexican frontier—California,
Arizona, New Mexico, and Texas. Almost without exception, the
only historians who have crossed provincial lines are those who have
studied explorers, trappers, or traders. In works on the Old Spanish
Trail, the fur trade, and the Santa Fe trade, historians such as LeRoy
and Ann Hafen, Robert Glass Cleland, and Max Moorhead have
followed the peregrinations of trappers and traders even when they
crossed the state line into alien archives.[2]

By and large, historians of the Mexican frontier have shown little
interest in following themes or answering historical questions which
lend themselves to a comparative approach. Works which discuss the
impact of Mexican colonization laws on Texas, for example, rarely
explain why those laws had slight influence on New Mexico, Arizona,
and California. Specialists in California history recognize that the
secularization of the missions was a major event of the Mexican period,
but rarely have they asked if it was important elsewhere on the frontier.
Nor have historians considered more sophisticated questions of comparative history such as the nature of Indian-white relations, social
mobility, class analysis, or demographic patterns.

It might be argued that the provincialism of historians is a justifiable
expression of the provincial frontier communities they are describing,
but it should be noted that some contemporary Mexicans took a
broader view. Men such as Francisco de Azcárate and Tadeo Ortiz y
Ayala saw the entire far northern frontier from California to Texas as
a distinctive region with common problems of defense against the so-
called *indios bárbaros* and against foreign powers—the United States
and Russia. From the vantage point of Mexico City, it was clear that
the border provinces were the most vulnerable in the republic, and

2. Hafen and Hafen, *Old Spanish Trail, Santa Fé to Los Angeles* (Glendale, 1954);
Cleland, *This Reckless Breed of Men: The Trappers and Fur Traders of the Southwest*
(New York, 1950) and Moorhead, *New Mexico's Royal Road: Trade and Travel on the
Chihuahua Trail* (Norman, 1958). The literature on the Texan–Santa Fe expedition,
such as Noel M. Loomis, *The Texan–Santa Fe Pioneers* (Norman, 1958), and Charles
McClure, "The Texan–Santa Fe Expedition of 1841," *New Mexico Historical Review*
48 (January 1973): 45–56, must also, of necessity, cross provincial boundaries.

yet they were also the least populated and most poorly defended; the entire region needed more troops, more colonists, and special incentives for economic development lest it be lost.[3] The historical literature on the Southwest would be enriched by studies which take this broad view of the region.

This is not to suggest that local history, or what Luis González has more aptly termed *microhistoria,* is inferior to regional or national history.[4] To the contrary, any fair-minded historian recognizes that sound, archivally based local studies must be done before launching into meaningful comparative work. Some questions are best understood in a regional or national context, however, and sufficient research to make synthesis possible has been accomplished in some areas. Daniel Tyler, for example, recently drew upon the surprisingly abundant literature on education in California, New Mexico, and Texas to produce a brief overview of the subject, and Ralph Smith has made a substantial contribution to our understanding of the Mexican War by explaining how Mexico had to fight wars on two fronts in 1846: one against the Apache and Comanche on its northern frontier and the other against the United States.[5] These, however, are exceptional studies. The literature in general has remained provincial.

Still another example of the unbalanced nature of the historiography of the Mexican frontier is that the literature on California far outweighs that on Arizona, New Mexico, and even Texas. Texas historians can be forgiven for taking second place, because Texas was part of independent Mexico for a scant fifteen years compared to California's twenty-five. Why, though, should California historiography be more extensive than that of New Mexico? The Mexican flag

3. For Azcárate's views see "Dictamen presentado a La Soberana Junta Gubernative del Imperio Mexicano, por la Comisíon de Relaciónes Exteriores, en 29 de diciembre del año de 1821 . . . ." in *Un programa de política internacional,* by Juan Francisco de Azcárate (Mexico, 1932). Ortiz de Ayala's views are best articulated in *Resúmen de la estadística del Imperio Mexicano, 1822* (1st ed. 1822; Mexico, 1968), and *México considerado como nación independiente y libre . . .* (1st ed. 1832; Guadalajara, 1952).

4. Luis González, *Invitación a la microhistoria* (Mexico, 1973).

5. Daniel Tyler, "The Mexican Teacher," *Red River Valley Historical Review* 1 (Autumn 1974): 207–21. Another example of moving beyond provincial lines is Tyler's "Anglo-American Penetration of the Southwest: The View from New Mexico," *Southwestern Historical Quarterly* 75 (January 1972): 325–38, which looks briefly at the New Mexican reaction to Anglo-American settlement in Texas. Ralph A. Smith, "Indians in American-Mexican Relations before the War of 1846," *Hispanic American Historical Review* 43 (February 1963): 34–64.

flew over both provinces for the same length of time and their stories seem to be of equal interest and merit. Moreover, the hispanized population of New Mexico far exceeded that of California prior to 1846. The answer to that question probably lies in events that occurred after, rather than during, the Mexican period and says much about the elitist nature of the historian's craft.

There is a saying in the West that "water does not run downhill. It runs toward money." To a large extent, that is true of historians as well. After the gold rush, California became the home of men with money and time to read, write, and buy books. It was in California that Hubert Howe Bancroft and his team amassed an extraordinary private archive, oral history collection, and produced thirty-nine hefty volumes on the history of the Pacific Coast of North America. New Mexico Territory had no counterpart to the Golden State's Bancroft. On the contrary, while Bancroft was spending large sums to preserve the historical record, New Mexico's governor, William Pile, apparently sold documents out of the state archives to raise funds.[6] Ultimately, Bancroft devoted seven of his thirty-nine volumes to California and only one volume to New Mexico and Arizona combined.[7]

Hubert Howe Bancroft, then, a product of California's affluence, tipped the balance of regional historiography toward California and, as Earl Pomeroy has noted, shaped the proportions of regional history to the present day.[8] The efforts of Lansing Bloom notwithstanding, the Mexican period in New Mexico has never been examined with the richness of detail and color that Bancroft achieved for California.[9] Nor is it likely that it ever will be. Many of the kinds of sources that

6. This event occurred in 1870. See Ralph Emerson Twitchell, *Leading Facts of New Mexico History*, 2 vols. (Cedar Rapids, 1911–12), II. 413.

7. Bancroft devotes nearly a third of volume II and all of volumes III and IV of his *History of California* (San Francisco, 1884–1890) to the period 1821–45, while he treats those years in one chapter of his *History of Arizona and New Mexico* (San Francisco, 1889). Bancroft also treated the social history of Mexican California in one volume, *California Pastoral, 1769–1848* (San Francisco, 1888), which concentrates on the Mexican period and for which there is no counterpart for any other southwestern state.

8. Earl Pomeroy, "Old Lamps for New: The Cultural Lag in Pacific Coast Historiography," *Arizona and the West* 2 (Summer 1969): 110.

9. The most detailed examination of the Mexican period in New Mexico is Lansing B. Bloom's "New Mexico under Mexican Administration, 1821–1846," published serially in *Old Santa Fe*, I and II (1913–1915).

Bancroft retrieved for California have been irrevocably lost to historians of New Mexico.

The historiography of the Mexican period is also unbalanced in the sense that United States historians hold a virtual monopoly on the field. The few Mexican writers who have interested themselves in the northern frontier have confined their investigations almost exclusively to the Texas revolt or to broader aspects of diplomatic history which led to the invasions by North Americans in 1846 and 1847, and have ignored other developments on the frontier.[10] United States dominance of the field, then, has occurred largely by default. Indeed, Mexican historians' slight interest in the frontier region during this era reflects their general lack of interest in national history during the years between 1821 and 1854. This period, Josefina Vázquez has noted, "has been almost systematically forgotten" by Mexican historians because it is a confusing, complex era of which Mexicans have not been proud.[11]

10. On the Texas Revolution, see for example, José C. Valadés, *Mexico, Santa Anna y la Guerra de Texas* (3rd ed., rev.; Mexico, 1965); Pablo Herrera Carrillo, "Las Siete Guerras por Texas," in the *Colección de Documentos para la historia de las guerras entre México y los Estados Unidos*, dirigida por Luis Chávez Orozco (vol. I; Mexico, 1959); and Miguel A. Sánchez Lamego, *Sitio y toma del Alamo, 1836* (Mexico, 1966). The standard account of diplomatic history during these years is Carlos Bosch García's *Historia de las Relaciones entre México y los Estados Unidos, 1819–1848* (Mexico, 1961), which should be supplemented by the more recent overview by Luis G. Zorrilla, *Historia de las Relaciones entre México y Los Estados de América, 1800–1958*, 2 vols. (Mexico, 1965). A detailed bibliography of Mexican–United States relations is in Daniel Cosío Villegas, *Cuestiones internacionales de México. Una bibliografía* (Mexico, 1966). Mexican historians continue to be attracted by the themes of manifest destiny and American expansion before the Mexican War. See, for example, *Anglia: Anuario/Estudios Angloamericanos*, V (Mexico, 1973). Most Mexican publications which treat the Southwest between 1821 and 1846 are more likely to consist of edited documents rather than be interpretative, secondary works. See, for example, Alfonso Teja Zabre, *Lecciones de California* (Mexico, 1962); Carlos Sánchez-Navarro, *La guerra de Tejas: Memorias de un soldado* (Mexico, 1938); and the reprinting of rare items by Vargas Rhea such as Ignacio Zuñiga's *Rápida ojeada al estado de Sonora, territorios de California, y Arizona. Año de 1835* (Mexico, 1948), and [Jean Louis Berlandier] *Viage a Texas en el año de 1828* (Mexico, 1948). The two-volume study by Vito Alessio Robles of *Coahuila y Texas desde la consumación de la independencia hasta el Tratado de Paz de Guadalupe Hidalgo* (Mexico, 1943) stands alone in Mexican historiography as an interpretative, scholarly study of political, economic, and social affairs in a province of Mexico's former frontier. Significantly, Alessio Robles relied heavily upon United States historiography, especially the work of Eugene Barker, for the Texas portion of his book. Alfonso Trueba, in works such as *California: Tierra Perdida*, 2 vols. (Mexico, 1956 and 1958), writes for a popular audience, and his work is not documented.

11. "La historiografía mexicana ha olvidado de manera casi sistemática todo el

The history of Mexico's far northern frontier, then, has been written almost entirely by United States historians, and one theme has
dominated their writing: American expansion. Historical literature
dealing with the Mexican frontier has centered on that theme and its
components: the expansion of American commerce into the region;
American colonization; the Texas Revolt of 1836; Texas's annexation
in 1845; the so-called Mexican War of 1846–48; and the Gadsden
Purchase of 1854. American expansion, which saw the United States
seize the heart of the North American continent and Mexico lose half
of her territory, is of extraordinary significance. The theme has dominated historical explanation to such a point, however, that the activities of Mexicans on their own frontier have been neglected and, in
the process, ethnocentricity has influenced scholarship.

A student looking through standard textbooks, for example, is
likely to gain the impression that Anglo-Americans were playing the
only game in town. One text on the Southwest discusses "The Mexican
Era" in three sections: first, "The Arrival of the Anglo Americans,"
second, "The Colonization of Texas, the Revolution, and the Republic," and third, "The Mexican War."[12] Similarly, a survey of early
California history treats the years 1837 to 1847 in a chapter entitled
"Waiting for Old Glory," and a text on New Mexico views the Mexican
era in chapters entitled "Enter the Americans" and "The Time of the
Gringo."[13] With the exception of texts on California,[14] most surveys
of the Southwest or of individual southwestern states reduce the Mexican period to a simple prelude to Texas independence and the United
States conquest.[15]

período que va de 1821 a 1854. El porqué es aventurado. Una primera razón es su
complicación y poco brillo. Es una etapa que todos consideramos negra. . . ." Josefina
Vázquez de Knauth, *Mexicanos y norteamericanos ante la guerra del 47* (Mexico, 1972),
11. The most recent attempt at a detailed synthesis of these years is *Orígenes de la
república mexicana* by José C. Valadés (Mexico, 1972).

12. Odie B. Faulk, *Land of Many Frontiers. A History of the American Southwest*
(New York, 1968).

13. Charles E. Chapman, *A History of California: The Spanish Period* (New York,
1921), and Warren A. Beck, *New Mexico: A History of Four Centuries* (Norman, 1962).

14. Reflecting the monographic literature, and influenced perhaps by the enormous detail uncovered by Bancroft, California textbooks usually devote a separate
chapter to "Mexican California." See, for example, the standard texts by John Caughey
and Andrew Rolle, and the newer works by Walton Bean, and Warren Beck and
David Williams.

15. See, for example, W. Eugene Hollon, *The Southwest Old and New* (New York,

Textbooks, of course, tend to reflect the monographic and periodical literature which also emphasizes United States expansion. The story of Thomas ap Catesby Jones's erroneous seize of Monterey in 1842, for example, has been retold in various books, and at least four articles on the subject have appeared in scholarly journals since 1954. The most recent author to examine the Jones fiasco noted that "very little new can be added to the basic story," then proceeded to prove his point.[16] Such an unnecessary display seems especially lamentable when there are fresh subjects of equal if not greater significance waiting to be examined.

Nowhere is the lopsided nature of historical writing on the Mexican frontier more evident than in respect to the fur trade, a subject that is, of course, closely related to the question of American economic expansion into northernmost Mexico. Scholarship on the fur trade had reached such a level of maturity by the mid-1960s that LeRoy Hafen and the Arthur H. Clark Company could launch a ten-volume series containing biographies of 292 individual trappers, many of whom operated in northern Mexico. Of necessity, Hafen's series on the mountain men and the fur trade of the Far West included some very minor figures. (I speak with authority on this matter, having contributed to the series sketches of some of the most minor of the mountain men.) In addition to the articles in the Mountain Men series, biographers have also produced book-length studies of trappers, some of whom are closely related to northernmost Mexico: Kit Carson, James

---

1967), and Lynn I. Perrigo, *The American Southwest: Its Peoples and Cultures* (New York, 1971) which provides the most balanced treatment. For Texas, see Rupert N. Richardson, *Texas, the Lone Star State* (2nd ed.; Englewood Cliffs, 1958), and Seymour V. Connor, *Texas: A History* (New York, 1971), both of which focus on American colonization in Texas and Mexican efforts to control that colonization. For Arizona, see Jay J. Wagoner, *Early Arizona: Prehistory to Civil War* (Tucson, 1974), which suggests that land grants and mountain men are the two major themes of the period.

16. James High, "Jones at Monterey, 1842," *Journal of the West* 5 (April 1966): 173–81. Earlier article-length treatments of this incident include: Frank A. Knapp, Jr., "Preludios de la perdida de California," *Historia Mexicana* 4 (octubre–diciembre 1954): 235–49; Lou Ann Garrett, "The Commodore's Decision," *Southern California Quarterly* 40 (December 1958): 337–52; and George M. Brooke, Jr., "The Vest Pocket War of Commodore Jones," *Pacific Historical Review* 31 (August 1962): 217–33. Of these four articles only Knapp's examines the Mexican reaction to the seizure in depth. The other three articles, although published subsequently, do not even cite Knapp.

Kirker, Antoine Leroux, Pegleg Smith, Antoine Robidoux, Old Bill
Williams, William Wolfskill, and Ewing Young among them.[17]

This is not to suggest that biographies of mountain men have
become excessive, but simply to note that historians have shown far
greater interest in Americans in northern Mexico than in Mexicans.
A recent detailed study of early Arizona, for example, recounts explorations by mountain men while completely ignoring the reopening of
the Anza trail from Tucson to Los Angeles by Captain José Romero
(1823–26).[18] In contrast to the plentiful biographies of one small group
of American adventurers and entrepreneurs, the mountain men, few
biographies of Mexican frontiersmen exist. There is no biography, for
example, of a single governor of Mexican California or New Mexico
save one article-length chronicle of the life of Luis Antonio Argüello,
governor of California between 1822 and 1825.[19] The number of book-
length biographies of Mexican frontiersmen can be counted on two
hands: two *tejanos* have been the subject of books (Martín de León
and José Antonio Navarro),[20] four *californios* (José de la Guerra,

17. Two recent biographies of Carson are Bernice Blackwelder, *Great Westerner*
(Caldwell, 1962), and M. Morgan Estergreen, *Kit Carson: A Portrait in Courage* (Nor-
man, 1962). The other men listed have had but one biographer to date: William C.
McGaw, *Savage Scene: The Life and Times of James Kirker, Frontier King* (New York,
1972); Forbes Parkhill, *The Blazed Trail of Antoine Leroux* (Los Angeles, 1965); Sardis
Templeton, *The Lame Captain: The Life and Adventures of Pegleg Smith* (Los Angeles,
1965); William S. Wallace, *Antoine Robidoux, 1794–1860* (Los Angeles, 1960); Alpheus
H. Favour, *Old Bill Williams, Mountain Man* (Norman, 1962); Iris Higbie Wilson,
William Wolfskill, 1798–1866: Frontier Trapper to California Ranchero (Glendale, 1965);
and Kenneth Holmes, *Ewing Young: Master Trapper* (Portland, 1967).

18. Wagoner, *Early Arizona*. In this case, specialized studies do exist of which
Wagoner was apparently unaware. See, for example, George William Beattie, "Reopening
the Anza Road," *Pacific Historical Review* 2 (March 1933): 52–71, and Lowell John
Bean and William Marvin Mason, *Diaries and Accounts of the Romero Expeditions in
Arizona and California, 1823–1826* (Palm Springs, 1962). Rufus Kay Wyllys also
ignored the Romero expeditions in his *Arizona: The History of a Frontier State* (Phoenix, 1950).

19. Raymond Kenneth Morrison, "Luis Antonio Arguello: First Mexican Gov-
ernor of California," *Journal of the West* 2 (April and July 1963): 193–204, 347–61.
A more valuable contribution, containing considerable new information, is C. Alan
Hutchinson's account of the life of governor José Figueroa prior to his arrival in
California. "General José Figueroa's Career in Mexico, 1792–1832," *New Mexico
Historical Review* 48 (October 1973): 277–98.

20. Arthur B. J. Hammett, *The Empresario Don Martín de León* (Waco, 1973),
and Joseph Martin Dawson, *José Antonio Navarro: Co-Creator of Texas* (Waco, 1969).
Walter Stuck, *José Francisco Ruiz* (San Antonio, 1943), is a pamphlet containing
twelve pages of text. It does not seem sporting to consider Lorenzo de Zavala a Tejano,

Mariano Vallejo, Agustín Zamorano, and Bernardo Yorba);[21] and three *nuevomexicanos* (Manuel Antonio Chaves, Antonio José Martínez, and Donaciano Vigil).[22] I am interested here only in enumerating these biographies, not in assessing their quality.[23]

This small list of biographies of Mexican frontiersmen does not include Franciscans; they seem to belong in a separate category. Franciscan historians have written a substantial number of biographical sketches of their predecessors of the Mexican era. Father Maynard Geiger has given us a masterful biographical dictionary of Franciscans in California and Fray Marion Habig has produced a similar, but more limited, work for Texas, while Fray Angélico Chávez has outlined the lives of many of the New Mexico Franciscans.[24] Only one book-length biography of a Franciscan of the Mexican period has appeared, however, and that is a brief study of García Diego, California's first bishop, 1840–46, written by Father Francis Weber (who is not a Franciscan).[25]

In the selection of subjects for biographies, then, our ethnocentrism is quite apparent. More often than not, Franciscans have written

his few significant months of residence in Texas notwithstanding. Raymond Estep has studied his life in *Lorenzo de Zavala: Profeta del Liberalismo Mexicano* (Mexico, 1952).

21. Joseph A. Thompson, *El Gran Capitán: José de la Guerra* (Los Angeles, 1961); Myrtle M. McKittrick, *Vallejo: Son of California* (Portland, 1944). The best biography of Vallejo is George Tays, "Mariano Guadalupe Vallejo and Sonoma," which ran serially in six issues of the *California Historical Society Quarterly* in 1937 and 1938; George L. Harding, *Don Agustín V. Zamorano: Statesman, Soldier, Craftsman, and California's First Printer* (Los Angeles, 1934); Terry E. Stephenson, *Don Bernardo Yorba* (Los Angeles, 1941).

22. Marc Simmons, *The Little Lion of the Southwest: A Life of Manuel Antonio Chaves* (Chicago, 1973). Pedro Sánchez, *Memorias Sobre la vida del Presbítero Don Antonio José Martínez* (Santa Fe, 1903). F. Stanley [Stanley Francis Louis Crocchiola], *Giant in Lilliput: The Story of Donaciano Vigil* (Pampa, Texas, 1963).

23. Hammett's "biography" of Martín de León, for example, is a pastiche of research notes, and F. Stanley's life of Donaciano Vigil does not deserve comment. The life of Padre Antonio José Martínez is fifty-four pages long and undocumented; no good biography of him exists.

24. Maynard Geiger, *Franciscan Missionaries in Hispanic California 1769–1848: A Biographical Dictionary* (San Marino, 1969); *The Zacatecan Missionaries in Texas, 1716–1834*, includes *A Biographical Dictionary* by Fr. Marion Habig (Austin, 1973), and is limited to padres from the College of Zacatecas; Fray Angélico Chávez's guide, *Archives of the Archdiocese of Santa Fe, 1678–1900* (Washington, 1957), provides bare bones biographical data for most New Mexico Franciscans.

25. Francis J. Weber, *Francisco García Diego: California's Transition Bishop* (Los Angeles, 1972). This is a greatly expanded version of a biography which Weber published in 1961 under a different title.

about Franciscans and secular Anglo-American writers have examined the activities of their countrymen. On those occasions when Americans have written about Mexican frontiersmen, their choice often seems influenced by the fact that their subject was either pro-American or cooperated with Americans, as was the case with José Antonio Navarro, Donaciano Vigil, and Mariano Vallejo. Vallejo's biographer, for example, is reluctant to abandon the idea that on the eve of the Mexican War Vallejo said of the Americans: "Look not therefore with jealousy upon the hardy pioneers who scale our mountains . . . but rather welcome them as brothers . . ." even though there is no sound evidence that Vallejo made such a statement.[26]

If our choice of subject reveals ethnocentrism, so too does our choice of source material. Writers have relied too heavily upon the valuable but imperfect observations of American visitors such as Richard Henry Dana, Josiah Gregg, and Mary Austin Holley for descriptions of Mexicans and Mexican society. We ought to be more cautious than ever in relying upon such sources, for Cecil Robinson and others have described the stereotypes and prejudices that clouded the judgment of those foreign visitors.[27] Recent studies by Janet Lecompte and Daniel Tyler demonstrate that North Americans recorded gossip and presented it as fact, and that historians have accepted those supposed facts and served them again to modern readers, unaware that they were perpetuating myths rather than writing history.[28]

Since many historians of the Mexican frontier have placed heavy reliance upon Anglo-American sources and themes, it is not surprising that they have not integrated regional history into Mexico's national history as well as they should. This is not entirely a result of ethnocentrism or happenstance. Charles E. Chapman, for example, saw little link between California and the rest of the Mexican Republic

26. McKittrick, *Vallejo,* 249. Bancroft, *California,* V: 41–47, 59–63, and Tays, "Vallejo," *California Historical Quarterly* 17 (June 1938): 164, have made convincing arguments that Vallejo never made such a speech.

27. Cecil Robinson, *With the Ears of Strangers: The Mexican in American Literature* (Tucson, 1963). See, too, my essay, "Stereotyping of Mexico's Far Northern Frontier," in Manuel P. Servín, ed., *An Awakened Minority: The Mexican-Americans* (Beverly Hills, 1974), 18–26.

28. Janet Lecompte, "Manuel Armijo's Family History," *New Mexico Historical Review* 48 (July 1973): 251–58; Lecompte, "The Making of a Villain: Manuel Armijo of New Mexico as Portrayed by Kendall and Gregg," paper presented to the Southwest Social Science meeting, Dallas, 1974; Daniel Tyler, "Gringo Views of Governor Manuel Armijo," *New Mexico Historical Review* 45 (January 1970): 23–46.

and concluded that "Strictly speaking, there was no Mexican period of California history," because Mexican influence on the frontier was so limited.[29] That conclusion seems incorrect. Writers such as George Tays, Adele Ogden, Frank Knapp, and C. Alan Hutchinson have made California history more intelligible by placing it in a national context. Hutchinson's 1969 study of the Híjar-Padrés colony in California is especially noteworthy for it not only provides fresh detail, but it also suggests a revisionist view of Governor José Figueroa and of the Mexican colonists who accompanied Híjar and Padrés.[30] Other writers who have studied regional events in a national context include historians of Mexican Texas such as Eugene Barker, Ohland Morton, and Joseph C. McElhannon, and New Mexico writers such as Lansing Bloom, Ward Alan Minge, and Daniel Tyler.[31]

Many questions of regional importance require additional research into national history in order to answer them with understanding. Despite all that has been written about Mexican colonization laws, for example, there appears to be no satisfactory account of the discussions and rationale behind that policy as it emerged in Mexico City and in Saltillo between 1821 and 1825. Similarly, although much has been written about the events leading up to the significant law of April 6, 1830, which prohibited further American colonization in Texas, there seems to be no satisfactory explanation for why the law

29. Chapman, *California*, 455.

30. Tays doctoral dissertation, "Revolutionary California: The Political History of the Mexican Period, 1822–1846," done at Berkeley in 1932, remains unpublished. For an example of his published work see "Captain Andrés Castillero, Diplomat: An Account from Unpublished Sources of His Services to Mexico in the Alvarado Revolution of 1836–1838," *California Historical Society Quarterly* 14 (September 1935): 230–63. Ogden's most substantial work is *The California Sea Otter Trade, 1784–1848* (Berkeley, 1941). For Knapp see "The Mexican Fear of Manifest Destiny in California," in Thomas E. Cotner and Carlos E. Castañeda, eds., *Essays in American History* (Austin, 1958), 192–208. Hutchinson is author of *Frontier Settlement in Mexican California: The Híjar-Padrés Colony and Its Origins, 1769–1835* (New Haven, 1969).

31. Barker distilled much of his research into *The Life of Stephen F. Austin, Founder of Texas, 1793–1836* (1st ed. 1926; Austin, 1969). Morton is author of *Terán and Texas: A Chapter in Texas-Mexican Relations* (Austin, 1948); McElhannon's "Imperial Mexico and Texas, 1821–1823," *Southwestern Historical Quarterly* 53 (October 1949): 117–50, is based upon his doctoral dissertation and is broadly conceived. Bloom, "New Mexico under Mexican Administration." Tyler and Minge have written doctoral dissertations at the University of New Mexico which remain to be published. Respectively: "New Mexico in the 1820s: The First Administration of Manuel Armijo" (1970), and "Frontier Problems in New Mexico Preceding the Mexican War, 1840–1846" (1965).

was repealed in 1833. On a broader canvas, the Mexican period saw the decay of the frontier church and military, the two most important frontier institutions in the Spanish period. Their decline cannot be understood as a purely regional event. Foreign visitors to the frontier, who reported on the ragtag uniforms and outdated equipment of the troops, and who ridiculed the moral lapses of the clergy, saw only the tip of the iceberg and had no way of fathoming its depth.

We need, then, to make far greater use of Mexican archival materials and of Mexican historiography if we are to avoid ethnocentrism and produce a balanced re-creation and explanation of the Mexican period. That task should be far easier for the present generation of historians because entire collections are now readily accessible on microfilm. The Bexar Archives and the Mexican Archives of New Mexico have been filmed in recent years, and projects continue in the north Mexican states, such as the filming of the archives of the State of Sonora at Hermosillo, with its valuable documentation on Arizona. Newspapers, too, such as those of Ciudad Chihuahua, continue to be made available on film through the active program at the University of Texas at El Paso.

Greater use of Mexican sources should improve our understanding of traditional topics. Much has been written about Indian policy in the Spanish period, for example, but only the surface has been scratched in the Mexican period despite the notable contributions of Sherburne F. Cook, C. Alan Hutchinson, Myra Ellen Jenkins, Ernest W. Winkler, Ralph A. Smith, and Edward Spicer.[32] The Mexican period was not simply an extension of the Spanish period in regard to Indian affairs,

32. Cook, *The Conflict between the California Indian and White Civilization*, parts I and II (Berkeley, 1943); Hutchinson, "The Mexican Government and the Mission Indians of Upper California, 1821–1835," *Americas* 21 (April 1965): 335–62; Jenkins, "The Baltasar Baca Grant: History of an Encroachment," *El Palacio* 68 (Spring and Summer 1961): 47–64, 87–105, and "Taos Pueblo and Its Neighbors, 1540–1847," *New Mexico Historical Review* 41 (April 1966): 85–114; Winkler, "The Cherokee Indians in Texas," *Quarterly of the Texas State Historical Association* 7 (October 1903): 95–165; for Smith see note 5; Spicer has made an admirable effort to synthesize the Mexican period in *Cycles of Conquest: The Impact of Spain, Mexico, and the United States on the Indians of the Southwest, 1533–1960* (Tucson, 1962). Indian-white relations in the Mexican period are touched upon in many studies of broader scope, but the period is usually treated in a pedestrian manner as in Charles L. Kenner, *A History of New Mexican–Plains Indians Relations* (Norman, 1969). Better than most is Frank McNitt, *Navajo Wars: Military Campaigns, Slave Raids, and Reprisals* (Albuquerque, 1972).

for new conditions arose: Indians achieved legal equality in the young republic; Indians, especially in California, developed new techniques for resisting Mexican encroachment; Indians throughout the region acquired guns, ammunition, and a new market for stolen goods from westward moving Anglo-Americans; and the crumbling military establishment on the Mexican frontier could not offer a defense as effective as that of the Spanish period.

Indian-Mexican relations during the Mexican period, then, possessed a dynamic of their own, unique to that time and place, but we know little about the processes involved or about answers to some basic questions. How, for example, could frontier officials continue to sign peace treaties with Indians as if they represented sovereign nations when the law regarded them as fellow Mexicans?[33] How could separate sections of the cemetery and of the church be reserved for Indians in Los Angeles as late as 1845 if they were equal before the law?[34]

In addition to illuminating traditional topics, Mexican sources suggest new paths of inquiry. Historians interested in the Southwest have thus far remained innocent of the kinds of questions that Clio's servants in European and American history have been asking about the nature of society, the family, disease, mortality, social and spatial mobility, crime and violence, land-man relationships, class structure, class conflict, and the relationship between kinship and political power. Some work in social history has been done in the Spanish period, but the Mexican years remain largely untouched except for work by social scientists and genealogists.[35] Indeed, the implicit assumption seems to

33. This question not only puzzles us in retrospect, but confused contemporaries as well.

34. W. W. Robinson, compiler, "The Indians of Los Angeles as Revealed by the Los Angeles City Archives," Southern California Quarterly 20 (December 1938): 161–62.

35. Especially noteworthy is Alicia V. Tjarks, "Comparative Demographic Analysis of Texas, 1777–1793," Southwestern Historical Quarterly 77 (January 1974): 293–338. Bancroft's California Pastoral (San Francisco, 1888), and Nellie Van der Grift Sánchez's Spanish Arcadia (Los Angeles, 1929) are episodic and meant to entertain more than to instruct, but are works of social history for which neither Arizona, New Mexico, or Texas have counterparts. Some basic data for social history has been published in the form of census reports and church records by J. Gregg Layne in California (see note 39), and Fray Angélico Chávez in New Mexico (see, for example, his "New Names in New Mexico, 1820–1850," El Palacio 64 (September–December 1957): 291–318, 367–80. Ward Alan Minge's translation of "The Last Will and Testament of Don Severino Martínez," New Mexico Quarterly 33 (Spring 1963): 33–

be that Mexican frontier society remained largely unchanged until the American conquest. A recent study by Leon Campbell, however, suggests that the period was a time of rapid mobility for the californios and there is reason to suppose that the brief Mexican era witnessed substantial institutional and societal change.[36]

Records of the Mexican period are often fragmentary and the statistical base is small, but it seems possible to draw some conclusions regarding frontier society from census, ecclesiastical, and judicial records. An examination of Los Angeles census records, for example, has led Richard Griswold to conclude that from 1781 on the pueblo was "a settlement of women, children and married men," with the ratio of males to females nearly equal. Violence and social disruption, Griswold argues, were less common than in youthful communities on the American frontier.[37] Between 1834 and 1845, however, Los Angeles averaged over two murders a year when its adult population was about a thousand.[38] In 1836, six percent of the women in Los Angeles were known prostitutes.[39] These figures suggest something other than a quiet

---

56, contains valuable information for social history, especially in regard to material culture, as does Lynn I. Perrigo, "New Mexico in the Mexican Period as Revealed in the Torres Documents," *New Mexico Historical Review* 29 (January 1954): 28–40. See, too, Frederick Chabot, *With the Founders of San Antonio: Geneology* . . . (San Antonio, 1931). Interpretive work in social history has been left largely to anthropologists who touch on the Mexican period in broader works, as did Frances León Swadesh in *Los Primeros Pobladores: Hispanic Americans of the Ute Frontier* (Notre Dame, 1974). With the exception of education, more has been written about medicine and disease than any other aspect of frontier society in the Mexican period. Much of that literature is episodic, but it includes such serious studies as J. Villasana Haggard, "Epidemic Cholera in Texas, 1833–1834," *Southwestern Historical Quarterly* 40 (January 1937): 216–30; Sherburne F. Cook, "Smallpox in Spanish and Mexican California, 1770–1845," *Bulletin of the History of Medicine* 7 (February 1939): 153–91; and Cook, "The Epidemic of 1830–1833 in California and Oregon," *University of California Publications in American Archaeology and Ethnology* 43 (May 1955): 303–36.

36. Campbell suggests that California's soldiery evolved into a ranchero class, but he does not recognize that this process occurred after 1822 in the main. "The First Californios: Presidial Society in Spanish California, 1769–1822," *Journal of the West* 11 (October 1972): 583–95.

37. Richard Griswold del Castillo, "La Raza Hispano Americana: The Emergence of an Urban Culture among the Spanish Speaking of Los Angeles, 1850–1880" (Ph.D. dissertation, University of California, Los Angeles, 1974), 26.

38. Index to Criminal Cases, Los Angeles, 1830–1846 (Juzgado de la primera instancia) in the California Historical Documents Collection, Huntington Library, San Marino, California.

39. J. Gregg Layne, "The First Census of the Los Angeles District. Padrón de la Ciudad de Los Angeles y su Jurisdicción. Año 1836," *Historical Society of Southern*

family town. At the same time that crime seems to have been on the upswing in Los Angeles in the 1830s and 1840s, males began to far outnumber females, leading one to suspect that a demographic change had undermined the traditional restraints of family life.[40]

Greater and wiser use of Mexican archives will not answer all of our questions about the past, but it may help free us of our all too quick acceptance of the exaggerated judgments of an Alfred Robinson, who maintained that murder was a daily occurrence in the Los Angeles area, or the romantic recollections of a Juan Bautista Alvarado who averred that prostitution did not exist in California before the Americans came.[41] "In my day," Alvarado asserted, "it was possible for some women to surrender to immoral love, but I can assure you that money did not have anything to do with their love affairs. Our women succumbed to the desires of the heart, but they never sold their caresses for a vile coin."[42] A social historian might someday resolve these contradictory statements, but in the meantime we should recall that the californios suffered from a notorious shortage of coin in Alvarado's day.

Earl Pomeroy once suggested that Hubert Howe Bancroft told more than we need to know about Spanish and Mexican California. Bancroft, Pomeroy quipped, brought about "the sudden shift from total neglect of early California history to total recall."[43] Historians who have dug deeply into the sources, however, and a new generation of students asking fresh questions about the past, make it plain that we have not achieved "total recall" or even a satisfactory understanding of Mexico's far northern frontier. Although many scholars have made substantial contributions, the Mexican period remains an open field for historical research. Its challenges will be met most effectively by

California Quarterly 18 (September–December 1936): 82–83. Fifteen of 250 women were identified as of *mala vida*, a term which usually signified a prostitute.

40. According to Griswold del Castillo's count, the ratio of males to females was 11:15 in 1781; 258–264 in 1830; 553–421 in 1836; and 627–500 in 1844. Griswold does not comment upon the widening ratio of the 1830s and 1840s which, along with judicial records, weakens his thesis that Los Angeles was a relatively nonviolent community until the Americans came. The entire question needs to be explored.

41. *Life in California* (1st ed., 1846; Santa Barbara, 1970), 105.

42. "History of California," 1876, 5 vols., ms. Bancroft Library, University of California, Berkeley, III: 52–53.

43. Pomeroy, "Old Lamps for New," 117.

historians who combine linguistic skill with the interdisciplinary training and impartiality necessary to understand this complex era when Mexico, the United States, and autonomous nations of native Americans vied for control of the regions that we know today as the American Southwest.

6

"From Hell Itself"
*The Americanization of Mexico's Northern Frontier**

In 1830, José Francisco Ruiz of San Antonio, one of the pillars of that small Mexican community, made a telling comment about the large influx of Anglo American colonists who were settling in Mexican Texas. Whereas the central government in Mexico City sought to restrict the flow of Anglo Americans into Texas, through the controversial Law of April 6, 1830, Ruiz wanted to welcome them: "I cannot help seeing advantages which to my way of thinking, would result," he said, "if we admitted honest, hard-working people, regardless of what country they come from . . . even hell itself." A decade later in Alta California, which then formed part of Mexico's northern frontier, Pablo de la Guerra of Monterey is said to have made a similar observation about the number of Yankees settling in California. The foreigners, De la Guerra said, "are about to overrun us, of which I am very glad, for the country needs immigration in order to make progress."

When war broke out between Mexico and the United States in 1846, foreigners did indeed overrun California, but not in the way

*The themes outlined in this essay are developed at greater length in my book, *The Mexican Frontier, 1821–1846: The American Southwest Under Mexico* (Albuquerque: University of New Mexico Press, 1982). Selected passages are reproduced with permission of the University of New Mexico Press; citations to all quotations that appear in this essay may be found in *The Mexican Frontier*. I prepared this essay to present at the Border Studies Symposium at the University of Texas, El Paso, on March 23, 1983, and read a Spanish version of it on the occasion of my induction into the Mexican Academy of History, on July 17, 1984. The English version was distributed in the *Border Perspectives* series of the Center for Inter-American and Border Studies at UTEP (October 1983), and is reprinted here with permission of the director.

that Pablo de la Guerra had envisioned. Armed forces from the imperialistic United States invaded California, and took possession of its principal towns, just as American forces seized the key settlements in New Mexico and southern Arizona during the war. There was no need for the United States to send troops into Texas, for that former Mexican province had rebelled in 1836 and entered the American union in 1845—an event that, in itself, contributed to the war between Mexico and the United States. When the shooting ended and the last signatures were put on the Treaty of Guadalupe Hidalgo, the United States had possession of half of Mexico, a region embracing not only the present border states from Texas to California, but Nevada, Utah, and half of Colorado as well.

To be sure, American forces had met resistance in New Mexico and California, but both provinces had fallen rather easily and no prolonged guerrilla struggle followed. How could invading armies conquer northern Mexico so easily, and why did the invaders meet so little resistance?

Part of the answer can be found in the dynamic nature of American expansionism, and this is the subject to which most American historians have devoted their attention. As a result, we have splendid studies of people such as Stephen Austin, Kit Carson, Charles Bent, and Thomas Oliver Larkin—those intrepid traders, trappers, and colonists who settled in northern Mexico and helped, often unwittingly, to prepare the region for an American conquest. American historians have also examined the forces that gave impetus to what came to be called Manifest Destiny and Mission, and the lurching, blundering policies—sometimes known as diplomacy—that led us into the war. But this represents only half of the answer. To understand why the Mexican North became the American Southwest with such ease between the Texas Revolt of 1836 and the Mexican-American War of 1846–47, it is also necessary to understand something of the nature of the Mexican frontiersman who acquiesed to the conquest—the Mexican counterparts to the Austins, Carson, Bents, and Larkins—and the dynamics of the Mexican society and institutions that lay behind the Mexican frontier. Here, historians are on shakier ground, for they enter into an era of Mexican history that, as Mexican historian Josefina Vázquez has put it, has been "almost systematically forgotten."

Although our knowledge of Mexico in this era lacks depth and precision, it does seem clear that the American conquest of the Mexican North was facilitated greatly, if not made possible, by Mexico's failure to tie her frontier to the rest of the nation through the building of strong institutional, economic, and even social ties. That Mexico failed to do this was not for lack of foresight or concern about the frontier, or because of the "natural inferiority" of Mexicans as some contemporary Anglo-Americans smugly imagined. Rather it was because of Mexico's extraordinary internal problems. Newly independent from Spain in 1821, Mexico had embarked on a bold new political and economic course that affected every aspect of life in the nation, including life on its remote frontiers.

At the same time that some Mexican *políticos* sought to implement profound political, economic, and social changes, they met a series of seemingly insurmountable obstacles: the destructive effects of the ruinous decade of civil war that had given life to the young nation; repeated economic crises; quarrels between church and state; the machinations of predatory and often illiterate army officers; the defiance of local leaders whose regional interests ran deeper than their allegiance to the nation; and the threats of foreign invasion. The magnitude of these problems overwhelmed Mexico's inexperienced and sometimes doctrinaire civilian leaders, who could neither bring order out of chaos nor maintain themselves in power. As governments came and went, policies toward the frontier often disappeared in the shuffle and continuity was lost. Key officials in Mexico City understood the urgency of frontier problems as only one of a series of urgencies.

Efforts at reform, then, bumped squarely into immense obstacles and sent shock waves across the young nation—reaching as far away as the northern frontier. There, they shook that region's already weak attachment to the rest of the nation and facilitated the Americanization of northern Mexico. Let us look at some examples, beginning in the political sphere.

Mexico's first national charter, the Constitution of 1824, envisioned a federal republic composed of states and territories that would be relatively autonomous like those of the United States. The underlying philosophy, as Lorenzo de Zavala explained in the preamble to the Constitution, was to allow local decision making in a nation characterized by "enormous differences of climate, temperature, and their consequent influence." For the northern frontier, however, the promise of political autonomy was not realized. Due to their sparse population, New Mexico and California became territories rather than states under the Constitution of 1824 and the document gave Congress the power to draw up regulations for the internal administration of the territories. Rather than leaving decisions to local lawmakers, Congressmen in Mexico City would decide what was best for California and New Mexico. But to make matters worse, Congress was preoccupied by more pressing concerns and failed to draw up internal regulations for the territories during those years that the Constitution of 1824 was in force (1824–1835). For lack of new laws, frontier administrators turned to old Spanish laws, and those posed peculiar problems. As Carlos Carrillo of California put it: "The laws of the Spanish Cortes . . . present many difficulties, doubts, and perhaps errors in their application, because they were made for other countries, for another kind of government, and for other circumstances very different from ours." Tired of waiting for Congress to act, some frustrated frontiersmen in New Mexico drew up a plan for statehood, proposing to name the territory the State of Hidalgo. Although the plan won the endorsement of many municipalities in New Mexico, the territorial assembly tabled it.

Under the Constitution of 1824, Texas also failed to achieve political autonomy. Texas entered the United States of Mexico tied to its larger and more populous neighbor to the south, Coahuila, as the single state of Coahuila y Texas. From the very beginning, when the state legislature infuriated them by abolishing their local legislature, *tejano* leaders entered into an adversary relationship with Coahuila politicians. Texas deplored the failure of the state government to address the unusual needs of the frontier and lamented the great distance that separated them from the state capital in Saltillo, described by one visitor as "ridiculously placed. . . . The distance from Saltillo to Nacogdoches in the north is about three hundred leagues, whereas lands laying fifteen leagues to the south of Saltillo no longer belongs to Coahuila y Texas." General Manuel Mier y Terán, who inspected Texas in 1828, termed the arrangement a "monstrosity," and the town council of San Antonio, in a memorial of 1832, blamed the lack of a responsive state government for the "paralysis" of Texas. An official inspector who visited Texas that year, Tadeo Ortiz, concluded: "I am certain that all of the ills of Texas date from its annexation to the State of Coahuila." Notwithstanding such general agreement that the arrangement had proved unworkable, Texas remained linked to Coahuila. Important decisions continued to be made in faraway Saltillo and the discontent generated by that lack of political autonomy became one of the many burrs under the saddle that led Texas to throw off Mexican rule in 1836.

In the mid-1830s, Mexico abandoned the federalist system, replacing the Constitution of 1824 with a conservative charter that made government even less representative and that consciously centralized decision making in Mexico City. For frontiersmen who had sought greater local autonomy, this was the last straw. In a stunning series of revolts between 1836 and 1838, Texas, Alta California, New Mexico, and Sonora (which then embraced present southern Arizona), declared against the central government. All except Texas soon returned to the fold, but resentments lingered and confidence in the central government waned as instability became the hallmark of Mexican politics. From 1833 to 1855 the presidency of Mexico changed hands thirty-six times! On the eve of the North American invasion, frontier *políticos* openly expressed discontent with the failure of the political system to respond to their needs: "Hopes and promises are only what [New Mexico] has received . . . from its mother country," Mariano Chávez wrote in 1844. Another New Mexican bitterly complained: "Mexico has never been able to protect us because, unfortunately, of continuous revolts . . . opportunism has smashed the union to pieces."

The forces that fed frontier disaffection and separatism were not just political. Thoughtful frontiersmen also witnessed a weakening of economic, military, cultural, and religious ties to Mexico in the years following Mexican independence from Spain.

The Catholic Church, represented on the frontier largely by the activities of Jesuits and Franciscans, had been a bastion of strength and a key institution for frontier expansion during most of the Spanish period. The missions, which had begun to decline in the late eighteenth century, collapsed completely under independent Mexico. In the view of some Mexican liberals, missions represented antiquated institutions that oppressed Indians by holding them forcibly and denying them the full equality accorded to other Mexican citizens. Missions also aided the Church in amassing wealth and property, some liberals reasoned, and abolishing missions would indirectly weaken Church influence in secular affairs. Although they had fallen from official favor, the missions might have held on had there been enough missionaries to staff them, but most of the missionaries were Spanish-born. In 1827 and 1829, during the xenophobic aftermath of the wars of independence against Spain, Mexico ordered Spanish residents to leave the Republic, with but few exceptions. Many of those who departed were priests. Thus, the Franciscan colleges that had staffed the frontier missions faced acute shortages of manpower. By the eve of the Mexican-American War, only ten Franciscans remained on the northern frontier, nine of them in California.

The dismantling of the missions and the rapid decrease of Franciscans on the frontier in the 1820s and 1830s left the way open for secular priests to replace the *friars*, but the opportunity was lost. Weakened by a shortage of funds and of clergy, the bishops of the secular Church found themselves unable to fill the void left by the departing Franciscans. By 1828, half the parishes in Mexico lacked priests and a disproportionate share of those empty parishes existed in rural and remote areas such as the frontier. Priests tended to avoid isolation, hardship, danger, and low salaries of the frontier and to gravitate toward more comfortable urban parishes. Perhaps with tongue in cheek, Antonio Barreiro of New Mexico proposed that priests ought to receive a reward for serving at a frontier hardship post. Those who ministered for ten years on the frontier, he suggested, should receive preference for a comfortable cathedral appointment in one of the nation's "civilized communities." But the problem seemed beyond simple remedy. As early as 1831, Antonio Barreiro reported that abandoned churches were falling into ruins in New Mexico and that many parishes received visits from priests only a few times a year. People could not attend Mass or receive the sacraments, he said, and "corpses remain unburied for many days. . . . How resentful must be the poor people who suffer such neglect!"

Curiously, many Anglo-American visitors to northern Mexico seemed blind to the declining influence of the Church and pronounced the frontiersmen a "priest-ridden" people, who behaved obsequiously toward their priests. In fact, however, the once-powerful Church on the Mexican frontier had become a paper tiger, its temporal and ecclesiastical power greatly diminished by the time of the United States invasion.

At the same time that Mexico's political and ecclesiastical authority over her frontier subjects eroded, her military supremacy over the frontier also slipped away. In many areas of the frontier, the decades following independence saw relations worsen with those autonomous tribes of seminomadic Indians who rejected Christianity and much of Hispanic culture—Indians the frontiersmen often termed *indios bárbaros* or *salvajes*. By 1846 the situation had deteriorated to the point that some areas of the frontier had less to fear from imminent war with the United States than they had from Indians who were better armed, better mounted, and more successful than ever at defending their lands and striking offensive blows deep into Mexico and stealing Mexican livestock. The sources of Indian firearms, and the markets for stolen Mexican livestock, were often unscrupulous AngloAmerican traders who had penetrated the High Plains and the Rockies of northern Mexico in the decades before the war. As one Mexican historian, Carlos J. Sierra, has reminded us, "the guides or pioneers of the so-called American West were spies in our territory and dealers in furs and arms—many of them were constant instigators of attacks on Mexican towns and villages."

Before the arrival of Anglo-American traders in the region, Mexican frontiersmen had a near monopoly over the Indian trade and used the Indians' commercial dependency to help maintain the peace. As control over trade shifted increasingly to the westward-moving Anglo Americans, however, its importance as a diplomatic tool for Mexican frontiersmen lessened, forcing them to rely more than ever on force of arms. Here, the timing was especially unfortunate for it seemed to frontiersmen that the Mexican military was weaker than it had been under Spain.

With a demoralized soldiery and a highly politicized officer corps, the Mexican army seemed unable and unwilling to engage hostile Indians on the frontier. Instead, like those clergy who preferred plush cathedrals to primitive frontier chapels, politically motivated officers kept their units concentrated near the centers of power—Mexico City or Veracruz—so they could be on the scene when a government tottered and opportunity beckoned. From the vantage point of the nation's capital, the defensive needs of the frontier were generally out of sight and out of mind. Seldom did newspapers note, as one did in 1827, the peculiarity of having well-equipped and well-dressed troops in Mexico City while Indian raids went unchecked in the north. Under these circumstances the frontier presidios, bastions of defense under Spain, declined under independent Mexico, and the burden of defense fell on the frontiersmen themselves, who organized ill-equipped militia to make forays against Indians.

Mexico's failure to provide resources or direction to carry out an effective Indian policy in the north added to the discontent of the frontiersmen. As Mariano Chávez of New Mexico bitterly complained in 1844: "We are surrounded on all sides . . . by many tribes of heartless barbarians, almost perishing; and our brothers, instead of helping us, are at each other's throats in their festering civil wars."

To these failures to shore up frontier defense, maintain a vibrant Church, and meet the political aspirations of frontiersmen, must be added Mexico's failure to integrate the frontier into the nation's economic system. Following Mexican independence, the rapid influx of foreigners, foreign merchandise, and foreign capital, together with access to new foreign markets, increased the tempo of activity in many areas of the once isolated and nearly moribund frontier economy. But the new pace of economic life did not always produce harmonious results. The frontier remained dependent upon outsiders, especially Americans, for manufactured goods, and foreigners came to dominate local commerce and industry. Trade deficits characterized the new arrangements; specie and investment capital remained in short supply; and some natural resources, especially beaver and sea otter, seemed threatened to the point of extinction.

Put simply, the pull of the vigorous American economy reached beyond the United States borders onto the neighboring Mexican frontier, as American economic colonialism quickly supplanted the old Spanish colonial structure after 1821. The American economy gave impetus to the economic growth of northernmost Mexico, but at the same time it pulled that region into the American commercial orbit and away from its own economically weak metropolis. Mexico's failure to exert a strong economic counterforce contributed to the growing sense of alienation of some of her frontiersmen. They could not mistake the new reality that the lines of commerce no longer ran just north and south as they had prior to Mexican independence.

The westward thrust of economic activity and population from the United States began to Americanize Mexican frontier society and culture well before the American military conquest of the region. American influence was strongest in East Texas, close to the American border. Speaking of the *tejanos* at Nacogdoches, one Mexican officer noted in 1828:

Accustomed to the continued trade with the North Americans, they have adopted their customs and habits, and one may say that truly they are not Mexicans except by birth, for they even speak Spanish with marked incorrectness.

American influence extended to San Antonio, too, where a Swiss scientist noted in 1828 that "trade with the Anglo-Americas, and the blending in to some degree of their customs, make the inhabitants of Texas a little different from the Mexicans of the interior." Indeed, as American influence spread throughout Texas, it seemed to one official, Juan Almonte, that it would be wise to make the whole state of Coahuila y Texas officially bilingual and to translate all laws and government acts into English.

Not just in Texas, but wherever Americans gathered in significant numbers—in Santa Fe, Taos, and in California's coastal communities—American influence was apparent to contemporaries. "These foreigners gradually modified our customs," California Governor Juan Bautista Alvarado would later recall.

As early as 1825, the governor of Chihuahua expressed the hope that contact with Americans "would produce the advantages of restraining and civilizing the New Mexicans, giving them the ideas of culture which they need to improve the disgraceful condition that characterizes the remote country where they live, detached from other peoples of the Republic." Whatever its benefits, however, American cultural influences also had seductive qualities that could further weaken the frontiersmen's ties to central Mexico, as one Mexico City newspaper warned in 1825:

Territorial limits are barriers too weak to stop the progress of the Enlightenment. Mexicans who live under poverty and ignorance on one side of the river cannot remain unaware of the fortune enjoyed by citizens of the United States who live on the opposite bank.

Nearly a decade later the struggling young Santa Fe newspaper, *El Crepúsculo de la Libertad*, took up the same theme of the danger inherent in America's cultural penetration of the region:

The reign of brute force has been replaced by that of reason. . . . We can be sure that the Americans will not take our land with bullets . . . their weapons are others. They are their industry, their ideas of liberty and independence. The stars of the Capitol of the North will shine without a doubt even more brightly in New Mexico where the darkness is most dense due to the deplorable state in which the Mexican government has left it.

Mexican officials also recognized the danger and expressed fear that the *californios* and *nuevomexicanos* would not resist if Americans tried to take over their respective provinces. Ties between Americans and Mexican frontiersmen may have begun with commercial alliances, but as Manuel Castañares, who knew California well, warned the central government in 1844, the sympathy that the frontiersmen had toward *norteamericanos* was based not only on their economic interests but also on "the much stronger ties of marriage and property. . . ." The californios, Castañares warned, regard the Americans "as brothers."

Some of the Mexican frontiersmen, then, seemed to have undergone a pattern of change similar to that of other frontier peoples— one which fits anthropologist Owen Lattimore's classic description of a "marginal" border population whose "political loyalty may be emphatically modified by economic self-interest in dealings with foreigners across the border." Although trade often brings frontier peoples into contact, their activities are not "limited to the economic," Lattimore argued. Frontier residents "inevitably set up their own nexus of social contact and joint interest."

Settlers on the Mexican frontier were no exception. The "ambivalent loyalties" that Lattimore found characteristic of border peoples were probably intensified in the Mexican Far North by the neglect of the central government, extreme distance from the nation's core, and by virulent regionalism—a key feature of Mexican life in the early part of the nineteenth century. Indeed, some contemporaries questioned whether Mexico existed as a nation or whether it was simply a collection of semiautonomous provinces. Loyalty to one's locality, one's *patria chica,* frequently took precedence over loyalty to the *patria,* or nation as a whole.

Ambivalent loyalties, exacerbated by the frontiersmen's growing contact with Europeans and Americans in the Mexican era, took its most extreme form in Alta California, the most isolated of the northern provinces. Even casual visitors to California noted the hostility and deep hatred that the californios held toward Mexicans from *"la otra banda,"* or "other shore," as californios termed central Mexico.

Mexican-born Governor José Figueroa noted in 1833 that the *califor-nios* looked upon Mexicans with the same animosity that Mexicans viewed Spaniards. Intensifying the hostility that many frontiersmen held toward residents of central Mexico was a knowledge that Mexican officials viewed frontier peoples with contempt and described them as uneducated rustics who lacked the training and competence to manage their own affairs. "The best of the Mexicans among us," one *californio* later recalled, "were far more insulting and offensive than any foreigner."

Thus, as the military forces of the expansionist United States moved into the Mexican North, they found a people who had already begun to be Americanized, and whose loyalties toward Mexico had become ambivalent. Mexico had tried to pull the Far North tightly to the center of the nation by building strong political, ecclesiastical, military, economic, and demographic links, but the center did not hold. The disaffected periphery had begun to drift away. America's political incorporation of the Mexican frontier in the mid-nineteenth century represented the culmination of a process as much as it did the inauguration of a new era.

7

American Westward Expansion and the Breakdown of Relations Between *Pobladores* and *"Indios Bárbaros"* on Mexico's Far Northern Frontier, 1821–1846 *

In the late eighteenth century, innovative policies and mutual interest had spun a delicate web of peace between Hispanic and Indian peoples in the "land of war," as far northern New Spain was sometimes called. By the time Mexico won independence in 1821, the strains of a decade of revolution had begun to tear apart that fragile fabric, and the new nation could not mend it.[1] In many areas of Mexico's Far North, from Texas to Alta California, the decades following independence saw relations worsen with those autonomous tribes of seminomadic Indians who rejected much of Hispanic culture—Indians whom the *pobladores*, or frontiersmen, variously termed *"indios bárbaros," "salvajes," "gentiles,"* or *"naciones errantes."* By 1846, the situation had deterio-

*This essay first appeared in the *New Mexico Historical Review* 56 (July 1981): 221–38, and is reprinted here with permission. One of the themes in the article is expanded upon in the same journal, in Donald W. Matson's letter to the editor and in my reply to him (57 [April 1982]: 203–8). This study would not have been possible without fellowship assistance from the National Endowment for the Humanities and the American Council of Learned Societies. Their help is gratefully acknowledged.
   1. A number of specialists have described the relative success of Spanish policies in bringing about detente in the late colonial period: Joseph F. Park, "Spanish Indian Policy in Northern Mexico, 1765–1810," *Arizona and the West* 4 (Winter 1962): 325–44; Odie B. Faulk, *The Last Years of Spanish Texas, 1778–1821* (The Hague: Mouton and Co., 1964), pp. 65–71; Sidney B. Brinckerhoff, "The Last Years of Spanish Arizona, 1786–1821," *Arizona and the West* 9 (Spring 1967): 5–20; Max L. Moorhead, *The Presidio: Bastion of the Spanish Borderlands* (Norman: University of Oklahoma, 1975), pp. 95–161.

rated to the point that some areas of the Mexican frontier had less to fear from an imminent war with the United States than they had from "savage" Indians who were better armed, better mounted, and more successful than ever at defending their lands and striking offensive blows deep into Mexico.

In Mexican Texas, many observers took the view that raids by Comanches and their occasional Wichita allies, such as Tawakonis and Wacos, had hindered expansion of the tejano settlements and left people living in fear of "total extermination," notwithstanding interludes of relative peace. By the mid-1830s, as Texas stood on the brink of separation from Mexico, bands of Comanches and smaller tribes kept the province in a state of constant agitation. In what is today Arizona, then the northern edge of Sonora, the Mexican frontier receded in the face of an Apache onslaught, with farms and ranches reduced to ashes and considerable loss of life. New Mexicans saw themselves threatened with ruin at the hands of "thirty or more tribes of wild Indians"—allowing for hyperbole and depending on how one counted. At the outbreak of war with the United States, New Mexicans were still trying to neutralize Navajos who had raided the Rio Grande settlements for decades. "The war with the Navajos," Governor Manuel Armijo wrote in 1845, "is slowly consuming us." In addition, an ugly incident in 1844 had infuriated the traditionally friendly Utes against the nuevomexicanos. In the years just prior to the American invasion, Ute attacks forced pobladores from small communities such as El Rito and Ojo Caliente to flee their homes.[2]

2. Andrew Anthony Tijerina, "Tejanos and Texas" (Ph.D. dissertation, University of Texas, Austin, 1977), p. 117; Report of Ramón Músquiz, Béxar, 1 October 1831, in Ildefonso Villarello, "El Departamento de Béjar del Estado de Coahuila y Texas," *Boletín del Seminario de Cultura Mexicana* 2 (September 1945): 81; *Representación dirijida por el ilustre ayuntamiento de la ciudad de Béxar al . . . Congreso del Estado* (Brazoria, Tex.: D. W. Anthony, 1833), p. 4. Gilberto Miguel Hinojosa, "Settlers and Sojourners in the 'Chaparral': A Demographic Study of a Borderlands Town in Transition, Laredo, 1775–1870" (Ph.D. dissertation, University of Texas, Austin, 1979), pp. 37, 59–62. Official correspondence of the mid-1830s in Texas abounds in statements of concern about Indian depredations and incidents of robberies and occasional murders. See, for example, Martín Perfecto de Cos to the Minister of War, Saltillo, 29 December 1834, in Guerra y Marina, Archivo General de la Nación, Mexico City (AGN), transcript, University of Texas, folder 331; John H. Jenkins, ed., *Papers of the Texas Revolution*, 10 vols. (Austin: Presidial Press, 1973), 1: 22, 36, 44, 49, 75, 78, 80, 115, 134, 152, 175–77, 264–65, 273, 311, 367; Robert C. Stevens, "The Apache Menace in Sonora, 1831–1848," *Arizona and the West* 6 (Autumn 1964): 220–22;

Of course, not all Utes, Navajos, Apaches, or Comanches raided Mexican settlements all of the time. None of these groups possessed a central political structure or functioned as a unit or as a "nation," notwithstanding Spanish and Mexican use of the term "nación" to describe them. As one military veteran characterized Apaches:

Each family forms a ranchería [a community] and all live independently of one another without recognizing a government. Hence, war with this horde of savages never has ceased for one day, because even when thirty rancherías are at peace, the rest are not.[3]

Thus, pobladores who enjoyed harmonious relations with one group of Apaches might have their livestock stolen by members of another band, or even by individuals from a friendly ranchería. Mexican officials struggled to sort out differences between "barbarians" and distinguish friend from foe, but usually without long-lasting results. Garbled reports, rumors, conflicting evidence, and rapidly shifting alliances in this turbulent era made the task nearly impossible.

No single Indian group in Alta California achieved the fearsome reputations of Apaches, Comanches, Navajos, or Utes, but members of smaller tribes raided California settlements with increasing intensity in the years before the war with the United States. Non-mission Indians from the interior, who enjoyed the relative security of the Sierras, the Tulare country, and the Central Valley, together with Indians who had abandoned the newly secularized missions, took the

Juan Estevan Pino, "Manifiesto," to the Congreso General, Santa Fe, 24 November 1829, Mexican Archives of New Mexico (MANM), State Records Center and Archives, Santa Fe (SRCA), reel 9, frame 1120; Report of the committee to investigate New Mexico's military situation, 30 January 1829, MANM, roll 9, frames 1082–86; Proclamation of Comandante José Caballero, Santa Fe, 9 September 1837, in Benjamin M. Read, Illustrated History of New Mexico (Santa Fe: New Mexican Printing Company, 1912), p. 381; Antonio Barreiro, Ojeada sobre Nuevo-México . . . (Puebla: Imprenta del José María Campos, 1832), in Three New Mexico Chronicles, ed. and trans. H. Bailey Carroll and J. Villasana Haggard (Albuquerque: Quivira Society, 1942), p. 74; Armijo quoted in Frank McNitt, Navajo Wars: Military Campaigns, Slave Raids, and Reprisals (Albuquerque: University of New Mexico [UNM] Press, 1972), p. 90; Ward Alan Minge, "Mexican Independence Day and a Ute Tragedy in Santa Fe, 1844," in The Changing Ways of Southwestern Indians: A Historic Perspective, ed. Albert Schroeder (Glorieta, N.M.: Rio Grande Press, 1973), pp. 107–22.

3. Ignacio Zúñiga, Rápida ojeada al estado de Sonora (Mexico: Juan Ojeda, 1835), p. 7, facsimile in Northern Mexico on the Eve of the United States Invasion: Rare Imprints . . . , ed. David J. Weber (New York: Arno Press, 1976).

offensive in the 1830s and raided coastal settlements regularly. Indians made life on the ranches insecure and put californios on the defensive by the 1840s. Few californios died at the hands of Indians in these years, but destruction was such that historian Hubert Howe Bancroft judged Indian raids as California's "most serious obstacle to progress and prosperity." The San Diego area was hit hardest. In the late 1830s and early 1840s, outlying ranches came under attack and had to be abandoned. The population of the town dropped from 520 in 1830 to about 150 in 1840, when one visitor described it as "almost deserted." By the time of the Mexican-American War, according to Thomas Larkin, an experienced observer, Indian attacks had become commonplace throughout California, causing some californios to desert their ranchos: "the Indians are losing all fear of the inhabitants and with their arrows have shot several of them during the years 1845 and 1846."[4]

Indian raids on more prosperous Mexican states below the present border also accelerated in the years prior to the Mexican War. In the 1840s some Comanches reportedly reached Zacatecas, nearly 500 miles south of the Rio Grande, and on one occasion a group was reported at Querétaro, some 135 miles north of Mexico's capital. The extent of Indian control over northern Mexico was described by the despairing Chihuahua legislature in 1846:

we travel the roads . . . at their whim; we cultivate the land where they wish and in the amount that they wish; we use sparingly things they have left to us until the moment that it strikes their appetite to take them for themselves.[5]

4. Hubert Howe Bancroft, History of California, 7 vols. (San Francisco: The History Company, 1884–90), 3: 361; Jessie Davies Francis, "An Economic and Social History of Mexican California, 1821–1846" (Ph.D. dissertation, University of California, Berkeley, 1935), concluded that "never a year went by without its raids and depredations" (p. 420); Alfred Robinson, Life in California (1846; reprint ed., Santa Barbara, Calif.: Peregrine Publishers, 1970), p. 12; Lucy Lytle Killea, "The Political History of a Mexican Pueblo: San Diego from 1825 to 1845," Journal of San Diego History 12 (July 1966): 24–32; Bancroft, History of California, 3: 611. Bancroft suggested that San Diego "more than any other part of California resembled . . . the Apache frontier, though the loss of life was much less" (4: 70); Thomas O. Larkin's Description of California, Monterey, 20 April 1846, in The Larkin Papers: Personal, Business, and Official Correspondence . . . , ed. George P. Hammond, 10 vols. (Berkeley: University of California Press, 1953), 4: 306.
5. Quoted in Ralph A. Smith, "Indians in Mexican-American Relations Before

Although the picture is far from complete, historians and contemporaries have provided vivid images of the devastating effects of Indian raids on areas of northern Mexico prior to the Mexican-American War. Explanations for the intensity and scope of those raids, however, remain murky. Part of the explanation, of course, lies within Indian communities themselves and may never be fully understood. Some historians have pointed correctly to Mexico's waning military strength as a reason for Indian military successes. Few historians, however, have understood the extent to which American expansion upset the delicate balance between independent Indian peoples and pobladores in Mexico's Far North, from Texas to California.

The breakdown of relations between Mexican frontiersmen and "indios bárbaros" owed much to the activities of unscrupulous traders from the United States. Writing in 1830, the liberal savant from Coahuila, Miguel Ramos Arizpe, explained why. Prior to the coming of the Americans, he said, Indians "did not have firearms except a small number of old muskets which they received as gifts from the Spaniards, with a very small supply of powder that hardly served them because of its bad quality." Indians thus remained "rather weak" and dependent upon Spaniards alone for trade. Americans, Ramos Arizpe said, broke that dependency by furnishing Indians good guns and "very exquisite powder." Thus fortified by their new trading partners, Indians raided Mexican settlements, taking livestock and even human captives who could be traded to the Americans for more arms and munitions as well as whiskey and other goods. Some contemporaries considered it a mistake to assume that Indians did more damage with guns than with bows and arrows, but most apparently believed firearms to be more effective, including Indians themselves. Perhaps more important than the weapons Americans furnished, however, was the market they provided for stolen property, thereby encouraging Indian

the War of 1846," *Hispanic American Historical Review* 43 (February 1963): 35–36, 62. Smith has described Indian raids on northern Mexico in a number of articles: see especially "Apache 'Ranching' Below the Gila, 1841–1845," *Arizoniana* 3 (Winter 1962): 1–17, and "Apache Plunder Trails Southward, 1831–1840," *New Mexico Historical Review* (NMHR) 37 (January 1962): 20–42. Other sources include David M. Vigness, "Indian Raids on the Lower Rio Grande, 1836–1837," *Southwestern Historical Quarterly* 59 (July 1955): 14–23; the excellent collection of documents and commentary by Isidro Vizcaya Canales, ed., *La invasión de los indios bárbaros al noreste de Mexico en los años de 1840 y 1841* (Monterrey: Instituto Tecnológico de Estudios Superiores, 1968); and Zúñiga, *Rápida ojeada al estado de Sonora.*

raids on northern Mexico. Little wonder that some of these American traders came to be charged with "land piracy," even by their countrymen.[6]

The pernicious impact of American traders on relations with neighboring Indian tribes had first troubled Spanish officials in the eighteenth century, and their concern increased after the United States acquired Louisiana in 1803. By the time of Mexican independence it was widely recognized that some Apaches and Comanches, and probably Wichita bands such as the Taovayas, stole horses and mules from tejanos and exchanged them for guns and ammunition with traders in Louisiana. Acting as middlemen, Comanches were also believed to be trading guns and ammunition with more westerly tribes. The problem became so alarming that in 1826 Mexico's secretary of state asked the United States minister in Mexico City to stop the "traders of blood who put instruments of death in the hands of those barbarians." Years later, when the United States had still not stopped the traffic in armaments, one high-ranking Mexican official wondered if it was United States policy "to use savage Indians to menace defenseless Mexicans in order to force them to abandon their lands or . . . request the protection of the United States government."[7]

As Americans moved farther west into Texas in the 1820s, some

6. Ramos Arizpe to Lucas Alamán, Puebla; 1 August 1830, Archivo de la Secretaría de Fomento y Colonización (ASFC), AGN, legajo 6, pt. 2 (1828–1831), expediente 43, West transcripts, University of Texas; Joseph Carl McElhannon, "Imperial Mexico and Texas, 1821–1823," *Southwestern Historical Quarterly* 53 (October 1949): 126. For the merits of bows and arrows over firearms, see José Agustín Escudero, *Noticias estadísticas del Estado de Chihuahua* (México: Juan Ojeda, 1834), p. 247.

7. For the late colonial period see Rupert N. Richardson, *The Comanche Barrier to South Plains Settlement* (Glendale, Calif.: Arthur H. Clark, 1933), pp. 58–59, 67–73, and Abraham P. Nasatir, *Borderland in Retreat: From Spanish Louisiana to the Far Southwest* (Albuquerque: UNM Press, 1976), pp. 57, 98; Sebastián Camacho, Secretary of State, to Joel R. Poinsett, 15 June 1826, Relaciones Exteriores, AGN, Mexico, transcript, Texas State Archives, Austin (TSA) (2-22/618); Lester G. Bugbee, "The Texas Frontier, 1820–1825," *Publications of the Southern History Association* 4 (March 1900): 109; Eugene C. Barker, *The Life of Stephen F. Austin: Founder of Texas, 1793–1836* (1926; reprint ed., Austin: University of Texas, 1969), pp. 48–49; Jean Louis Berlandier, *The Indians of Texas in 1830*, ed. John C. Ewers (Washington: Smithsonian Institution Press, 1969), p. 48; José Francisco Ruiz, *Report on the Indian Tribes of Texas in 1828*, ed. John C. Ewers, trans. Georgette Dorn (New Haven, Conn.: Yale University Library, 1972), pp. 14, 16; Elizabeth Ann Harper [John], "The Taovayas Indians in Frontier Trade and Diplomacy, 1779–1835," *Panhandle-Plains Historical Review* 26 (1953): 58–69, and correspondence with the author; Juan N. Almonte to the Secretary of State, 10 December 1830, ASFC, legajo 8, expediente 65, transcript, TSA (2-22/640).

of their more unscrupulous countrymen spared Comanches and other Indians the inconvenience of hauling furs and stolen Mexican property all the way to Louisiana. Texas officials, for example, had reason to believe that some residents of Stephen Austin's colony carried on a "clandestine trade" in arms and ammunition with Indians. Mexican officials could also read in the American press about itinerant peddlers from the United States, such as a group from Kaskaskia, Illinois, who entered Texas in 1826 "on a trading adventure to the Cumancha Indians." Reports that Texas officials offered a $1,000 reward for every American trading illegally with Indians apparently did not deter these merchants, and the harmful effects of their activities in Texas were no secret. One Louisiana newspaper reported in 1826 that Americans carried on "an extensive and often very lucrative trade" with the Comanches,

one of the most hostile nations in America, who are continually at war with the Mexicans, and who will remain so long as they are supplied with goods, in return for the horses and mules, of which they rob the inhabitants of the Province [of Texas].[8]

Dealing with Indians was sufficiently lucrative in Texas that some Americans set up trading posts along the Red River where it formed the boundary with the United States. Texas officials believed that these traders not only furnished arms and ammunition to Indians, but also incited them to attack Mexican settlements. One trader, Holland Coffee, who had established a post on the upper Red River in 1833, met with some Comanches, Wacos, and Tawakonis in 1835 and "advised them to go to the interior and kill Mexicans and bring their horses and mules to him and he would give them a fair price," according to James Bowie. By 1838, one Texas newspaper reported, American traders in Texas faced stiff competition for the "immense booty" that "the

8. Francisco Ruiz to Antonio Elosúa, 1 August 1830, translated in *Papers Concerning Robertson's Colony in Texas*, ed. Malcolm D. McLean, 7 vols. to date (Fort Worth and Arlington: Texas Christian University Press and the University of Texas at Arlington, 1974–), 4: 335; Stephen Austin to Ramón Músquiz, Austin, 24 August 1829, in *The Austin Papers*, ed. Eugene C. Barker, 3 vols. (Washington, D.C. and Austin: U.S. Government Printing Office and University of Texas Press, 1924–28), 2: 250; *Little Rock Arkansas Gazette*, 21 November 1826, reporting on a party apparently led by Pierre Menard; see, too, *Little Rock Arkansas Gazette*, 16 January 1827 and 27 January 1829; *Natchitoches Courier*, 15 May 1826, quoted in the *Little Rock Arkansas Gazette*, 25 July 1826.

most powerful of the most savage nations of North America" brought
back from Mexico. Much of the lucrative Indian trade, the paper said,
was being siphoned off by merchants from Arkansas and Missouri,
some of whom traded as far west as Santa Fe.[9]

The report was correct. The opening of the trail between Missouri
and Santa Fe to legal trade in 1821 facilitated the importation of
American guns and munitions to Taos, Santa Fe, El Paso, and more
remote locations. Far from the eyes of Mexican officials, armaments
could be traded to Apaches, Comanches, and other tribes in West
Texas, Chihuahua, and Sonora. As early as 1823 New Mexicans learned
that Americans had furnished guns and ammunition to Navajos, and
by the late 1820s New Mexicans recognized that American armaments
had shifted the balance of power to the Indians.[10]

By the early 1830s Apache attacks extended beyond New Mexico
to Chihuahua. Officials there, too, viewed Americans as a major source
of the trouble. In prohibiting all trade with Indians, Chihuahua officials specified that Anglo Americans found trading arms, powder, or
lead with Apaches would be executed. In 1835 Governor Albino Pérez
of New Mexico attempted to cooperate with Chihuahua officials and
ordered strict regulation of trade with "indios bárbaros." He, too,
singled out norteamericanos as the chief suppliers of arms, but he also
noted that some New Mexicans followed the Americans' "corrupt and
noxious example." Whether or not they had been corrupted by the
Americans, some pobladores continued a long tradition of trading

9. James Bowie to Henry Rueg, Natches, 3 August 1835, in Jenkins, *Papers of
the Texas Revolution,* 1: 301–2; similar complaints about an American trader appear
in Peter Ellis Bean to Domingo de Ugartechea, Béxar, 21 April 1835, and Rueg to
the jefe político of Béxar, 18 May 1835, in Jenkins, *Papers of the Texas Revolution,* 1:
80, 115–16; *The Telegraph and Texas Register,* quoted in the *Arkansas Gazette,* 28
February 1838, in Ralph A. Smith, "Mexican and Anglo-Saxon Traffic in Scalps,
Slaves, and Livestock, 1835–1841," *West Texas Historical Association Year Book* 36
(October 1960): 102–13. For an interesting glimpse at Torrey's Post, near present
Waco in 1838, see Howard R. Lamar, *The Trader on the American Frontier: Myth's
Victim* (College Station: Texas A&M University Press, 1977), pp. 13–16.

10. Santiago Monroy to Governor Bartolomé Baca, Xemes, 20 February 1823,
in Lourdes Lascuraín Orive, "Reflexiones sobre Nuevo México y su integración a los
Estados Unidos de Norteamérica," in *El Destino Manifesto en la historia de la nación
norteamericana, 6 ensayos* (México: Editorial Jus, 1977), p. 49. Pino, "Manifiesto,"
24 November 1829; Manuel de Jesús Rada, *Proposición hecha al Soberano Congreso
General de la Nación por el diputado del territorio de Nuevo México* (México: Imprenta
de C. Alejandro Valdés, 1829), p. 3, facsimile in Weber, *Northern Mexico.*

stolen goods with the very Indians who raided their settlements. Chihuahua officials even suspected one New Mexico governor, Manuel
Armijo, of furnishing guns to Apaches. New Mexicans known as
comancheros, who traveled out to the Plains to trade with Comanches
and other tribes, acquired an especially unsavory reputation following
the Mexican-American War, but little is known of their activities
during the Mexican era. Americans, then, had no monopoly on illicit
trade, but they did possess the most desirable arms and ammunition.[11]
    Repeated orders by Pérez and other officials did little to check
gunrunners or curb illicit trade in New Mexico. Governor Armijo
openly expressed skepticism about the effectiveness of trade embargoes
without adequate troops, but even if New Mexicans had succeeded in
patrolling their vast territory, Americans would have escaped the net.
In the mid-1830s Americans had begun to build trading posts outside
Mexican jurisdiction in present Colorado. First and foremost of these
isolated emporiums was Bent's Fort, on the United States' side of the
Arkansas, built in 1832 or 1833. After 1835, forts Vásquez, Jackson,
and Lupton opened for business on the South Platte—all in American
territory, but close enough to Mexico that the rifles and ammunition
they sold to Indians proved very troublesome.[12]
    These American trading centers earned the condemnation of the
dynamic *cura* of Taos, Antonio José Martínez. In a printed memorial
to President Antonio López de Santa Anna in 1843, Martínez accused
American traders of contributing to the moral decay of Indians and
of encouraging Indian depredations on New Mexico. Indians stole

11. Decree of 16 October 1835, Santa Fe, Ritch Papers, no. 153, Huntington
Library, San Marino, California (HEH); Circular from the Palacio del Gobierno del
Estado, Chihuahua, February 1835, cited in David J. Weber, *The Taos Trappers: The
Fur Trade in the Far Southwest, 1540–1846* (Norman: University of Oklahoma Press,
1971), p. 222; Escudero, *Noticias estadísticas del Estado de Chihuahua*, pp. 245–46;
Ward Alan Minge, "Frontier Problems in New Mexico Preceding the Mexican War,
1840–1846" (Ph.D. dissertation, UNM, 1965), p. 62; Josiah Gregg, *Commerce of the
Prairies*, ed. Max L. Moorhead (1844; reprint ed., Norman: University of Oklahoma
Press, 1954), p. 203; Charles L. Kenner, *A History of New Mexican-Plains Indian
Relations* (Norman: University of Oklahoma Press, 1969), pp. 78–97; Vizcaya Canales,
La invasión, pp 55–59.
12. Printed circular, Juan Andrés Archuleta, Santa Fe, 21 February 1843, in the
María G. Durán Collection (SRCA); Minge, "Frontier Problems," pp. 55–58, 60–
62; Weber, *The Taos Trappers*, pp. 210–11. According to tradition, the Bents furnished
weapons to their Indian customers. George Bird Grinnell, *By Cheyenne Campfires*
(Lincoln: University of Nebraska Press, 1971), pp. 34–35, reference courtesy of George
Phillips, University of Colorado.

livestock from New Mexico, Martínez charged, in order to exchange it at the American posts for liquor. Americans also led some "idle and ill-intentioned" New Mexicans astray as well as Indians, the padre asserted. Equally distressing, Indians killed buffalo in immense quantities to obtain hides that they traded with Americans. Buffalo, Martínez warned, were not only becoming scarce, but would soon become extinct as a species and the *"naciones bárbaras,"* who depended upon buffalo for their survival, would turn more and more toward New Mexico to "rob and pillage." A few years after Martínez issued this prediction, New Mexico hunters had to travel more than 250 miles to find buffalo, but obtained so little meat that they consumed it all on the journey home.[13]

One of the most dramatic examples of the impact of American traders on traditional trading patterns and alliances is the case of the Utes. Occupying lands to the northwest of the New Mexico settlements, Utes had been rather consistent allies of New Mexicans throughout the first decades of the nineteenth century. In the late 1830s, however, Antoine Robidoux, an American of French ancestry who had become a Mexican citizen, built trading posts on the Gunnison River, in present Colorado, and on the Uintah River, in today's Utah. At those posts Robidoux traded guns and ammunition for pelts, and from the late 1830s on, tensions between Utes and New Mexicans increased. In 1844, when they became alienated from New Mexicans, Utes no longer depended on the *pobladores* for trade and possessed the means to launch a devastating series of attacks. Robidoux's activities alone did not cause the Ute "war," of course, but New Mexico officials rightly suspected that Robidoux contributed substantially to their problems with Utes.[14]

By 1844 when Utes stepped up their raids on New Mexico, Robidoux was not the only American supplying them with arms and munitions. A desultory group of American traders had settled at places like Pueblo, Hardscrabble, and Greenhorn in the Upper Arkansas Valley on the eastern edge of the Front Range of the Rockies and wantonly

13. *Esposicion* [sic] *que el Presbitero Antonio José Martínez, Cura de Taos en Nuevo México, Dirije al Gobierno del Exmo. Sor. General D. Antonio López de Santa-Anna. Proponiendo la civilisación de las naciones barbaras . . .* (Taos, N.M.: J.M.B., 1843), p. 4, facsimile in Weber, *Northern Mexico.* Donaciano Vigil to the Assembly, Santa Fe, 18 June 1846, MANM, roll 41, frames 330–39.

14. Weber, *The Taos Trappers,* pp. 213–17.

exchanged firearms for stolen Mexican livestock. Utes maintained harmonious relations with these Americans while simultaneously raid-ing New Mexico. One New Mexico officer was not far off the mark in describing the American traders as "protectors" of the Utes.[15]

The Ute example is not an isolated case. Other tribes, such as the band of Apaches known today as White Mountain, also raided Mex-ican settlements and befriended American merchants. It is under-standable, then, that by 1846, just prior to the war with the United States, one New Mexican could lament that "the lot of the Indians around New Mexico has improved at the time that ours has worsened."[16]

Indian raids on New Mexico increased not only as a result of the activities of American traders, but also due to demographic pressures from westward-moving American settlers. In a report to Congress in 1826, forty-six-year-old Juan Bautista Pino, a former alcalde of Santa Fe and one of several sons of the venerable Pedro Bautista Pino, New Mexico's delegate to the 1812 Spanish Cortes, explained the situation as many New Mexicans must have understood it. The growing pop-ulation of North Americans, he said, had forced Kiowas and their allies toward the west. They in turn pushed other tribes toward New Mexico so that "in time we will probably have them on top of us." "These [Indian] Nations are like balls in a row," Pino explained. When the first receives a "strong impulse it is passed along until it reaches the last." The source of the "strong impulse" Pino identified as "the wise and practical policy adopted by the government in Washington." The "active" Americans, Pino believed, had expanded their border rapidly by purchasing land from Indians and pushing them toward northern Mexico. When he wrote in the fall of 1829, Pino had prob-ably learned from American traders of strong sentiment in the United States for the removal of Cherokees and other "civilized tribes" from the southern states to beyond the Mississippi—sentiment that helped

15. José María Chaves to Juan Andrés Archuleta, Campo de operaciones, Taos, 18 June 1845, MANM, roll 39, frames 626–27; Janet Lecompte, *Pueblo, Hardscrabble, Greenhorn: The Upper Arkansas, 1832–1856* (Norman: University of Oklahoma Press, 1978), pp. 163–65, 74–75, 146; and George P. Hammond, ed., *The Adventures of Alexander Barclay, Mountain Man* (Denver: Old West Publishing Company, 1976), p. 71.

16. Grenville Goodwin, *The Social Organization of the Western Apache* (Chicago: University of Chicago Press, 1942), p. 94. Vigil to the Assembly, Santa Fe, 8 June 1846.

put Andrew Jackson in the White House in 1829 and that resulted in passage of the Indian Removal Act early in the following year.[17]

By the 1830s the influence of westward-moving American traders was felt in California, with its abundance of mules and horses. Governor Manuel Victoria reported to Mexico City in 1831 that "the interior valleys are being overrun by foreigners, who come in great numbers to corrupt the gentiles, and to steal." Horse thieves, among whom were traders from New Mexico, Victoria reported, "have begun trading with the gentiles, the fugitive Christians and the Neophytes of the missions and it results that the Indians of the mountains and the Tulares steal horses from the missions and ranchos in order to sell them." Victoria's successor, José de Figueroa, also recognized and deplored the influence of the foreigners. He prohibited foreigners from trapping in California and put a complete embargo on trade with "heathen Indians." To enforce these restrictions he ordered presidial officers at San Diego, Santa Barbara, and Monterey to patrol the coastal ranges and interior valleys. The program met modest success. Raids quieted for a few years, but resumed again in 1837, after Figueroa's death.[18]

Californios had no prior experience with foreign interlopers from the east until the first years after Mexican independence. In 1826, trapper Jedediah Smith became the first American to find his way across the continent to California, and he and the trappers who followed him found California horses as valuable a trade item as furs. Domesticated California horses, which Smith purchased at $10 a head, brought $50 at the trapper's annual mountain rendezvous in 1827.

17. Pino, "Manifiesto," 24 November 1829; Ronald N. Satz, *American Indian Policy in the Jacksonian Era* (Lincoln: University of Nebraska Press, 1975), pp. 11–31.

18. Manuel Victoria, quoted in Sardis W. Templeton, *The Lame Captain: The Life and Adventures of Pegleg Smith* (Los Angeles: Westernlore Press, 1965), p. 101; see, too, Narciso Durán, 3 October 1833, quoted in Zephyrin Engelhardt, *The Missions and Missionaries of California*, 4 vols. (San Francisco: James H. Barry Co., 1908–15), 3: 494. Figueroa to the Minister of War and Navy, Monterey, 12 April 1833, and Figueroa, decree concerning robbers of horses and other livestock, 18 November 1833, quoted in Sherburne F. Cook, "Expeditions to the Interior or California's Central Valley, 1820–1840," *Anthropological Records* 20 (February 1962): 188; Bancroft, *History of California*, 3: 197, n. 25; Eleanor Lawrence, "Horse Thieves on the Spanish Trail," *Touring Topics* 23 (January 1931): 23; LeRoy R. and Ann W. Hafen, *Old Spanish Trail* (Glendale, Calif.: Arthur H. Clark Co., 1954), pp. 227–58; Mariano Guadalupe Vallejo to the governor, Sonoma, 20 July 1838, in *Comunicaciones del Gen. M. G. Vallejo* (Sonoma; n.p., 1837–39), a volume of imprints in the Bancroft Library (BL).

Not all American trappers demonstrated Smith's scruples about obtaining California horses legally. Some American trappers enlisted the aid of Indians to raid California ranches, and other trappers turned to horse thieving in the late 1830s and 1840s as the fur trade fell on hard times. Among the better known mountain men-turned-horsethieves were "Peg-leg" Smith, "Old Bill" Williams, Joseph Walker, Jim Beckwourth, and Jean Baptiste Chalifoux. Much of the stolen California stock was driven east to New Mexico or sold at trading posts such as Bent's Fort. From there, some animals might be driven on to Missouri. By the 1840s, however, the increased traffic of Americans bound for Oregon seemed to move the market for stolen California livestock much farther west. California officials believed that American settlers in Oregon provided Indians with guns in exchange for stolen cattle and horses.[19]

Nuevomexicanos, who first brought woven goods from Santa Fe to Los Angeles beginning in 1830, also sought California horses and traded stolen stock with Indians in exchange for liquor. Merchants from New Mexico won such a bad reputation that Governor Figueroa felt obliged to ask the governor of New Mexico for help: "Every man coming from that territory is believed to be an adventurer and a thief," he wrote. California officials took stern measures to regulate the New Mexico traders, treating them as if they were foreigners.[20]

19. Hafen and Hafen, *Old Spanish Trail*, pp. 228, 236; John C. Ewers, ed., *Adventures of Zenas Leonard, Fur Trader* (Norman: University of Oklahoma Press, 1959), p. 113; Francisco Catillo Negrete, *Informe y propuestas que hace al Supremo Gobierno para la prosperidad y seguridad de la Alta California, su Comisionado . . .* [1836] (México: Vargas Rea, 1944), p. 10; Janet Lecompte, "Jean Baptiste Chalifoux," in *The Mountain Men and the Fur Trade of the Far West*, ed. LeRoy R. Hafen, 10 vols. (Glendale, Calif.: Arthur H. Clark Co., 1965–72), 7: 65–70; Templeton, *The Lame Captain*, pp. 103–58; Alpheus H. Favour, *Old Bill Williams: Mountain Man* (1936; reprint ed., Norman: University of Oklahoma Press, 1962), pp. 100–117; Lecompte, *Pueblo, Hardscrabble, Greenhorn*, pp. 150–54; George Verne Blue, ed. and trans., "The Report of Captain La Place on His Voyage to the Northwest Coast and California in 1839," *California Historical Society Quarterly* 18 (December 1939): 320; Manuel Castañares, "Exposición," 1 September 1844, in Castañares, *Colección de documentos relativos al departamento de Californias* (México: Imprenta de la Voz del Pueblo, 1845), p. 31, facsimile in Weber, *Northern Mexico;* Juan Bautista Alvarado also recalled that Indians received weapons from Russians at Fort Ross, "Historia de California," 1876, 5 vols. (Manuscript, BL), 3: 33.

20. Quoted in Bancroft, *History of California*, 3: 396; Eleanor Lawrence, "Mexican Trade Between Santa Fe and Los Angeles, 1830–1848," *California Historical Society Quarterly* 10 (March 1931): 30, and Hafen and Hafen, *Old Spanish Trail*, pp. 155–94.

In addition to New Mexicans, Americans, and California Indians who plundered their livestock, California *rancheros* also found themselves victimized by Indians from outside the province. Navajos, for example, reportedly stole cattle near Los Angeles in 1834. Nez Perces, Yakimas, and Cayuses from the north raided the Sacramento Valley. Utes, associated with Anglo Americans, apparently learned the way to California during these years and drove stolen livestock from the West Coast to New Mexico where they traded with foreigners and Mexicans. Walkara, the most notorious of the Ute leaders, is believed to have worked with Peg-leg Smith to make off with 1,200 animals at Mission San Luis Obispo in 1840. Walkara continued to lead raids into California well after the United States conquest in 1846, selling the stolen stock to Mormons in Salt Lake City.[21]

Indians who traveled farthest to raid California settlements were Delawares and Shawnees. Driven from their ancestral homes in the United States, bands of some of these displaced tribes took refuge in East Texas, along with displaced Creeks, Kickapoos, Cherokees, and Choctaws (groups that originally lived in such states as Wisconsin, Delaware, Pennsylvania, Georgia, Tennessee, Alabama, and Mississippi). Mexican officials generally welcomed these refugees from America, hoping they would form a buffer against both Anglo-Americans and the "indios bárbaros." Some of these Indians did become allies of Mexicans. Some English-speaking Shawnees and Delawares, on the other hand, teamed up with American trappers and adventurers, stealing horses in northern Mexico and as far west as California where officials corrupted the name *Shawnees* to *Chaguanosos*.[22]

Thus, from Texas to California, those unscrupulous Anglo Americans, who armed and displaced Indians, contributed enormously to Mexico's difficulties in controlling autonomous northern tribes. The difficulty was compounded because independent Mexico tried to continue the pragmatic Spanish policy of "purchasing" a peace through the use of trade and distribution of presents and did not attempt to control Indians with military force alone. Mexican officers continued

21. Bancroft, *History of California*, 3: 359, n. 22; Favour, *Old Bill Williams*, p. 104; Minge, "Frontier Problems," p. 65; Hafen and Hafen, *Old Spanish Trail*, pp. 237, 248, 251–57.

22. Ernest W. Winkler, "The Cherokee Indians in Texas," *Southwestern Historical Quarterly* 7 (October 1903): 95–165, treats one of the groups in depth; Weber, *The Taos Trappers*, p. 224; Bancroft, *History of California*, 4: 76–77.

the Spanish tradition of distributing gifts, such as tobacco, sugar, knives, cloth, mirrors, buttons, spoons, shirts, medals, and other manufactured items, purchased from a special "allies fund." The same fund was used to feed and entertain visiting delegations of Indians.[23]

Purchasing a peace brought some positive results. In New Mexico and Texas some Apaches and Comanches apparently spared those provinces from more serious raids because they served as convenient entrepôts for goods taken from wealthier provinces to the south. On the local level, individual pobladores put self-interest first and traded with those Indians with whom the larger nation was at war. As one anthropologist has written: "Trade has facility to survive when all other means of communication cease."[24]

As trade shifted increasingly to the westward-moving Anglo Americans, however, it became less effective as a diplomatic tool for Mexicans. Donaciano Vigil, an officer of unusual education who would become governor of New Mexico following the American conquest, summed up the situation clearly in the spring of 1846. During the Spanish period, he said, the application of the velvet glove—trade, gifts, and alliances—had made the iron fist less necessary. The coming of Anglo-Americans, however, had lessened Indian dependency on Mexicans and made it more necessary than ever to rely on the iron fist.[25]

Historians have often noted that defensive alliances, military strategies, and distribution of presents that worked for Spain in the late eighteenth century lost their effectiveness under independent Mexico. Few historians, however, have understood the extent to which American westward expansion made Mexico's task more difficult. Indeed, the Mexican government viewed American traders as so pernicious

23. Many sources refer to the continued use of this fund. See, for example, Minge, "Frontier Problems," pp. 51, 199; Tijerina, "Tejanos and Texas," p. 78. Continuity from the Spanish period is a theme in Daniel Tyler's "Mexican Indian Policy in New Mexico," NMHR 55 (April 1980): 101–20.

24. Shirley Hill Witt, "Migration into San Juan Pueblo, 1726–1968" (Ph.D. dissertation, UNM, 1969), p. 44. For examples of informal trade, see Vizcaya Canales, *La invasión*, p. 45; Kenner, *New Mexican-Plains Indian Relations*, p. 73. Frances León Swadesh, *Los Primeros Pobladores: Hispanic Americans of the Ute Frontier* (Notre Dame, Ind.: University of Notre Dame Press, 1974), pp. 20, 24–25; Berlandier, *Indians of Texas*, p. 31, n. 3, pp. 47–48; Benjamin Lundy, *The Life, Travels and Opinions . . .* (Philadelphia: William D. Parrish, 1847), p. 53; Papers relating to illegal trade with Apaches, 1846, MANM, roll 41, frames 548–60.

25. Vigil to the Assembly, 18 June 1846.

by the time of the Mexican-American War that it pressed the United States for protection from them in the Treaty of Guadalupe Hidalgo. But American traders continued to provide means and incentives for Indians, especially Apaches, to attack northern Mexico well into the 1850s.[26]

26. See, for example, Stevens, "The Apache Menace in Sonora," pp. 211–22; Edward H. Spicer, *Cycles of Conquest: The Impact of Spain, Mexico, and the United States on the Indians of the Southwest, 1533–1960* (Tucson: University of Arizona Press, 1962), p. 240; Walter Prescott Webb, *The Great Plains* (Boston: Ginn, 1931), p. 137; J. Fred Rippy, "The Indians of the Southwest in the Diplomacy of the United States and Mexico, 1848–1853," *Hispanic American Historical Review* 2 (August 1919): 364; Joseph F. Park, "The Apaches in Mexican-American Relations, 1848–1861, A Footnote to the Gadsden Treaty," *Arizona and the West* 3 (Summer 1961): 129. A study by a Mexican historian, which appeared while this article was in press, contains conclusions similar to mine; "the guides or pioneers of the so-called American West were spies in our territory and dealers in furs and arms—many were constant instigators of attacks on Mexican towns and villages. . . ." (Carlos J. Sierra, *Los indios de la frontera* [México: Ediciones de la Muralla, 1980], p. 40).

8

Refighting the Alamo
Mythmaking and
the Texas Revolution *

If we had some way to measure it, I think that it might be proved
that more ink than blood has been spilled over the Texas Revolution
in general, and the Alamo in particular. And with much less effect,
for although the war has ended, the ink continues to flow. Over three
decades ago William C. Binkley ended his short book of essays on *The
Texas Revolution* with the cautionary note that "the last word concerning the meaning or significance of the Texas Revolution has not
yet been said."[1] He was, of course, correct. Just as he did not say the
last word, neither did those of us who wrote or spoke about the
rebellion on its 150th anniversary, in 1986.

Perhaps this is as it should be. Not only does each generation have
a need to rewrite history, but major events in particular invite frequent
reinterpretation to make them meaningful to the sensibilities and
concerns of new generations. And the Texas rebellion *was* a major
event, representing a turning point for Mexico and the United States,
as well as for Texas. For Mexico it seems to mark the beginning of a
series of dismal setbacks that culminated with the United States invasion of 1846 and that resulted in the loss of half of Mexico to the
United States. For the United States, which would annex Texas nine

*In a shorter form, this essay had its origins as a lecture that I prepared for a
symposium, "Alamo Images: Changing Perceptions of a Texas Experience," sponsored
by the DeGolyer Library at Southern Methodist University, November 16, 1985. I
subsequently expanded that lecture to present at the opening of an exhibition of
Texana at the Beinecke Rare Book and Manuscript Library, Yale University, April
25, 1986. It is published here for the first time.
  1. (Baton Rouge: LSU Press, 1952), p. 132.

years after its successful rebellion, the Texas Revolution marked a turning point in the Americans' long and unsuccessful efforts to purchase Texas from Mexico and another large step in the fulfillment of what Americans perceived to be their manifest destiny—a continental nation with harbors on the Pacific.

The importance of the Texas struggle for independence has been widely recognized. Joe Frantz, a shrewd and much admired historian at the University of Texas, did not exaggerate when he wrote in his popular history of Texas that "to southwesterners the Alamo ranks alongside Lexington and Concord. . . ."[2] In James A. Michener's *Texas*, a novel written as a sesquicentennial event, one character does exaggerate somewhat when he notes that "the geographical shape of the *United States* today was ensured by the heroic actions of a few Texicans [*sic*] who resisted General Santa Anna's brutal oppressions. . . ."[3]

As *fact*, then, the Texas struggle for independence was, and has been regarded as, an event of sufficient importance for Texas and for two nations to merit the spilling of considerable ink. Nonetheless, much of the Texas writing about the events of 1836, and about the Alamo in particular, seems designed to magnify and romanticize this significant series of events.

Professor Frantz, for example, did exaggerate when he characterized the Texas rebellion as an event of which Texans can be proud because "a group of upstart Anglos defeated a sometimes brilliant general leading an army of a nation whose roots are a century older than those of the United States and in which in 1835–1836 was at least the equivalent of the United States in size and in strength."[4] Nearly every one of Frantz's assertions in this statement seems somewhat overblown.

First, it was not just "upstart Anglos" in Texas who defeated Mexican forces, but those Anglos had the help of Texas Mexicans, too. Second, Santa Anna may have been a "sometimes brilliant general," but most writers find him rather consistently flawed. As his most recent biographer put it: "his strategic planning . . . *always* seemed to omit something important.[5] Third, although the roots of Spanish colonialism in Mexico run a century deeper than the roots of English

---

2. *Texas: A Bicentennial History* (New York: W. W. Norton and Co.), p. 70.
3. (New York: Random House, 1985), p. 419. Emphasis added.
4. Frantz, *Texas*, p. 72.
5. Oakah L. Jones, Jr., *Santa Anna* (New York: Twayne Publishers, 1968), p. 157. Emphasis added.

colonialism in North America, we should remember that when Mexico achieved its independence in 1821, the United States had already been a nation for forty years. Two generations of political stability gave the Americans a tremendous advantage over a chaotic young Mexico, whose economy and politics were in shambles at the time of the Texas revolt. Fourth, Mexico was not the equivalent of the United States in size and in strength, as Frantz argues. A ruinous decade of warfare against Spain had brought Mexico into nationhood in 1821 with her population literally decimated (a tenth of the population, mostly young men of fighting age, had lost their lives). Mexico's population in 1821 was some 6,200,000, and remained at that level for decades. In contrast, at nearly 9,600,000, the population of the United States was half again as large as Mexico's in 1821. Moreover, the United States population grew with extraordinary speed due to immigration, reaching over 17,000,000 in 1840—three times the population of Mexico.[6] Finally, it is important to remember that much of the Mexican population consisted of Indians who did not identify themselves with the nation, or even speak the national language.

Mexico, then, did not quite have the advantages over the "upstart Anglos" in Texas that Professor Frantz suggested it did. The military achievements of Texans in 1836 were impressive enough, however, that there is no need to lose sight of the fact that Mexico in the mid-1830s was in extraordinary disarray and that some Mexicans raised doubts as to whether or not Mexico actually existed as a nation.[7]

We do not, of course, need to single out Professor Frantz for examples of exaggeration of the Texas achievements of 1836. If we move from the so-called Revolution to the Alamo itself, we have splendid essays by Walter Lord, Perry McWilliams, and, most recently, Paul Hutton and Susan Schoelwer, to remind us that a number of the cherished stories about the Alamo have no basis in historical fact, but have moved out of the earthly realm of reality into the stratosphere

6. David J. Weber, *The Mexican Frontier, 1821–1846: The American Southwest Under Mexico* (Albuquerque: University of New Mexico Press, 1982), p. 159. The 1840 United States Census listed the population of the United States at 17,069,453: *Statistical Abstract of U.S.: 1987* (Washington, D.C., 1986), p. 8.

7. See, for example, Dennis E. Berge, ed. and trans., *Considerations on the Political and Social Situation of the Mexican Republic, 1847* (El Paso: Texas Western Press, 1975), p. 45.

of myth.[8] Nonetheless, the sniping of scholars, no matter how true their aim, seems too feeble to bring these myths crashing down to reality.

On March 6, 1986, 150 years after the carnage ended, a number of Texas history buffs from across America gathered in San Antonio to remember the fall of the Alamo. In commemoration of the battle that raged in and around the walls of the former Spanish mission compound, participants reenacted the famous scene in which Colonel William Barret Travis supposedly traced a line in the dirt and said: "Those of you who are willing to stay with me and die with me, cross this line."[9]

Although reenactment of this dramatic moment brought tears to the eyes of some onlookers, there is no convincing evidence that Travis uttered his famous speech or that he drew such a line. Historians have repeatedly made this point. Nor is there convincing evidence to support the common notion that the defenders of the Alamo knew *from the first* that their situation was hopeless. To the contrary, they prepared for the battle with remarkable indecision and lassitude; only a swollen river prevented Santa Anna from launching a surprise attack while the Alamo's defenders enjoyed themselves at a fandango.[10] Although Colonial Travis's slogan was "Victory or Death," in the early stages of the siege he clearly expected victory. From his first call for help on February 24 through March 3, just three days before the Alamo fell, Travis believed that the Alamo could be defended if, as he expected, additional support arrived.[11] Nor were the defenders of the Alamo— nearly 200 men—hopelessly outnumbered by Mexican troops. At the beginning of the siege Santa Anna's army numbered about 1,500. By the time of the assault, some 2,600 Mexican soldiers had arrived, not

8. Walter Lord, "Myths and Realities of the Alamo," *The American West* 5 (May 1968): 18–25. Perry McWilliams, "The Alamo Story: From Fact to Fable," *Journal of the Folklore Institute* 15 (September–December 1978): 221–33; Paul Andrew Hutton, "Introduction," and Susan Prendergast Schoelwer, "Heroes Forgotten and Familiar," in Schoelwer et al., *Alamo Images: Changing Perceptions of a Texas Experience* (Dallas: DeGolyer Library and SMU Press, 1985), pp. 8–17, 104–62.

9. *New York Times*, March 7, 1986.

10. Tom W. Gläser, "Victory or Death," in Schoelwer, *Alamo Images*, p. 79.

11. For Travis's optimism as late as March 3, see Walter Lord, *A Time to Stand* (New York: Harper & Brothers, 1961), pp. 141–43, 203; Lord, "Myths and Realities of the Alamo," 21; and Archie P. McDonald, *Travis* (Austin: Jenkins Publishing Company, 1976), p. 171.

the 5,000 to 6,000 that is often suggested.[12] Many of the Mexican soldiers were bewildered Indian conscripts who did not even speak Spanish. Woefully ill-equipped, they were no match for superior Texas artillery and long rifles. Travis, then, had reason to remain confident of victory until toward the end, when it became clear that no help from fellow Texans would be forthcoming.

Finally, let us remember that it is by no means certain that all of the defenders died in an heroic fight to the finish. Strong evidence suggests that Mexican troops captured Davy Crockett and a half a dozen others (they may even have surrendered), and Santa Anna ordered them executed. The evidence for this comes from Mexican sources. As one of my former professors used to remark, rather ethnocentrically, we do not know what happened at the Alamo because no one who was there survived. There were some survivors, of course, the preponderance in the victorious Mexican army. The idea that Mexican sources indicate that Crockett died at the hands of an executioner rather than fighting to his last breath, has come to public attention from time to time, but has not won widespread acceptance for it seems to tarnish a hero. In 1978 historian Dan Kilgore received scorching mail when he stirred the embers of that controversy in a book entitled *How Did Davy Die?* One newspaper called it "a commie plot to trash our heroes."[13] More recently, Paul Hutton won similar opprobrium when, in an otherwise worshipful piece, he, too, suggested that Davy might not have died fighting. One angry Texan associated Hutton with Communists, while another unappreciative reader from Tennessee questioned his manhood and described him as a "gutless

12. Richard G. Santos, *Santa Anna's Campaign Against Texas, 1835–1836* (Salisbury, N.C.: Texian Press, 1968), pp. 60–61, 71, 79, who concludes that "Santa Anna did not have over 2,591 men in San Antonio and that the assault group was composed of 1,400 men" (p. 79). See, too, Gläser, "Victory or Death," p. 97. A pamphlet given to tourists at the Alamo as late as 1979 (and perhaps yet today) tells of the defenders withstanding "the onslaught of an army which ultimately numbered 5,000 men." James W. Pohl and Stephen L. Hardin, "The Military History of the Texas Revolution: An Overview," *Southwestern Historical Quarterly* 89 (January 1986): 276, 278, repeat the 6,000 figures, although they reveal the confusion surrounding this question when they state that Santa Anna's loss of 600 men in the assault on the Alamo reduced his force "by about one-fourth" (p. 291). The later statement would suggest that the authors believe that Santa Anna's army numbered about 2,400.

13. Hutton, "Introduction," in Schoelwer, *Alamo Images*, p. 16.

wonder."[14] If doubts about Hutton's politics and masculinity were not enough, another critic accused him of committing "blasphemy." Arguing that students need heroes, a Texas history teacher told Hutton: "I will *never* teach my students what you wrote. A real Texan would not. . . . You wrote that the evidence of Crockett's surrender came from a Mexican diary. Well that isn't good enough."[15]

On the other hand, some Texans have been able to maintain their sense of humor and keep these matters in perspective. As the story goes, when Senator John F. Kennedy visited the Alamo he was surrounded by large crowds and asked his host, Maury Maverick, if they might escape the crush by going out the back door. "There is no back door," Maverick is said to have replied, "that's why there were so many heroes."[16]

The lore surrounding the battle of the Alamo provides the clearest examples of how the Texas rebellion, like so many major events, has been romanticized to take on meanings that transcend the event itself and its principal characters reduced to caricature—to heroes and villains. In certain kinds of history, and in American popular culture, the Texas fight for independence has come to represent a triumph of Protestantism over Catholicism, of democracy over despotism, of a superior white race over a degenerate people of mixed blood, of the future over the past, of good over evil. Heroes of the Texas revolt are portrayed as committed republicans fighting for the noblest of motives (the blood of Davy Crockett, one historian has written, was shed upon "a holy altar").[17] The conflict over Texas has been reduced to nothing more than a conflict of two incompatible cultures. And the rebellion itself, which was a uniquely successful version of the separatist movements and rebellions that broke out all over Mexico at this time, has been elevated to the status of a "revolution"—a designation that few,

14. Paul Andrew Hutton, "Davy Crockett, Still King of the Wild Frontier," *Texas Monthly* 14 (November 1986): 122–30, 244–48. Viola I. Stewart to the Editor of *Texas Monthly*, Uvalde, Texas, November 8, 1986; Virginia Byrd to Paul Hutton, Algood, Tennessee, October 31, 1986. Copies of both letters in my possession.

15. Jean Mangano to Paul Hutton, Mission, Texas, November 5, 1986, copy in my possession.

16. This story, told by Richard Santos of San Antonio among others, appears in Schoelwer, *Alamo Images*, p. 115.

17. For analysis and examples, see especially Stephen Stagner, "Epics, Science, and the Lost Frontier: Texas Historical Writing, 1836–1936," *Western Historical Quarterly* 12 (April 1981): 172, quoting James M. Morphis, *History of Texas . . .* (New York: 1874), pp. 193–94.

if any, modern social scientists would apply to a revolt that did not seek a profound restructuring of society.[18]

What are the sources of these exaggerated notions about the Texas rebellion? Certainly one source was wartime propaganda—myths invented to stir people to action during conflict. Writing just after the fighting ended, for example, Stephen Austin explained the conflict as "a war of barbarism and of despotic principles, waged by the mongrel Spanish-Indian and Negro race, against civilization and the Anglo-American race."[19] That refrain echoed in nineteenth-century Romantic historiography, and its reverberations can be heard yet today in American popular history and popular culture.[20]

Still another source of distorted versions of the events of the Texas rebellion is almost certainly the well-known proclivity of Texans to embellish upon a story—to stretch the truth. There is a cartoon that represents a Texas variation of the story of George Washington and the cherry tree. It shows young George Washington and his father in Texas.

"I cannot tell a lie father," George says, "I chopped down the cactus."

"Well George, we're going back to Ol' Virginia," his father replies. "If you can't tell a lie, you'll never make a true Texan."

Even in an audience of Texans, I do not think I would find much argument about Texans' tendency to exaggerate, and that may explain in part why we have such grandiloquent versions of the events of 1836. Ironically, the reverse is also true. The Texas war for independence may also explain why Texans exaggerate. Historian Joe Frantz of the University of Texas has argued that the "real genesis [of Texas tendency

18. See, for example, Thomas H. Greene, *Comparative Revolutionary Movements* (Englewood Cliffs, N.J.: Prentice-Hall, 1974), pp. 116–17, 128.

19. Called to my attention by Arnoldo de León, *They Called Them Greasers: Anglo Attitudes toward Mexicans in Texas, 1821–1900* (Austin: University of Texas Press, 1983), p. 12, who mistakenly attributes the quote to a letter from Austin to Mary Austin Holley, August 21, 1835. The quote is actually in Stephen F. Austin to L. F. Linn, New York, May 4, 1836, in Eugene C. Barker, ed., *The Austin Papers*, vol. 3 (Austin: University of Texas, 1926), p. 345.

20. For analysis and examples, see especially Stagner, "Epics, Science, and the Lost Frontier," pp. 165–81, and Don Graham, "Remembering the Alamo: The Story of the Texas Revolution in Popular Culture," *Southwestern Historical Quarterly* 89 (July 1985): 35–66.

toward braggadocio] lies in the Texas Revolution" itself, and his argument seems plausible.[21] The simple fact that Texas became an independent nation as a result of the rebellion has given Texans enormous pride—perhaps too much pride. Historian T. R. Fehrenbach carried this idea to Texas-size proportions when he wrote, apparently without tongue in cheek: "The great difference between Texas and every other American state in the 20th century was that Texas had a history. Other American regions merely had records of development."[22]

But it is more than a traditional big brag that has led Texans to exaggerate the events of 1836 and to make mortal men into heroes of mythological proportions. This certainly reflects a more universal tendency—the tendency to write pietistic history and to use the past as a kind of Rorschach test, seeing wistfully in the past what we wish to see about ourselves in the present. In the interest of creating a usable past, all peoples seem to engage in the making of myths and passing them off as historical fact. In this country, we begin at an early age to be exposed to such historical figures as Santa Claus, and to learn to tell the truth from the homily about George Washington and the cherry tree. No matter that this fabled episode of the cherry tree did not occur—that the story is a lie. No matter that our teachers lied to us in order to teach us to tell the truth. History was being employed toward good ends. So, in many respects, have the tales of the Alamo been exaggerated to serve particular ends.

Rather than trying to read our present-day concerns into the past, let us try to reconstruct the past and look briefly at the coming of the Texas rebellion as contemporaries might have seen it. What did it mean to them? Certainly there was less heroism, less altruism, less patriotism, less clarity of purpose, and less unity than most of us might imagine. Instead, much as today, events moved along more quickly than contemporaries could grasp them and most Anglo Americans and Mexicans in Texas pursued their private lives, wishing that the entire affair would go away.

Let us look first at the proposition that the Texas rebellion represented a clash of cultures, rendering it nearly inevitable. This line

21. Frantz, *Texas*, p. 72. See, too, D. W. Meinig, *Imperial Texas: An Interpretive Essay in Cultural Geography* (Austin: University of Texas Press, 1969), p. 38.

22. *Lone Star: A History of Texas and the Texans* (New York: Macmillan, 1968), p. 711.

of argument was advanced by some Anglo Texans at the time of the revolt and has continued to receive the support of some scholars.[23]

Certainly it is easy to view the revolt as an "ethnic" conflict, for in some respects it was. Between 1821, when Mexico became independent, and 1836 when the armed struggle between Mexico and Texas began, perhaps 35,000 Anglo Americans had flocked across the border and into Mexican Texas, outnumbering the Mexican Texans, or tejanos, by a ratio of ten to one.[24] The Anglo Americans, so the argument goes, could not adapt to Mexican culture. Historians have identified a number of sources of cultural friction.[25]

First, Anglo Americans were required to become Catholics, and were not permitted to hold Protestant services.[26]

Second, Anglo Americans, some 75 percent of whom were southerners, were shocked when Mexico prohibited slavery in 1829. Mexicans seemed to have little respect for private property.[27]

Third, Anglo Americans could not tolerate the lack of a jury system and deplored the Mexican system of justice in which alcaldes made decisions on the merits of a case.

Fourth, Anglo Americans could not abide the lack of local autonomy in Texas—of home rule. Since 1824 Texas had been subservient to a larger and more populous state, Coahuila. Both Coahuila and Texas had been joined together as the single state of Coahuila y Texas. Control of state government rested squarely in the hands of officials in the distant state capital at Saltillo, and Coahuila's larger population assured that the state legislature would be controlled by representatives from Coahuila.

23. For an example contemporary with events, see the "Committee of Vigilance and Public Safety for the Municipality of San Augustín, Texas, December 22, 1835, quoted in David J. Weber, ed., *Foreigners in Their Native Land: Historical Roots of the Mexican Americans* (Albuquerque: University of New Mexico Press, 1973), pp. 105–8. For a modern historical interpretation, see Fehrenback, *Lone Star,* pp. 153, 168.

24. Weber, *Mexican Frontier,* p. 177. The "ethnic conflict" quote is from Fehrenbach, *Lone Star,* p. 168.

25. The classic statement of these cultural differences is Samuel H. Lowrie, *Culture Conflict in Texas* (New York: Columbia University Press, 1932), although he was not the first to explain them. See, too, for example, Eugene C. Barker, *Mexico and Texas, 1821–1835* (Dallas: P. L. Turner Co., 1928). Lowrie and Barker, however, concluded that political differences constituted the chief cause of the revolt.

26. The best elaboration of this question is William S. Red, *The Texas Colonists and Religion, 1821–1836* (Austin: E. L. Shettles, 1924), who saw religious differences as a cause of the Texas Revolution.

27. The percentage comes from Lowrie, *Culture Conflict in Texas,* pp. 32, 35.

Fifth, many Anglo Americans could not abide Mexicans them-selves. Stephen Austin, on visiting Mexico City in 1822–23, wrote in private correspondence that "the people are bigoted and supersti-tious to an extreem [sic], and indolence appears to be the order of the day." "To be candid the majority of the people of that whole nation as far as I have seen them want nothing but tails to be more brutes than apes." Many years after the bloody days at the Alamo and San Jacinto, one pioneer who had settled in Texas in 1827, Noah Smith-wick, echoed Austin's sentiments. "I looked upon the Mexicans as scarce more than apes," Smithwick recalled.[28]

Anglo Americans made no attempt to conceal their sense of supe-riority from Mexicans. In 1819, two years before Mexico won her independence from Spain, the Spanish minister who was negotiating with John Q. Adams what became the transcontinental treaty, char-acterized Americans as an "arrogant and audacious" people who believed themselves "superior to all the nations of Europe," and who were convinced "that their dominion is destined to extend . . . to the isthmus of Panama, and hereafter, over all the regions of the New World."[29] At the dawn of Mexican independence, in 1821, a Mexican Committee on Foreign Relations warned the government that unless Mexico could populate its northern borders, hordes of North Amer-icans would descend on the fertile province of Texas "Just as the Goths, Ostrogoths, Alans, and other tribes [of barbarians] devastated the Roman empire."[30] As this last statement suggests, many Mexicans believed themselves superior to the uncultured, brash, and barbaric Anglo Americans.

On the surface, then, the two cultures seemed incompatible and, even more important, the fact that some Anglo Texans *believed* the two cultures to be incompatible, contributed to Texas independence. Indeed, there seems little reason to doubt that profound cultural dif-ferences, including American racism, contributed to the Texas rebel-lion and gave it a special virulence.[31]

Nonetheless, it would be easy to exaggerate the importance of

28. The quotes from Austin and Smithwick are in David J. Weber, "'Scarce more than apes': Historical Roots of Anglo-American Stereotypes of Mexicans in the Border Region," in Weber, ed., *New Spain's Far Northern Frontier: Essays on Spain in the American West* (Albuquerque: University of New Mexico Press, 1979), pp. 297–98, 296.

29. Quoted in Weber, ed., *Foreigners in Their Native Land*, p. 55.

30. Quoted in Weber, *Mexican Frontier*, p. 161.

31. For a more narrow political viewpoint, that seems to dismiss cultural differ-

cultural differences, incorrectly identifying them as the principal cause of the rebellion. *Within* Texas itself, relations between Mexicans from Texas and the Anglo-American newcomers were generally amicable.[32] A few Anglo Americans had settled in the Mexican communities of San Antonio and Goliad, where they became assimilated. In the main, however, the two groups lived essentially apart, separated by considerable distance. Most Anglo Americans lived in East Texas and most Mexicans in the area of San Antonio and Goliad. As a result, Anglo Americans enjoyed a good deal of autonomy. Differences in religion, philosophy, or what we have come to call "lifestyles," did not become major irritants.[33]

The alleged "religious conflict" offers a case in point. Some writers have argued that Anglo Americans chaffed at the lack of religious freedom in Texas. In practice, the law requiring immigrants to become Catholics was never enforced. The Mexican government failed to send priests to minister to the Anglo-American colonists, as the Colonization Law of 1824 required, so the colonists were not obliged to practice Catholicism. Nor was the government ever so efficient that it investigated the private or quasi-public worship that went on in East Texas homes, where most Anglo Americans lived far from the watchful eye of Mexican officials.

Indeed, there is some evidence to suggest that Mexico's refusal to allow non-Catholics to worship openly (at least in theory) served as a screening device that kept the most devout or dogmatic Protestants out of Texas. Those who did filter through were less inclined to be irritated by strictures on their religious lives. Indeed, many of those

---

ences, see Seymour V. Connor, *Texas: A History* (New York: Thomas Y. Crowell, 1971), pp. 118–22.

32. Lowrie, *Culture Conflict in Texas*, p. 118.

33. For an elaboration of this view, and reference to further sources, see Weber, *Mexican Frontier*, pp. 254–55. In a paper entitled "Race, Revolution, and the Texas Republic: Toward a Reinterpretation," delivered at the annual meeting of the Texas State Association in Austin, March 7, 1986, James E. Crisp identified Arnoldo de León and myself with the point of view that the "clash of cultures" and Anglo-American racism made the Texas Revolution "virtually inevitable," a phrase that neither of us, to my knowledge, has used. De León, *They Called Them Greasers*, takes the position that "racism was not the cause of the Texas Revolution," but he clearly sees it as contributing to it (p. 12). Neither of us sees cultural differences as *the* cause of the rebellion, although we both see those differences as *a* cause (see, for example, Weber, *Foreigners in Their Native Land* (pp. 88–89).

early pioneers who entered Texas may have come precisely because of the lack of religious restraints and the absence of protestant preachers.

Put simply, the Mexican government never forced Catholicism on the Anglo-American colonists in Texas. To the contrary, in 1834, two years before the revolt broke out, the state of Coahuila y Texas went so far as to guarantee that "no person shall be molested for political and religious opinions provided the public order is not disturbed." Freedom of worship never became an important issue among the foreigners in Mexican Texas and, notwithstanding Anglo-Texan wartime propaganda, the issue of freedom of worship did not directly cause the Texas revolt in 1836.[34]

The idea that cultural conflict caused the Texas rebellion has contributed to the notion that the struggle itself was fought along ethnic lines, pitting *all* Mexicans against *all* Americans in Texas. This was decidedly not the case. Tejanos, for example, contributed substantially to the resistance against centralist forces in the fall of 1835, in the wave of hostilities that preceded Santa Anna's march into Texas. The Texas forces that laid siege to General Martín Perfecto de Cos in San Antonio in the fall of 1835 included as many as 160 *tejanos,* among them companies led by Colonel Juan Nepomuceno Seguín of San Antonio, Plácido Benavides of Victoria, and a group of rancheros from Goliad. The next spring, seven tejanos died inside the Alamo, fighting alongside Anglo Americans *against* Santa Anna. Colonel Seguín and the Second Company of Texas Volunteers, which he raised, performed valuable scouting services prior to the fall of the Alamo and contributed to the defeat of Santa Anna at San Jacinto. (Indeed, Seguín and one Antonio Cruz would have died defending the Alamo had they not been sent on a dangerous ride through enemy lines to seek help from Colonel James Fannin at Goliad.) Tejanos also participated in the famous "Consultation" at San Felipe on November 7 of 1835, which endorsed a conditional declaration of Texas independence. Four months later José Antonio Navarro and Francisco Ruiz, both Texas-born, signed the declaration of Texas independence at Washington-on-the-Brazos.[35]

34. Weber, *Mexican Frontier,* pp. 79–80.
35. This paragraph, along with the following discussion of the role of the *tejanos* and the divisions among Anglo Americans in Texas on the eve of the revolt, derives

Thus, the sides did not divide up uniformly along ethnic lines. The issues that caused men to take to arms in 1835–36 may have had to do more with the culture of politics than with the politics of culture. And both tejanos and Anglos *within* Texas found much about politics with which they could agree. Let us look at some areas of agreement.

Elites in the predominantly *tejano* communities of San Antonio and Goliad had apparently *shared* Anglo-American concerns about the need to improve the system of justice and to achieve greater autonomy by separating Texas from Coahuila. Many *tejano* leaders even saw slavery as a necessary evil for Texas if the underpopulated and beleaguered province was going to prosper. Nor, it would appear, did the large influx of Anglo Americans into Texas trouble the tejanos as much as it did the Mexican government. For the tejano *elite*, Anglo-American immigrants meant economic growth. From the *local* perspective Anglo Americans were a necessary evil, and Mexican officials in Texas opposed national laws that would restrict the number of Anglo-American immigrants.

From a *national* perspective, however, officials in Mexico City saw Anglo Americans as aggressive and expansionistic, and as a clear and present danger to Texas. There was no doubt that the United States government wanted Texas. The United States had advanced the absurd claim that Texas was part of the Louisiana Purchase. When that claim could not be sustained, the United States had sought to purchase Texas. Mexico, of course, declined to sell the national patrimony, and Mexican statesman Lucas Alamán feared that the Americans' next strategy would be to take Texas from Mexico by peopling it with Americans. As Alamán wrote in 1830: "Where others send invading armies . . . [the North Americans] send their colonists."[36]

As events would demonstrate, Alamán's fears were quite rational. If Mexican leaders *in Texas* shared those concerns, they subordinated them to their economic interests and called for more immigration to make Texas grow. Francisco Ruiz of San Antonio put it squarely when

from my previous work: *The Mexican Frontier*, pp. 245–55; *Foreigners in Their Native Land*, pp. 88–93, and *Troubles in Texas, 1832: A Tejano Viewpoint from San Antonio*, David J. Weber, ed., Cochita Hassell Winn and Weber, trans. (Dallas: Wind River Press for the DeGolyer Library, 1983). Arnoldo de León has analyzed the variety of historical interpretations of the role of the *tejanos* in "Tejanos and the Texas War for Independence: Historiography's Judgment," *New Mexico Historical Review* 61 (April 1986): 137–46.

36. Quoted in Weber, *Mexican Frontier*, p. 170.

he wrote in 1830: "I cannot help seeing advantages which, to my way of thinking, would result if we admitted honest, hard-working people, regardless of what country they come from . . . even hell itself."[37]

The evidence is scanty, but it appears that the Anglo Texans and the Mexican-Texan elite shared a number of common concerns. No matter how much mutual interests might tie them together, however, once the fighting began it must have been agonizing for tejanos to decide whether to remain loyal to Mexico or to join forces with Americans and take up arms against fellow Mexicans. Although they might agree with Anglo Texans on certain issues, the idea of separation from Coahuila, much less independence from Mexico came to hold less attraction for tejanos in the mid-1830s than it had in the 1820s. Anglo Americans, who vastly outnumbered tejanos by the early 1830s, would surely dominate the state and tejanos would become, to paraphrase Juan Seguín, "foreigners in their native land."[38] When, however, Coahuila fell into anarchy in the mid-1830s and Santa Anna's centralist dictatorship replaced Mexico's federalist Republic, tejano leaders must have wrung their hands over their unhappy alternatives— domination by Anglo Americans or domination by the centralist dictatorship.

The hard choice must have divided some families. We know, for example, that Gregorio Esparza, who died fighting alongside Americans inside the walls of the Alamo, had a brother, Francisco, who fought on the Mexican side. Most tejanos, however, probably responded like any residents of a war-torn land. They looked first to their families' welfare, fought on neither side, cooperated overtly with the group in charge at the moment, and hoped for an end to the nightmare.

The same may also be said for most Anglo Texans, who had no desire to fight over political issues until Mexican forces threatened their lives and property. Until autumn of 1835, Anglo Americans in Texas were divided between groups that had come to be called the "war party" and the "peace party." Both parties sought greater political autonomy for Texas in order to enable Texans to adopt measures that would make Texas more attractive to immigrants from the U.S.— measures such as more favorable tariffs, an improved judicial system, and the maintenance of slavery. While they agreed on the goals, the

37. Quoted in ibid., p. 176.
38. Quoted in Weber, *Foreigners in Their Native Land*, p. 178.

peace and war parties disagreed about the means to achieve them. The "peace party," of which the *empresario* Stephen Austin was the most influential representative, wanted Mexico to grant Texas a divorce from its unhappy and unequal marriage with Coahuila. The radical war party, led by ambitious and sometimes angry young men such as William Barret Travis (who a few years earlier had abandoned a wife and law practice in Alabama after killing a man), sought independence from Mexico itself.

Until the autumn of 1835, the "war party" remained a decided minority, its actions repudiated by most responsible Texans of both Anglo and Mexican background. Then, Mexico committed the blunder of sending troops into Texas under the direction of Santa Anna's brother-in-law, Martín Perfecto de Cos. In part, Mexico had been provoked into that action by the attack on a small Mexican garrison at Anahuac in June of 1835, led by Travis and thirty-some radicals. At first, Anglo-American communities throughout Texas repudiated that attack and professed loyalty to the government, but when Anglo Americans learned that Mexican troops would be sent to Texas, public opinion swung away from the "Tories," as Travis called the peace party, and over to the "war party." Even the foremost Texas "Tory," Stephen Austin, became convinced of the necessity of armed resistance. His private correspondence reveals that by the autumn of 1835 he had come to believe that Texas "must, and ought to become a part of the United States."[39]

Although Anglo Americans in Texas achieved unity of purpose by the fall of 1835, that unity disappeared again after General Cos's forces were defeated in San Antonio. In the spring of 1836, Anglo Americans were in disarray once again, both before, during, and after the tragic events at Goliad and the Alamo.

Clearly, then, the Texas struggle for independence was not a simple conflict of Mexicans versus Anglos, of Mexican culture versus American culture, of democracy versus despotism, or of good versus evil. It was not a conflict in which issues were so clearly drawn that men of good will united readily to fight for principles greater than themselves. That such men existed, I have no reason to doubt, but it should

39. Travis and Austin quotes appear in Weber, *Mexican Frontier*, pp. 249 and 250, respectively.

be remembered that many Anglo Americans who came to Texas had
more interest in fleeing the law than in changing the law; that they
came to Texas for personal gain. Pragmatism rather than principle,
self interest rather than political democracy, had driven a disproportionate share of Anglo Americans to Texas in search of opportunity.
And the unbridled pursuit of self-interest on the part of some Anglo
Americans, rather than the quest for liberty, may have helped to bring
on the Texas rebellion. The story is a complicated one, but Professor
Malcolm McLean has developed a strong case, in his monumental
series, *Papers Concerning Robertson's Colony in Texas*, that land spec-
ulation by certain Anglo Americans, and their manipulation of the
state government in Saltillo, helped win the wrath of the federal
government, bring Mexican troops into Texas, and provoke the Texas
revolt.[40]

If cheap land and opportunity attracted to Texas some unscrupulous
men (and, lest I be charged with sexism, unscrupulous women), so,
too, did the fear of the debt collector and the sheriff in the United
States push a good many American lawbreakers and criminals toward
Texas—James Bowie and William Barret Travis among them. Early
travelers to Texas often commented on the high number of murderers
and thieves in Texas. Indeed, Texas enjoyed such a reputation as a
refuge for criminals from the United States that in 1835 a Louisiana
newspaper observed that if a war between Mexico and Texas broke
out, a great many Texans would die and "the world would lose many
bad citizens and the devil would gain some faithful servants."[41] When
the fighting with Mexico did break out, not all of these early Anglo
Texans had liberty on their minds. A visitor described one Texan who
enjoyed "fighting simply for the love of it, he cared less for the result
than for the pleasurable excitement that it produced."[42]

I have not had time to develop these ideas thoroughly and convincingly, but I hope that I have at least succeeded in suggesting that

40. Malcolm D. McLean, comp. and ed., *Papers Concerning Robertson's Colony
in Texas* (Arlington: University of Texas at Arlington Press, 1974–1987 and ongoing):
10: 65–80; 11: 49–51, 60. I do not find McLean's thesis convincing, but it is provocative.
41. Mark E. Nackman, *A Nation Within a Nation: The Rise of Texas Nationalism*
(Port Washington, N.Y.: Kennikat, 1975), p. 9, quoting the *Louisiana Gazette*.
42. *Louisiana Gazette* quoted in Nackman, *A Nation Within a Nation*, p. 7.

in a historical event as complicated as the Texas struggle for independence, there are few heroes or villains, but rather men and women much like us, looking after their day-to-day interests and responding to a variety of impulses. By writing romanticized history that magnifies men and events, that simplifies a complicated story of a struggle for political and economic power into an ethnic conflict, and that makes Anglo Americans in the past more altruistic, courageous, patriotic, and united than they were, we not only distort the past, but we diminish ourselves. We come to believe that our own generation, when compared to the giants of yesteryear, is unprincipled and decadent.

Many of the giants of yesteryear—both heroes and villains—are, of course, creatures of our own making, invented to serve salutory ends. First, they provide us with a way to avoid abstractions and complicated issues and to focus instead on the personal, the concrete, the easily understood. As historian Michael Meyer, writing about the villain, has explained: "it is much easier to prepare a diatribe against an antihero than to fathom the actual dynamics of an age."[43] Second, by conjuring heroes of mythic proportions and keeping their memories alive, we hope to offer lessons in morality to the young, or to inspire the young with patriotism and pride. And such lessons have been well learned. As one Texas-educated young man, Lyndon B. Johnson, wrote in his college newspaper, "Down with the debunking biographer. . . . Hero worship is a tremendous force in uplifting and strengthening . . . let us have our heroes. Let us continue to believe that some have been truly great."[44]

Myths are, of course, important to a people. As historian William McNeill has reminded us in a recent essay, myths play an essential role in binding a people together and in serving as a basis for common action.[45] The question, however, is whether a myth is useful or pernicious; whether it drives people to constructive common action or to collective foolishness or disgrace. Perhaps these two extremes are not mutually exclusive, but the mythology surrounding the Alamo has served as rationalization for aggressive behavior toward Mexico and

---

43. Michael Meyer, "Antiheroism in the Mexican Revolution," *The Mexican Forum* 5 (October 1985): 9.

44. Doris Kearns, *Lyndon Johnson and the American Dream* (New York: Harper & Row, 1976), p. 64, quoting the *College Star*, July 17, 1929.

45. "The Care and Repair of Public Myth," in McNeill, *Mythhistory and Other Essays* (Chicago: University of Chicago Press, 1986), p. 25.

Mexicans that runs counter to our finest national ideals. In the immediate aftermath of the Texas revolt, the enshrinement of the Alamo
as a holy place and the popular sanctification of its defenders as martyrs
helped reinforce and intensify two complimentary articles of faith
among Anglo Americans: belief in the moral superiority of Anglos and
the degeneracy of Mexicans.[46] From those antipodal myths, which ran
strongest among Anglo residents of Texas, it followed that Mexico's
conquest by its morally superior neighbor might redeem her benighted
citizenry. Their faith affirmed by the windy rhetoric of their elders,
young American men of the mid-1840s swallowed the myth of a holy
war against Mexico. Entering a fantasy world of promised glory and
heroism against a foe they believed to be inferior, many young Americans marched to the Halls of Montezuma. One out of eight never
returned.[47]

It may be that by *manufacturing* heroes from the past we do not
necessarily "uplift and strengthen" the present generation, as young
LBJ supposed, or add to patriotism and pride. Instead, we may only
succeed in adding to our self-loathing and cynicism, for as mere human
beings we cannot live up to the impossible standards that we set for
ourselves when we invent heroes who are larger than life.

Distorted renditions of the past may be even more dangerous when
those who have confused myth with reality come to shape our public
policy. It was that same hero-loving young Texas schoolboy, Lyndon
B. Johnson, who, when he grew up to become president, said that it
was "just like the Alamo" when he sent Marines into the Dominican
Republic in 1965 in violation of the charter of the Organization of
American States and the principle of nonintervention. And it was
LBJ who also saw the Vietnam quagmire as "just like the Alamo"—a
place where stout defenders needed Americans to come to their aid.
He compared Vietnam to a hunt in the woods which must end, in
Davy Crockett fashion, "with that coonskin on the wall." And it was
LBJ, with what some historians have termed as his "Alamo complex,"
who could not bring himself to negotiate his way out of that great

46. For the role of writers of history in fashioning the myth, see Stagner, "Epics,
Science, and the Lost Frontier," especially pp. 166–72.
47. For a vivid study of popular American attitudes toward the war, see Robert
W. Johannsen, *To the Halls of the Montezumas: The Mexican War in the American
Imagination* (New York: Oxford University Press, 1985). For total casualties see K.
Jack Bauer, *The Mexican War, 1846–1848* (New York: Macmillan, 1974), p. 397.

struggle to make democrats of illiterate peasants in faraway rice paddies of Vietnam. LBJ had come to believe in the myths of American exceptionalism and American omnipotence—in a past that never was. Forgetting about the War of 1812 and the Korean War (wars that we neither won nor lost), LBJ did not want to be remembered, in the words of historian Thomas A. Bailey, as "the first President of the United States who failed to win a war for which he was responsible."[48]

Now I would not want to push this argument too far. I am not saying that LBJ's romantic view of the Alamo and its heroes was the sole cause of protracted U.S. involvement in Vietnam, but I do wonder what a president who brought to the White House a different set of myths—a different historical sensibility—would have done under the same circumstances.

In any event, it is statements such as LBJ's "just like the Alamo," that make me uneasy whenever someone says "history teaches us" such and such a thing, for I know that I am about to hear history being called upon to teach whatever that person wishes it to teach. This is not to say that we cannot draw lessons from the past, and use the past to inform our judgment about the present and future, but to do so realistically, we must be realistic and clearheaded about the past.[49] We must see historical figures and events as they *were* and not magnify them or romanticize them into something that we *wish* they had been. The Texas rebellion is no exception.

48. Bailey "Mythmakers of American History," *Journal of American History* 15 (June 1968): 19. Quotes from LBJ in this paragraph come from Bailey's splendid essay, pp. 10, 19. See, too, Richard Maxwell Brown, *Strain of Violence* (New York: Oxford University Press, 1975), pp. 296–97 for an interesting discussion and further references to LBJ's "Alamo Complex."

49. For case studies of the uses and misuses of argument by historical analogy by policymakers, and a primer for how to use historical examples wisely, see Richard E. Neustadt and Ernest R. May, *Thinking in Time: The Uses of History for Decision-Makers* (New York: The Free Press, 1986).

9

"Scarce More than Apes"
Historical Roots of Anglo-American Stereotypes of Mexicans in the Border Region*

Many nineteenth-century, Anglo-American visitors to what is today the southwestern United States (defined for present purposes as the four border states of Alta California, Arizona, New Mexico, and Texas), depicted the Mexican residents of that area in the most unflattering terms. Mexicans were described as lazy, ignorant, bigoted, superstitious, cheating, thieving, gambling, cruel, sinister, cowardly half-breeds. As a consequence of their supposed innate depravity, Mexicans were seen as incapable of developing republican institutions or achieving material progress.[1] These opinions of Mexicans, some of which endure to the present, are familiar to most Southwesterners and can be found in the writings of many early Anglo-American writers. One example will suffice. Thomas Jefferson Farnham, a New England attorney who toured Alta California in the early 1840s, described the californios thus:

There never was a doubt among Californians that they were at the head of the human race. In cowardice, ignorance, pretension, and dastardly tyranny, the reader has learned that this pretension is well founded.

Thus much for the Spanish population of the Californias; in every way a

*This essay is reprinted with permission from *New Spain's Far Northern Frontier: Essays on Spain in the American West, 1540–1821,* David J. Weber, ed. (Albuquerque: University of New Mexico Press, 1979; reprint edition, SMU Press, 1988).

1. This is the picture that emerges from such studies as Cecil Robinson, *With the Ears of Strangers: The Mexican in American Literature* (Tucson: 1963), and David T. Leary, "The Attitudes of Certain United States Citizens toward Mexico, 1821–1846" (University of Southern California, 1970).

poor apology of European extraction; as a general thing, incapable of reading or writing, and knowing nothing of science or literature, nothing of government but its brutal force, nothing of virtue but the sanction of the Church, nothing of religion but ceremonies of the national ritual. Destitute of industry themselves, they compel the poor Indian to labor for them, affording him a bare savage existence for his toil, upon their plantations and the fields of the Missions. In a word, the Californians are an imbecile, pusillanimous, race of men, and unfit to control the destinies of that beautiful country. . . .

No one acquainted with the indolent, mixed race of California, will ever believe that they will populate, much less, for any length of time, govern the country. The law of Nature which curses the mulatto here with a constitution less robust than that of either race from which he sprang, lays a similar penalty upon the mingling of the Indian and white races in California and Mexico. They must fade away. . . .[2]

Not all Americans who came to the Mexican frontier shared Farnham's passionate contempt for Mexicans, but many did and they expressed their feelings in no uncertain terms. Charles Bent, a merchant who became prominent in New Mexico in the 1830s and 1840s and took a Mexican woman as his common-law wife, wrote that "the Mexican character is made up of stupidity, obstinacy, ignorance, duplicity, and vanity."[3] Noah Smithwick, who settled in Texas in 1827, later recalled that "I looked on the Mexicans as scarce more than apes."[4] This image of Mexicans as subhuman creatures was shared by a Santa Fe trader who preferred not to consider Mexicans as part of "humanity," but to classify them separately as "Mexicanity."[5]

If Anglo Americans had portrayed individual Mexicans in a negative fashion, we might think little of it, for surely there were Mexicans, just as there were Anglo Americans, who fit the description.

2. Thomas Jefferson Farnham, *Travels in California* (1st ed., 1844; Oakland, California: 1947), pp. 147–48, 161.

3. In an article sent to Manuel Alvarez (a Spaniard), Taos, March 30, 1845, quoted in Ward Alan Minge, "Frontier Problems in New Mexico Preceding the Mexican War, 1840–1846" (Ph.D. dissertation, University of New Mexico, 1965), p. 309. Harold H. Dunham, "Charles Bent," in *The Mountain Men and the Fur Trade of the Far West*, ed. LeRoy R. Hafen, 10 vols. (Glendale, Calif., 1965), 2: 44.

4. Noah Smithwick, *The Evolution of a State: or, Recollections of Old Texas Days* (1st ed., 1900; reprint, Austin: 1935), p. 45.

5. Richard L. Wilson, *Short Ravelings from a Long Yarn, or Camp Sketches of the Santa Fe Trail*, ed. Benjamin F. Taylor (1st ed., 1847; reprint, Santa Ana, Calif., 1936), p. 120.

When such characterizations are applied to an entire people, however, they clearly are no longer based on empirical evidence and cannot be regarded as valid generalizations. Sweeping generalizations, which either have no basis in fact, or which are based on "overgeneralizations of facts," are known as stereotypes.[6] Negative stereotypes are, of course, an obstacle to communication and understanding for they are usually expressions of prejudice which, as Walter Lippman once put it, "precedes the use of reason."[7]

Stereotypes need not always be negative, of course. In describing Mexicans as a peculiarly depraved people, for example, early Anglo-American writers, who were almost always males, frequently took pains to exempt Mexican women from their disparaging remarks. Hence, the negative stereotype applies to the male half of the Mexican population; the feminine half has enjoyed a positive image. "The men of northern Mexico," wrote one early American settler in Arizona, "are far inferior to the women in every respect." Similarly, an English visitor to Alta California in 1842 concluded that women were "by far the more industrious half of the population."[8]

Male visitors to the Mexican frontier, who usually had not seen a woman for several months, were frequently impressed with the beauty, kindness, and flirtatiousness of Mexican women. In forming this positive stereotype, American males allowed their hormones to overcome their ethnocentrism. Indeed, one visitor to New Mexico put aside his characteristic chauvinism to pronounce Mexican women "more beautiful" than their counterparts in the United States.[9] Another young American traveler in New Mexico carried a stereotype to its extremes by asserting that "women is women the whole world over, no matter where she is found."[10]

6. In this article I am following Gordon Allport's widely accepted distinction between a stereotype and a valid generalization. *The Nature of Prejudice* (Cambridge, Mass., 1954), pp. 190–91.

7. Quoted in Rosemary Gordon, *Stereotype of Imagery and Belief as an Ego Defence* (Cambridge: 1962), p. 5. Psychologists give Lippman considerable credit for popularizing the term *stereotype*.

8. Charles D. Poston, *Building a State in Apache Land* (Tempe: 1963), p. 75. Sir George Simpson, *Narrative of a Journey Round the World*, 2 vols. (London: 1847), 1: 381.

9. Lansing Bloom, ed., "Santa Fe and the Far West in 1841," *New Mexico Historical Review* 5 (1930): 300.

10. Lewis H. Garrard, *Wah-To-Yah and the Taos Trail* (Palo Alto, Calif., 1968), p. 194.

Americans found some things to dislike about Mexican women, to be sure, but in general their high regard for Mexican women stands in sharp contrast to their contempt for Mexican men. Francis Parkman, traveling in the Far West in 1846, revealed this dichotomy in American thinking clearly if unconsciously when he termed Mexican women "Spanish" and Mexican men "Mexicans."[11]

How did a negative stereotype of Mexican males develop? There are many approaches to that question which cannot be explored in a brief paper. As a historian, I would like to suggest that the answer has larger dimensions than usually suggested by southwestern writers. One popular explanation, implied more often than it is stated, is that a negative stereotype of Mexicans developed as a result of the contacts made between Mexicans and Anglo Americans in the border region in the two and a half decades before the so-called Mexican War.

There is no doubt that Anglo Americans' first significant contact with Mexicans occurred in the border region. Anglo-American trappers, traders, and settlers first entered Texas, New Mexico, and Alta California in the 1820s, after Mexico achieved independence from Spain and relaxed restrictions against foreigners. The Anglo Americans who entered northernmost Mexico in the 1820s, 1830s, and 1840s, it is said, came to know an area of Mexico that was backward politically, economically, and culturally. Thus, it has been suggested, Anglo Americans formed a mistaken notion of what *all* Mexicans were like on the basis of contact with relatively *few* Mexicans in the border region.[12]

Writers who have taken this position have found support from a contemporary Mexican visitor to the frontier, General Manuel Mier y Terán, who, after inspecting Texas in 1828, reported to President Guadalupe Victoria:

It would cause you the same chagrin that it has caused me to see the opinion that is held of our nation by these foreign colonists [i.e., Anglo

11. Quoted in James H. Lacy, "New Mexico Women in Early American Writings," *New Mexico Historical Review* 34 (1959): 41.
12. This argument was put forth by Cecil Robinson, *With the Ears of Strangers*, pp. 29–30 and Samuel H. Lowrie, *Culture Conflict in Texas, 1821–35* (New York: 1935), pp. 82, 88. Herbert E. Bolton, in a more generalized essay, advanced a similar thesis. See "Defensive Spanish Exploration and the Significance of the Borderlands," in *Bolton and the Spanish Borderlands*, ed. John Francis Bannon (Norman: 1964), pp. 33–34.

Americans], since, with the exception of some few who have journeyed to our capital, they know no other Mexicans than the inhabitants about here, and excepting the authorities . . . the said inhabitants are the most ignorant of negroes and Indians.[13]

As literary historian Cecil Robinson summed up the situation, "Early American writers and chroniclers in dealing with Mexico generally mistook a part for the whole thing."[14]

I would like to suggest that no such mistake occurred. On the contrary, many Anglo-American writers held a contemptuous view of Mexican males wherever they encountered them. General Mier y Terán, for example, would have been even more chagrined had he known the private views that Stephen Austin expressed about Mexicans during a visit to Mexico City in 1822–23. Austin wrote that: "the people are bigoted and superstitious to an extreem [sic], and indolence appears to be the general order of the day." "To be candid the majority of the people of the whole nation as far as I have seen them want nothing but tails to be more brutes than the apes."[15]

It could be said that Austin's previous experience in Texas had predisposed him to dislike Mexicans wherever he found them. This was not the case with Joel Roberts Poinsett, who never set foot in what is today the Southwest.[16] In 1822 Poinsett visited Mexico for the first time, traveling to Mexico City by way of Vera Cruz. In his well-known Notes on Mexico, Poinsett pronounced Mexicans in general to be lazy.[17] The Indians and mixed-bloods were "indolent," he said, and the "lazy" creoles "are not remarkable for their attainments, or for the strictness of their morals." He described the upper class as a complacent, self-satisfied group. The clergy, Poinsett said, had too great an influence in society, and the people were superstitious.[18] Just

13. Mier y Terán to Guadalupe Victoria, Nacogdoches, June 30, 1828, in Allaine Howren, "Causes and Origin of the Decree of April 6, 1830," Southwestern Historical Quarterly 16 (1913): 395.

14. Robinson, With the Ears of Strangers, p. 29.

15. To James Brown Austin, July 8, 1822, and June 13, 1823, quoted respectively in Lowrie, Culture Conflict, p. 89, and William S. Red, Texas Colonists and Religion, 1821–36 (Austin: 1924), p. 43.

16. See J. Fred Rippy, Joel R. Poinsett, Versatile American (Durham, N.C.: 1935).

17. J. R. Poinsett, Notes on Mexico, Made in the Autumn of 1822 . . . (London: 1825), p. 37. At one point Poinsett departs from his generalization to indicate that the "labouring class" in cities, towns, and countryside is "industrious" (p. 163).

18. Ibid., pp. 161, 162, 112.

as visitors to the frontier would note, Mexicans practiced terrible vices of gambling and smoking, and gave little thought to the future. Poinsett found the people to be generally ugly, and one can only wonder if this was because he had also discovered them to be "swarthy."[19] Compared to most of his contemporaries, Poinsett's observations tended to be sophisticated. The well-traveled Poinsett showed some awareness of his prejudices and tried, but often failed, to avoid overgeneralizing.[20]

More typical was another visitor to Mexico in 1822 whose notes, describing a journey from Tampico to Mexico City, appeared in the appendix to Poinsett's work. This anonymous traveler dismissed all Mexicans with the characteristic stereotype:

Their occupation seems to consist, principally, in removing fleas and lice from each other, drinking pulque, smoking cigars, when they can, and sleeping.[21]

On a return visit to Mexico in 1825, Joel Poinsett brought with him a young secretary, Edward Thornton Tayloe, another person who had had no previous contact with Mexicans. Tayloe quickly judged the residents of Mexico City, including the upper class, to be superstitious and lazy. Not as gallant as some of his contemporaries, Tayloe singled out upper-class women, especially, as "idle and useless." "They can do naught but eat, sleep, smoke or talk, or visit the theatre." The Mexicans, Tayloe wrote, were ignorant, vicious, thieving, and incapable of governing themselves as republicans. In fact, Mexicans had no virtues whatsoever. "Should I attempt to find them out," Tayloe wrote, "I fear I shall fail."[22]

These remarks by a necessarily small sample[23] of Anglo-American visitors to Mexico City in the early 1820s seem to indicate that Anglo Americans did not, as Cecil Robinson said, mistake "a part" of Mexico "for the whole thing." A negative stereotype of Mexicans was articulated very early, almost as soon as foreigners began to get a good look

19. Ibid., pp. 160, 100, 174, 51.
20. See, ibid., p. 88.
21. Ibid., Appendix, p. 7.
22. C. Harvey Gardiner, ed., *Mexico, 1825–1829. The Journal and Correspondence of Edward Thornton Tayloe* (Chapel Hill, N.C.: 1959), pp. 54, 69, 116, 55.
23. The writings of Poinsett and Tayloe are the only book-length descriptions of Mexico by Anglo Americans to be published in the 1820s. See C. Harvey Gardiner, "Foreign Travelers' Accounts of Mexico, 1810–1920," *The Americas* 8 (1952): 321–51.

at Mexico City after 1821.[24] The relative uniformity of the stereotype suggests the possibility that the observers were making valid generalizations—that Mexicans were lazy, ignorant, bigoted, superstitious, cheating, thieving, gambling, cruel, sinister, cowardly half-breeds, incapable of self-government or material progress. Yet, a closer look at American thought suggests that the stereotype was based not so much on direct observation or experience with Mexicans, but was in large part an extension of negative attitudes toward Catholic Spaniards which Anglo Americans had inherited from their Protestant English forebears.

During the colonial period, English colonists on the Atlantic Coast had almost no contact with Mexicans or other Latin Americans. Nonetheless, seventeenth-century Protestant New Englanders, such as Samuel Sewall and Cotton Mather, took a jaundiced view of Catholic Latin America, based largely on what they had read in literature from England. Sewall believed that Mexican culture was doomed to fall before a triumphant Protestantism and hoped that Mexico would hasten the process by revolting against Spain. Mather took the trouble to learn Spanish in order to write a missionary tract for Spaniards in the New World, designed "to open their eyes and be converted . . . away from Satan to God."[25]

Anti-Spanish views inherited from England were far more complex than simple anti-Catholicism, however. The English colonists also believed that Spanish government was authoritarian, corrupt, and decadent, and that Spaniards were bigoted, cruel, greedy, tyrannical, fanatical, treacherous, and lazy. In attempting to respond to these charges, Spanish historians have found it convenient to give them a pejorative label: The Black Legend. Not surprisingly, in defending themselves from the "blackening" effect of this "Legend," Spaniards have often gone to the other extreme of whitewashing Spain of all faults, giving rise to what Spain's detractors called a White Legend.

The origins of the Black Legend are complex. Some of its roots lie in the New World where Spanish conquistadors have been viewed

24. Such views continued to be articulated by visitors to Mexico City in the 1830s and 1840s, as David Leary's dissertation suggests. By that time, of course, these views could have been influenced by reports about Mexicans on the frontier.

25. Harry Bernstein, *Making an Inter-American Mind* (Gainesville: 1961), pp. 6–10. See also Stanley T. Williams, *The Spanish Background of American Literature*, 2 vols. (New Haven, Conn.: 1955), 1: 9, 18.

as the apotheosis of evil. Interestingly, Spain's enemies drew much of their inspiration from the self-critical writings of Spaniards themselves, most notably Bartolomé de las Casas, who was widely read in England and in her American colonies. In this literature, Spaniards were depicted as grasping adventurers who came to the New World, not to seek liberty or better homes for their families as did the English, but to search for treasure and to live in idleness on the sweat of enslaved aborigines. This image remained alive. In 1821, the same year that Mexico won independence from Spain, Henry Clay told Congress that if Anglo Americans moved into Texas "it will be peopled by freemen and sons of freemen, carrying with them our language, our laws, and our liberties." Should Texas remain part of Mexico, however, Clay warned that "it may become the habitation of despotism and slaves, subject to the vile domination of the Inquisition and of superstition."[26]

For our purposes, suffice it to say that Mexicans, the descendents of the Spanish conquistadors, inherited the reputation of their fore-fathers. As Phillip Wayne Powell recently put it: "We [Anglo Americans] transferred some of our ingrained antipathy toward Catholic Spain to her American heirs."[27]

Powell is one of the few historians to take note of this connection between the Black Legend and anti-Mexicanism,[28] but one does not need to read too carefully in the writings of Anglo-American visitors to the Mexican frontier to find evidences of the Black Legend. One of the most explicit statements comes from young Lewis Garrard, who visited New Mexico during the Mexican War. After briefly charac-terizing the New Mexican males as alternatively "servile," and "vil-lainous," he explained the reason for their depravity in terms which

26. Quoted in Joseph Carl McElhannon, "Imperial Mexico and Texas, 1821–1823," *Southwestern Historical Quarterly* 53 (1949): 137.

27. Philip Wayne Powell, *Tree of Hate: Propaganda and Prejudices Affecting United States Relations with the Hispanic World* (New York: 1971), p. 118. Mr. Powell's work is the best history of the Black Legend in English. *The Black Legend: Anti-Spanish Attitudes in the Old World and the New*, ed. Charles Gibson (New York: 1971), contains well-chosen selections of anti-Spanish writing.

28. The only other writers who have made this connection are Cecil Robinson, in discussing the notion that Mexicans are unusually cruel (*Ears of Strangers*, p. 190), and Harry Bernstein, who says that the Black Legend "became Americanized under the name of Manifest Destiny" (*Making an Inter-American Mind*, p. 4). Powell and Bernstein were both trained in Latin American history. Historians of Manifest Destiny, such as Federick Merk and Albert K. Weinberg, who were trained in United States history, seem to be unaware of the depth of anti-Latin feeling in the United States, or else believe it unimportant.

show clearly the influence of the Black Legend. "The extreme degradation into which they are fallen," Garrard observed, "seems a fearful retribution on the destroyers of [the] Aztec Empire."[29]

In addition to the Black Legend, Anglo Americans found one other element to despise in Mexicans—racial mixture. Color-conscious Anglo Americans were nearly unanimous in commenting upon the dark skin of the "swarthy" Mexican *mestizos* who, it was generally agreed, had inherited the worst qualities of Spaniards and Indians, resulting in a "race" still more despicable than that of either parent group.[30] In suggesting that Anglo Americans were racists, I am not trying to ignore the racist nature of Mexican society. We do not have time to elaborate on this matter and for present purposes I simply want to suggest that a belief in the Black Legend, combined with a belief in the inferiority of mixed-bloods, enabled Anglo Americans to predict erroneously what Mexicans would be like (that is, to construct a stereotype) even before coming into significant contact with them. Not surprisingly, the Anglo Americans' expectations were fulfilled.

Anglo-American stereotypes of Mexicans, then, did not originate in the border region. Indeed, as early as 1822 the Mexican minister in Washington recognized that Anglo Americans viewed Mexicans as "inferiors."[31] There can be little doubt, however, that the growing number of travelers, merchants, trappers, and settlers who entered northernmost Mexico after 1821 nourished the stereotype and through writing and conversation, encouraged its growth throughout the United States.

To understand better the nature of Anglo-American stereotypes of Mexicans, let us examine how one of its components functioned—that is, the frequent charge that Mexicans were lazy.

Disparaging remarks regarding Mexicans' lack of initiative were widespread, and were especially abundant in literature describing the border region. Typical was a visitor to San Antonio who observed in 1837 that "The life of the Mexican here is one of unconcerned indolence and ease. As long as he is satisfied with a bare living for the

29. Garrard, *Wah-To-Yah and the Taos Trail*, p. 194.
30. For a discussion of this theme see Robinson, *With the Ears of Strangers*, pp. 67–74. In addition to those writers cited by Robinson, explicit statements about the evils of miscegenation are found in the writings of men such as Rufus B. Sage, Thomas James, and Thomas J. Farnham.
31. Manuel Zozaya, quoted in McElhannon, "Imperial Mexico and Texas," p. 137.

present, there is no reason that he should give himself much trouble about the future."[32] Many writers expressed their disdain for Mexicans' work habits in more colorful terms. Albert Pike, visiting New Mexico in 1831, found the nuevomexicanos "a lazy gossipping people, always lounging on their blankets and smoking the cigarrillos—living on nothing and without labor."[33] How Mexicans lived on nothing, Pike does not trouble himself to explain. An American resident of California told his readers that "you might as well expect a sloth to leave a tree, that has one inch of bark left upon its trunk, as to expect a Californian to labor, whilst a *real* glistens in his pocket."[34] Richard Henry Dana likened laziness in California to an endemic disease, terming it "California Fever," which, he said, might spare the first generation but which "always attacks the second."[35] As an enduring monument to the laziness of Mexicans, there is said to be a gravestone somewhere in California which bears the inscription: "Aquí reposa Juan Espinosa. Nunca en su vida hizo otra cosa."[36] ("Here rests Juan Espinosa. Never did he do anything else.")

Contemporary accounts of the laziness of Mexican frontiersmen are abundant, then, and even include accusations made by officials from Mexico City and Mexican or Spanish-born clergy who had their own reasons for labeling the frontiersmen lazy.[37] Some historians have

32. Andrew Forest Muir, ed., *Texas in 1837: An Anonymous Contemporary Narrative* (Austin: 1958), p. 104.

33. Albert Pike, *Prose Sketches and Poems Written in the Western Country (With Additional Stories)*, ed. David J. Weber (Albuquerque, 1967), p. 247.

34. Alfred Robinson, *Life in California* (1st ed., 1846; Santa Barbara, Calif., 1970), p. 99.

35. Richard Henry Dana, Jr., *Two Years Before the Mast*, ed. John Haskell Kemble (1st ed., 1840; 2 vols.; Los Angeles: 1964), 1: 172.

36. Quoted in Thomas Workman Temple II, "Our Heritage from the Days of the Dons," *Southern California Quarterly* 40 (1958): 70.

37. See, for example, José María Sánchez, "Trip to Texas in 1828," trans. Carlos E. Castañeda, *Southwestern Historical Quarterly* 29 (1926): 250–51; and Governor Juan Bautista Elguézabal, A Description of Texas in 1803," ed. and trans. Odie B. Faulk, *Southwestern Historical Quarterly* 66 (1963): 513–15. For California, see C. Alan Hutchinson, *Frontier Settlement in Mexican California. The Híjar-Padrés Colony and Its Origins, 1769–1835* (New Haven: 1969), pp. 81, 138, 346–47. It is not my purpose here to analyze the reasons why some Franciscans and upper-class Mexicans viewed frontiersmen as lazy. Manuel P. Servín has provided a good explanation of the case of the Franciscans in "California's Hispanic Heritage: A View into the Spanish Myth," *The Journal of San Diego History* 19 (1973): 1–9.

It is interesting to note that *peninsulares* frequently regarded Mexicans as lazy (see, for example, Christon Archer, "The Key to the Kingdom: The Defense of Veracruz,

taken these contemporary accounts at face value and perpetuated the stereotype of Mexican indolence.[38] Yet, it is not only possible to refute the charge that Mexican frontiersmen were lazy, but there is reason to suppose that Mexicans on the frontier were energetic pioneers who worked as hard, if not harder, than their compatriots in the more "civilized" areas of central Mexico. With the exception of Alta California, it was more difficult to exploit Indian labor on the frontier than in central Mexico; frontiersmen had to work with their own hands. For example, the *encomienda* (a system of distributing Indian labor), was unsuccessful and short-lived in the Borderlands, operating only in seventeenth-century New Mexico.[39] Hard work by colonists from Mexico was necessary in some areas of the frontier to provide defense against hostile Indians. Moreover, hard work was probably rewarded on the frontier, where there seems to have been greater social mobility than in central Mexico.

The idea that Mexican frontiersmen were industrious has been suggested by historians such as Silvio Zavala and France Scholes, and anthropologist Miguel León-Portilla.[40] It was also mentioned by contemporaries such as Miguel Ramos Arizpe in Texas, Pedro Bautista Pino in New Mexico, Alexander von Humboldt, the German savant and traveler, and Zebulon Montgomery Pike, the "lost pathfinder."[41]

1780–1810," *The Americas* 27 [1971]: 427, 430) while Mexicans regarded *peninsulares* as generally "disdainful of applying themselves to work which they look on as too servile." Benito María de Moxó, quoted in Hugh Hamill, *The Hidalgo Revolt, Prelude to Mexican Independence* (Gainesville: 1966), p. 30.

38. See, for example, Odie B. Faulk, *Land of Many Frontiers. A History of the American Southwest* (New York: 1968), p. 79; and Charles E. Chapman, *A History of California: The Spanish Period* (New York: 1921), pp. 391–92.

39. Charles Gibson, *Spain in America* (New York: 1966), p. 190.

40. Zavala, "The Frontiers of Hispanic America," in *The Frontier in Perspective*, ed. Walker D. Wyman and Clifton B. Kroeber (Madison: 1965), pp. 36–58. Scholes, "Civil Government and Society in New Mexico in the Seventeenth Century," *New Mexico Historical Review* 10 (1935): 98. León-Portilla, "The Norteño Variety of Mexican Culture: An Ethnohistorical Approach," in *Plural Society in the Southwest*, ed. Edward H. Spicer and Raymond H. Thompson (New York: 1972), pp. 110–11. Not all historians, of course, would agree. Two recent works that suggest opposite conclusions are Hutchinson, *Frontier Settlement in Mexican California*, p. 399; Lynn I. Perrigo, *The American Southwest: Its Peoples and Cultures* (New York: 1971), pp. 416–17.

41. For Ramos Arizpe and Von Humboldt, see Zavala, "The Frontiers of Hispanic America," pp. 48–49. For Pino, see his comments about paupers in Mexico in H. Bailey Carroll and J. Villasana Haggard, eds., *Three New Mexico Chronicles* (Albuquerque: 1942), pp. 27–28.

Pike, for example, termed the inhabitants of New Mexico "the bravest
and most hardy subjects in New Spain," because of "their continual
wars with the savage nations who surround them," because of their
isolation from the rest of New Spain, and because they lacked gold
and silver, a source of easy wealth.[42]

It is possible, then, that Mexicans on the frontier were not lazy
and were perhaps even harder working than their countrymen to the
south.[43] Nevertheless, Anglo-American visitors generally described
frontier Mexicans as lazy. How can this be explained? The Black
Legend, which identified Spaniards as lazy, offers part of the explanation. An understanding of Anglo-American attitudes toward racial
mixture also adds to the explanation, for Anglo Americans generally
regarded persons of mixed blood as lazy. In 1844, for example, Thomas
Jefferson Farnham described the complexion of upper-class Californians as "a light clear bronze; not white . . . not remarkably pure in
any way; a lazy color."[44] Still a third explanation needs to be considered. Psychologists tell us that we stereotype ethnic groups in part
because "in them we may perceive our own shortcomings."[45] According
to Maurice Janowitz and Bruno Bettelheim, "ethnic hostility is a projection of unacceptable inner strivings onto a minority group."[46] The

42. "Pike's Observations on New Spain," in Donald Jackson, ed., *The Journals of
Zebulon Montgomery Pike with Letters and Related Documents*, 2 vols. (Norman: 1966),
2: 58. Among the few Americans who agreed with Pike's analysis in later years was
John Fox Hammond, who thought the New Mexicans indolent, but nonetheless more
industrious than "the inhabitants of lower Mexico." See *A Surgeon's Report on Socorro,
New Mexico, 1852* (Santa Fe: 1966), pp. 26–27.

43. Poinsett and Tayloe suggest this possibility in their observations on Mexico.
Poinsett found rural Mexicans generally more virtuous than city dwellers (*Notes on
Mexico*, pp. 266–67, 163, 175). Both men offered something of a "reverse frontier
thesis." As Poinsett put it, "where nature has done much, man is indolent," and he
added: "To no part of the world has nature been more bountiful, and in no part of
it is there so little of comfort among people" (p. 181; see also Tayloe, *Mexico*, p. 69).
This environmental explanation for indolence was popular through much of the
nineteenth century in describing Anglo-American residents of Texas, too. See Marilyn
McAdams Sibley, *Travelers in Texas, 1761–1860* (Austin: 1967), p. 100. A more
detailed analysis of the question of indolence on Mexico's far northern frontier would
need to distinguish between regions of the frontier. See, for example, how Pike's
description of Texas differed from his description of New Mexico (*The Journals*, 2:
58, 80).

44. Farnham, *Travels*, p. 142.

45. Allport, *Nature of Prejudice*, p. 200.

46. Quoted in ibid., p. 199. See, too, the fine discussion of this question by Joan
W. Moore and Alfredo Cuéllar, *Mexican Americans* (Englewood Cliffs, N.J.: 1970),
p. 5.

ethnic group, in other words, becomes our alter ego. Examined in this context, the Anglo-American observation that Mexicans were lazy may tell us more about the rigorous work ethnic of nineteenth-century Americans than it does about Mexican culture.

The fact that many Anglo Americans blamed the economic and cultural underdevelopment of Mexico's far northern frontier on the "indolent" character of the Mexican settlers not only reveals a bias, but is simplistic. Better explanations for underdevelopment could have been found by looking into historical, geographical, and economic circumstances that contributed to the relative backwardness of the region. Indeed, had they looked more closely, Anglo Americans might have found that underdevelopment was not as much a result of the supposed laziness of Mexican frontiersmen, but instead, the frontiersmen's lack of initiative was a result of underdevelopment and of peculiar frontier conditions. As one astute Franciscan, José Señán, summed up the situation of the californios; "I have good reason to accuse the settlers of laziness, but there is equally good reason to excuse them in large part. Their lack of enthusiasm for their work is not surprising, inasmuch as they regard most of it as fruitless." In a province dominated by the military, Señán explained, a settler was prohibited from selling grain or other surplus crops to anyone except the quartermaster at "absurdly low prices" fixed by law, "while being charged exorbitantly for whatever goods he can procure." Clothing, farm implements, and household goods were in short supply and soldiers had first preference at purchasing them. Even if the settlers had cash, then, "there would be no place to spend it."[47] The situation in Texas was similar, according to Fray Mariano Sosa, who saw the lack of a market for agricultural goods as destroying "incentive to raise larger or better crops."[48]

Whereas some padres blamed the military system for economic stagnation and lack of incentive among the frontier settlers, some settlers, especially in California, criticized the padres for monopolizing Indian labor and the best lands.[49]

47. Señán to the Viceroy, the Marqués de Branciforte, May 14, 1796, in *The Letters of José Señán, O.F.M. Mission San Buenaventura, 1796–1823*, trans. Paul D. Nathan, ed. Lesley Byrd Simpson (San Francisco: 1962), pp. 3–4.

48. Sosa to Governor Manuel de Salcedo, May 26, 1810, quoted in Carlos E. Castañeda, *Our Catholic Heritage in Texas, 1519–1936*, 7 vols. (Austin: 1936–1958), 5: 429.

49. See, for example, José Bandini, *A Description of California in 1828*, trans. and ed. Doris M. Wright (Berkeley: 1951), pp. 6–7. See, too, Robinson, *Life in California*, p. 152.

Those who truly understood the rugged conditions of life on the frontier and the legal restrictions on trade and commerce, then, were not so quick to label frontiersmen lazy. Indeed, some knowledgeable officials expressed admiration for the frontiersmen's tenaciousness and initiative. As Governor Manuel Salcedo wrote of the *tejanos* in 1809: "one . . . marvels at how the most of them cultivate their lands without the necessary farming tools, . . . how some have built houses without artisans . . . how in this poverty they have been able to dress themselves and their families."[50]

For most Anglo-American observers, however, there was no need to look too closely for explanations of lack of economic progress on the Mexican frontier. The stereotype of Mexican laziness constituted a sufficient explanation. Historians of the border region need to be reminded, then, that Anglo Americans did not necessarily see what they said they saw. This contention may be unprovable, but it is not unreasonable. A stereotype, psychologist Gordon Allport tells us, "may interfere with even the simplest rational judgments."[51]

This discussion of the historical roots of Anglo-American stereotypes is not solely of academic interest, for stereotypes have had a profound impact on Mexican–United States relations and on the treatment of Mexicans and Mexican Americans in the United States. The stereotype of the inferior Mexican lay behind the arrogant sense of cultural and political superiority, known in United States history as Manifest Destiny, that led to the United States' seizure of half the Mexican Republic in 1846–47. The stereotype of the inferior Mexican has been used to the present to justify efforts to "Americanize" Mexicans in the southwestern United States, replacing their "folkways," with "superior" Anglo-American culture. Stereotypes have also helped Anglo Americans rationalize their exploitation and mistreatment of Mexican and Mexican-American workers in the fields and factories of the border region. Those who seek to improve the economic conditions of Mexicans in United States, or to make relations between

50. Nettie Lee Benson, ed. and trans., "A Governor's Report on Texas in 1809," *Southwestern Historical Quarterly* 76 (1968): 611.
51. Allport, *Nature of Prejudice*, p. 190. For a different view of this question, see David J. Langum, "Californios and the Image of Indolence," *Western Historical Quarterly* 9 (1978): 181–96; and my commentary and his reply, *Western Historical Quarterly* 10 (1979): 61–69.

Mexicans and Anglo Americans more harmonious, need to be reminded that deeply rooted stereotypes stand as a formidable obstacle to progress. We have come a long way since Noah Smithwick thought that Mexicans were "scarce more than apes," but we have not come nearly far enough.[52]

52. For a discussion of stereotypes in the late nineteenth and early twentieth centuries, as well as a good guide to sources on this question, see the recent article by José E. Limón, "Stereotyping and Chicano Resistance: An Historical Dimension," *Aztlán* 4 (1973): 257–70.

Examples of the ways in which stereotypes have been used to justify imperialism and to exploit Mexicans are abundant. For historical treatments see the overview by Carey McWilliams, *North from Mexico: The Spanish-Speaking People of the United States* (New York: 1948), and my own *Foreigners in Their Native Land: Historical Roots of the Mexican Americans* (Albuquerque: 1973).

Index

absolutism, Spanish, 37, 38
Alamán, Lucas, quoted, 145
Alamo, battle of, 136–38;
  commemoration, 136; historical
  literature on, 135; myth of, 149–50
"Alamo complex," 150
"Alamo Images" symposium (1985),
  133n
Albuquerque, 48
Alessio Robles, Vito, 44n37, 46n47
alliances, Indian-Mexican, 126
"allies fund," 131
Allport, Gordon, quoted, 166
Almaraz, Félix D., 74n59
Almonte, Juan, 113
Alta California, 37, 44–45, 48, 61,
  105, 109, 114–15, 119–20
Alvarado, Juan Bautista, quoted, 103,
  113
America, as earthly paradise, 5
American Airlines, 60
American Historical Association, 33,
  36
Americanization, of northern Mexican
  frontier, 112–14
America, The, 28n28
Anderson, Clinton P., 16
Anglo Americans: inability to adapt to
  Mexican culture, 141–42; initial
  contact with Mexicans, 156–57;

Mexican view of, 142, 145; role in
  Texas Rebellion, 144–47
Annales school, 46
anthropologists, 28, 31–32, 49, 62,
  102n35, 131
anti-Catholicism, in colonial period,
  159–60
anti-Mexicanism, 153–55, 160–61,
  166–67
anti-Spanish views, in colonial period,
  159–60
Antilia, Seven Cities of, 2–3, 8
Anza trail, reopening of, 96
Apache Indians, 91, 118, 119, 122,
  124, 127, 131
Arawak Indians, 4
archives, Mexican, importance of,
  100–103, 137
Arenal, pueblo of, 10
Arizona: Hispanic frontier of, 49n58;
  historical studies of, 91, 96; under
  Mexican rule, 108, 109; during
  Mexican War, 106; as part of
  Mexican frontier, 90, 100, 118; as
  part of Pimería Alta, 66
Arizpe, Miguel Ramos de, 44
Armijo, Manuel, 125; quoted, 118
army, Mexican, 111, 121, 136–37
Arroyo, Luis Leobardo, quoted, 71
Ascención, Fray Antonio de la, 13